Jargon

THE LANGUAGE LIBRARY

EDITED BY DAVID CRYSTAL

JARGON

ITS USES AND ABUSES

WALTER NASH

BLACKWELL

Oxford UK & Cambridge USA

First published 1993

Blackwell Publishers
108 Cowley Road
Oxford OX4 1JF
UK

238 Main Street
Cambridge, Massachusetts 02142
USA

British Library Cataloguing in Publication Data
A CIP catalogue record for this book is available from
the British Library.

Library of Congress Cataloging-in-Publication Data
Nash, Walter.
    Jargon: its uses and abuses/Walter Nash.
      p.   cm. – (The language library)
    Includes bibliographical references and index.
    ISBN 0-631-18063-X (alk. paper)
    1. English language – Jargon – Dictionaries.   2. English language – Usage –
    Dictionaries.   3. English language – Jargon.   4. English language – Usage.
    I. Title.   II. Series.
    PE 1585.N37   1993
    427'.003 – dc20   92-36120
                                                                                   CIP

Typeset in 10 on 11½ pt Sabon
by Best-set Typesetter Ltd., Hong Kong
Printed in Great Britain by TJ Press, Padstow, Cornwall.

This book is printed on acid-free paper

Contents

My Readers will soon observe what a great Compass of real and useful Knowledge this Science includes; Wherein, although Nature, assisted by a Genius, may be very instrumental, yet a strong Memory and constant Application, together with Example and Precept, will be highly necessary: For these Reasons I have often wished, that certain Male and Female Instructors, perfectly versed in this science, would set up Schools for the Instruction of young Ladies and Gentlemen therein.

Jonathan Swift, *Polite Conversations*

Preface

My book is called *Jargon*, but 'Jargoning' (a word that keeps turning up in this text) might have been a more accurately descriptive title. As an academic study, jargon is for lexicographers, whereas jargoning, being jargon on the move or jargon in action, is for students of style – or rather, *styles*: literary styles, journalistic styles, official styles, commercial styles, social styles, professional styles – varieties of language, written or spoken, in diverse functions, with diverse pretensions.

From this, readers may conclude that I have no ambitions or qualifications in lexicography, and should understand that the glossary in Part II of this text is designed to be no more than an amplifying commentary on themes discussed in Part I – a 'glossary of furthermores'. I have to confess to amassing material and examples in a rather casual way: by reflecting on my own usage, making smuggled jottings in the course of a day's social and professional encounters, taking notes during television broadcasts, but above all by trawling (as current jargon puts it) through broadsheet newspapers. Unfortunately, it would take a squad of eager amanuenses, a regular hive of programmed honey-bees, to keep up with the jargoning output of the British press, and my store of old newspapers has consequently grown, mound by mound, until I am in the diurnal doghouse because of the unsightly condition of my study and also because of my unreasonable reluctance to give up any part of this collection for firelighting and other domestic duties. I now surrender it all to the flames and the floorwashing, sad for the dozens of unrecorded examples, the missed passages that might have amplified many a point had I roused myself to transcribe them, but on the whole glad of the houseroom.

This is not a subject on which a decently warm human being can write with complete academic detachment, and I must own up to some splenetic outbursts – notably in reference to time-share salesmen, literary theorists, and political sophisters of every muddy and mendacious colour. In this I claim the privilege of the elderly; as the years advance, rage is the only fun left. Otherwise I hope that I have controlled my tendency to be frivolously opinionated – the more so since the writer does not exist who can claim to compose a page without somewhere falling into something perceived by someone as jargon. In many pages of this book I have ventured into parodies of jargoning; but there must be many more in which I have unconsciously taken to jargoning on my own account, and I can only ask the reader to take notice and take warning.

WN

Part I

*Taking On Board Relevant Insights Into
an Ongoing Situation*

'Somehow it seems to fill my head with ideas – only I don't know
exactly what they are!'

Alice

'Clear your *mind* of cant.'

Dr Johnson

1

Introduction

(I)
'MOBLED QUEEN' IS GOOD — OR IS IT?

Nobody has a good word for jargon, as one might have for its neighbour, slang, or its distant cousin, metaphor. Writers or speakers are never praised for their assured command of rousing cliché, stunningly eloquent shop talk, vivid, arresting gobbledygook. Jargon is a species of crime against language and clear thinking, typically described by such adjectives as 'incomprehensible', 'pretentious', and 'dreary'. As for the perpetrators of this offence, they are always other people. Apart from occasional lapses into stereotyped expression — the pardonable consequence of creative fatigue — I never use jargon. I speak plainly; *you*, I fear, sometimes have unnecessary recourse to technical terms; but *he* — *she* — *they* — are neckfast in cant and conundrums, which is why our journalism, our political language, indeed all our discourse, is in such a wretchedly tainted condition. You can hardly turn on the TV news without wondering where John Bunyan went, and whatever happened to Standard English.

I find it not at all unpleasant to become angry about jargon. It is a therapeutic source of amusement and rage, just as long as you can assure yourself that others are to blame, and that this deplorable linguistic malady is quite beyond your own responsibility and control, like a disease that strikes only the uncleanly. But let us from time to time be a little prudent in our prejudice. What if it should turn out that we are all jargon makers and jargon users, and that jargon is necessarily involved in the growth and change of language? That we are consumers of jargon as we are eaters of sliced bread? What if we are obliged to confess, shamefully, that there are times when we actually enjoy it — within reason, of course? Think of the inter-office memo; think of the annotated wine-list or the elaborated menu; think of the patter of importunate salesfolk; think of the spouting of sportspersons; think of the stuff educationists come out with; think, if you can, of literary criticism; think of the speeches of the nearly-great and the almost-good, the presidents and prime ministers and prime movers of our destinies – think on these things, and if you have never once laughed, or relished a portentous phrase ('mobled queen' is good, says Polonius), or even fallen into the habit of portentousness, think yourself peculiar. In short, what if we conclude that jargon, though doubtless a bad practice – shoddy – oh, certainly – corrosive – mind-sapping – may nevertheless have intelligible and sometimes pardonable motives? And what, in any case, do we mean by this slippery term?

(II)
THE MEANINGS OF JARGON

The dictionaries on my shelf offer several senses of the word. One of the oldest is 'babbling', or meaningless phonation – the twittering of birds, the chatter of apes, the lallation of babes in their bassinets. Another is 'hybrid language', or pidgin; the lingo used in the nineteenth century by Americans and Europeans trading with the Chinook Indians in the north-west of the United States was actually known as *the Jargon*. Yet another sense is 'secret language', the code that baffles the beak, the snoop, the nosey-parker, the nark, the alien: schoolboy slang, mess-deck and barrack-room talk, cockney patter, 'eggy-peggy' (cagan yagou ragead thagis?) and 'pig-Latin' (ellway ancay ouyay eadray isthay?). All these, however, have become incidental to the two senses in which the word is now most commonly used.

In one of these senses, 'jargon' denotes the terminology of some pro-fession, occupation, or pursuit. Every activity has its occupational terms, many of which cross the bounds of technical usage and enter into common parlance. We may speak of a 'standard' language, but the history of English is full of examples of the common idiom drawing on the resources of technical or occupational varieties. An interesting (if, no doubt, obvious) fact about these 'resources' is that they do not remain quite the same from one generation to the next. They change gradually, in phases, as society changes, as technologies and customs and institutions change. The language is thus forever coloured by the social history of the people.

Take an instance. Currently, a powerful idiomatic influence is the almost universal activity of using computers. Most of us know what is meant, for example, when we are told that a computer is 'down'; this is a way of saying that the machine is out of order, or not in operation. Consequently, if we hear that the computer is 'up and running', we understand that it is operable ('up') and going about its programmatic business ('running'). Now if, as a person habitually reliant on computers, I were to remark on my up-and-running plans for a book, or observe that my brain, having been down for months, was up and running at long last, a purist might accuse me of jargon-making because I would have taken an expression out of its legitimate occupational sphere and put it to work in contexts where 'ordinary' English would serve equally well.

What might I say to that? I might argue, in the first place, that my invention was a harmless pleasantry; and furthermore, that the transference of usage from a particular sense to a general domain is one of the means by which language grows and changes. I am only doing the sort of thing that Shakespeare did, and generations of speakers before him. In the course of such changes, parent expressions are lost or forgotten while their offspring increase and flourish. As common usage, rather than as an occupational phrase, 'up and running' is coloured by notions of alacrity, vigour, and physical fitness, suggesting the image of the athlete more than that of the computer and its programs. It could easily be taken as a description of the sprinter rising from the blocks. This colouring can be detected in some recent uses of the expression, for example this:

'They've convinced me that it's an up-and-running entity, a goer', she said of the paper that was launched in February. (*UK Press Gazette*)

or this:

While they may or may not have killed off the restaurant, another blow fell in January, when *The Times* referred to its 'closure' while it was still up and running, or at least limping. (*Independent*)

'Goer' in the first example is the word that suggests a shift of connotation; in popular usage, a 'goer' is someone with get-up-and-go, or a flighty woman, or a spirited horse, or a stout-hearted whippet, or a good second-hand car – someone or something *viable*, imbued with possibilities, and in that sense 'an up-and-running entity'. In the second quotation, the non-occupational use of 'up and running' is emphasized by the playful 'limping'. In each instance there is an indication that the writer is aware of using the expression in an irregular or transferred sense.

Obsessional activity – our commitment to the occupations and pursuits that frame and inform our lives – is a primary source of jargon, but not the only one, and probably not the most productive. What we now generally think of as 'jargon' has other, even more fertile sources, in pretentiousness, in the emulation of fashionable trends, in the wish to be on the inside and the woe of being on the outside. There is a social origin of jargon which has less to do with pursuing a profession than with the masquerade of assuming a role and striking an accredited pose. It produces expressions like the following, noted by me in the course of ten minutes during an academic committee meeting: 'operating in the tutorial situation'; 'maximizing feedback'; 'managerialism'; 'corporate image';

'range of proven teaching strengths'; 'package of proposals'; 'involving students in the decision-making process'; 'developing entrepreneurial skills'. An observer might conclude from these words and phrases either that the scholars using them were anxious to be perceived (and to perceive themselves) as smart-suited businessfolk, or that they chose to talk in this ready-mixed style because on the whole it is easier than having to make your own phrases. You can, if you like, maximise feedback from your package of proposals, after accessing students to the decision-making process all the way across the board; or you can develop and enhance entrepreneurial skills ('enhance' is good) with a view to targeting pre-selected overseas markets; or you can agree that the appropriate managerial strategy in the context of developments off-campus would involve the design of an operational package offering a full range of options backed by proven teaching strengths. You can shuffle the words and cut the phrases to the admiration of all, and your brain need never once be up and running.

2

A Jargoning Taxonomy

(III)
SHOP TALK IS ONE THING...

Any study of this subject needs to take some account of the interplay of *shop talk* and *show talk*; jargon links the callings people follow with the impressions they try to create. Of the two, shop talk, the phraseology of pursuits, invites the more sympathetic consideration, because even if we are sometimes baffled and irritated by technical terms – 'terms of art', our ancestors would have called them – we can nevertheless understand that over the centuries mere shop talk has usefully and even pleasurably enlarged the general vocabulary of English.

There is no mystery about this process of enlargement. Some word or phrase in regular occupational service is used by the practitioner with reference to objects or activities outside the sphere of working life. In this way it becomes a form of slang, or even a sub-species of metaphor. By and by it is taken up, often for the sake of show-talking, by members of the general public, who conspire to neglect the specific source of the term, using it ever more loosely, until at length it becomes so well established as standard idiom that its original sense is lost. This process can be traced in the history of some of our commonest words and idioms. Lexicographers and old salts apart, how many people are precisely aware of the military or maritime origins of 'forlorn hope', or 'taken aback', or 'under way' (which our journalists now write 'underway'), or 'making headway'?[1] A further question is why these particular expressions should have won acceptance while their occupational companions have been left behind. We do not speak, in general English, about 'making sternway' ('Johnny's making sternway with his sums'), and while landlubbers may confess themselves 'completely taken aback' only ancient mariners know that the appropriate style is to be 'taken *flat* aback'. It is a little mysterious. By what processes of supply and demand do samples of other people's shop talk get into the public market?

I am led to reflect on a personal example. Some years ago I shared a course of lectures – in General Linguistics – with a colleague whose comings and goings never seemed to coincide with mine; such were our timetable arrangements that the presence of one of us apparently required, as if by some demographic law, the absence of the other. Referring to this one day, he pleasantly observed 'We are allomorphs in complementary distribution'. He meant that we were like the farcical Box and Cox, who took it in turns to occupy a lodging-house bed, but for my amusement and his own diversion he expressed the idea in the technical language of linguistics. It is an example of an 'in-joke'; the question is whether its language could ever get 'out', to a wider, non-specialist audience? 'Allomorph' (= 'different form', 'variant representation') is the kind of technical term that resists translation beyond occupational bounds. It is unlikely that Mrs Jones will ever tell Mrs Brown, 'Bert's the dead spit of the Prince of Wales, oh, yes, they could be allomorphs'. 'Complementary distribution', on the other hand, has its possibilities. One can imagine contexts in which the phrase would be whimsically apt, since bodies or objects might be said to be in complementary distribution when the functional presence of one implies the absence of the other. The night sister and the day sister in a hospital ward are in complementary distribution; my shoes (when I leave the house) and my slippers (on my return) are in complementary distribution. The possibilities multiply, but jokily, without seriously claiming a place, or a need, for the phrase in common usage; for which reason, I suppose, it will probably remain a piece of shop talk, not readily transferable into current jargon.

There is a middle ground of jargoning usage, lying between the narrow domain of technical terminology and the general territory of accepted idiom. Words here are not wholly 'in' and not completely 'out'; they keep, distinctively, their original meanings, even while they are developing new associations. This is awkward and treacherous country. In it you may find, as of recent decades, the occupational talk of the space explorers: 'launch pad', 'lift-off', 'into orbit', 'window', 'splashdown', 'countdown', 'all systems are go'. These expressions have become familiar enough for us to use them in extended reference to things generally analogous to the rocket engineers' launching procedures – that is, to the execution of any plan or venture. We may have a 'countdown to the summit conference', and even a 'countdown to Christmas'; in the old aeroplane age we got enterprises 'off the ground', whereas we now 'have lift-off'; and politicians with schemes to promote or election dates to fix look for a 'window of opportunity'. Yet common though such transferred usages may be, we have not quite come to the stage of forgetting the parent sense – as we are now forgetful of the origin of 'forlorn hope' or 'under way' – and thus there will be times when the use of these phrases in non-technical contexts will strike us as audacious and even illicit. If we read that 'The Kingman report was the launch-pad for current ideas about the teaching of English', or 'All systems are go for the implementation of the Government's fiscal reform proposals', it may seem to us that this language is wanting in decorum. Perhaps we will not choose to put it quite in that way, since 'decorum' is not a word in general use in the shops and thoroughfares and on the 5.20 out of St Pancras. We are more likely to tell ourselves, 'This is a load of jargon'.

Yet often it is not the phrases themselves that invite censure, so much as the habit of indiscriminately thrusting them into congested company, one jostling with another. The coupling of 'All systems are go' with 'implementation of . . . fiscal reform proposals' is a rather obvious example. The stylistic contrast between the free-and-easy 'all systems are go' and the high-collared 'implementation of fiscal reforms' is too abrupt, making the sentence seem jargon-ridden at both ends. Composite jargon of this kind is a ludicrous exercise. 'All systems are go' is a piece of shop talk that may occasionally find a useful place in our household chatter; but that place is not in combination with pretentious constructions like 'implementation of fiscal reform proposals'. By and by, the teeth are set on edge. Shop talk is one thing . . .

(IV)
. . . BUT SHOW TALK IS TOO MUCH

Nothing provokes resentful mockery more quickly than the aping of flashy words and fashionable phrases. This kind of jargon – show talk – is as old as snobbery and as common as insecurity. Shakespeare knew it, and detested it. Here he is, in the fifth act of *Hamlet*, with his tetchy prince at the mercy of an incomprehensible courtier:

Osric:	The king, sir, hath wager'd with him six Barbary horses: against the which he has imponed, as I take it, six French rapiers and poniards, with their assigns, as girdle, hangers, and so; three of the carriages, in faith, are very dear to fancy, very responsive to the hilts, most delicate carriages, of very liberal conceit.
Hamlet:	What call you the carriages?
Horatio (aside to Hamlet):	I knew you must be edified by the margent ere you had done.
Osric:	The carriages, sir, are the hangers.
Hamlet:	The phrase would be more german to the matter, if we could carry cannon by

our sides: I would it might be hangers
until then.

Osric is a jargonist of the first rank, a smooth-operating, gobbledygooking
man-about-Elsinore, with all the latest words and wondrous phrases in his
repertoire (note 'impone', 'assigns', 'responsive', 'delicate', 'conceit'). In
their previous exchanges, Hamlet has done fairly well, even managing to
baffle his conversational opponent with some inventions of his own; but
'carriages' is too much. Guns are borne on carriages and swords are
carried on hangers, and it is absurdly pretentious to speak otherwise. Now
notice Horatio's part. His wry interpolation, 'I knew you must be edified
by the margent ere you had done', is a shop-talking response to Osric's
show-talking display. His role here is not that of the subject addressing
his prince, but of the undergraduate talking to his fellow-student. (They
are both attending the University of Wittenberg.) The language is academic
shop: 'margent' (= 'margin') has the occupational meaning of 'commentary
on a text'. With this aside to Hamlet, Horatio is being privately witty in
the language of the truth-seeking scholar; the implication that Osric's
frothy verbiage might deserve a commentary is ironic and contemptuous,
and the clear hint to Hamlet is not to waste his time in trying to cope with
such nonsense. A little later, Hamlet says that Osric and his kind have
'only got the tune of the time, and outward habit of encounter', an apt
description of the social importance of show talk. A modern Osric might
say that he explores current approaches and strategies for maximizing
interactional skills in culturally loaded situations.

To play the tune of the time calls for some virtuosity in word-forming
and phrase-making. There are grammatical symptoms of jargoning. It is
not uncommon, for instance, for words ordinarily treated as abstract non-
count nouns, that is, nouns not usually given a plural form – 'strength',
'skill', 'initiative' – to be used as countables, with implications of concrete
and specific reference: 'proven teaching strengths', 'study skills', 'diplomatic
initiatives'. Another symptom of the grammar of jargoning is the tendency
to form denominal verbs – verbs derived from nouns. Recent examples of
this are 'target', 'access', and 'trial'. One targets for specific discussion
areas that have been accessed as a result of current initiatives (you choose
to talk about things other people are talking about); one anticipates
positive feedback after projects have been trialled (you hope that when
your ideas are tested they will go down well). Powerful action is suggested,
'to target' seeming weightier than 'to aim at', 'access' more strenuous than
'open' or 'make available', 'trial' a stride ahead of 'test'. There is a cult
of muscular meanings, in which prefixes and suffixes become important
agents. Prefix elements commonly suggest, in relation to their bases,
directive energy rather than mere direction; thus 'on', 'through', 'over',
and 'out', in 'ongoing', 'throughput', 'overkill', 'outsource'. A favourite
suffix is *ize*, as in 'maximize', 'regularize', 'privatize'; the purport of the

suffix varies, but in these examples it clearly has the sense of 'doing something', 'making', 'putting into effect'. Having targeted your areas and trialled your pilot projects, you prioritize your agenda and then proceed to maximize your throughput, relying on feedback to monitor the danger of overkill. This is sinewy stuff; but as the late John Wayne reportedly observed, a man's gotta do what a man's gotta do.

And one thing you gotta do, what indeed you must attempt at every opportunity, if jargoning is your game, is to find out how to talk about things without using their simplest names. The sergeant-instructor in Henry Reed's poem 'Judging Distances' gives excellent advice on this matter. 'Whatever you do', he tells his class of recruits, 'don't call the bleeders *sheep*'. By no means call them sheep (call them disposable agrarian assets if you like); and never let an *area* shrink to a 'point', or reduce a *situation* to an 'event', or otherwise nominate a spade a spade, but whenever possible use one of the many fashionable expressions, large in implication and loose in import, which are the essential lexicon of modern jargon. Some current stalwarts are 'area', 'dimension', 'concept' (like Osric's 'conceit'), 'operation', 'package', 'perception', 'situation', 'strategy', 'syndrome'. Such vogue words (or mode words, or buzz words – and there are dozens more for us to muse over) are commonly supported by vogue phrases, clichés from the smart speaker's repertoire: eg. 'take on board', 'across the board', 'at the end of the day', 'in the last analysis', 'in terms of'. The skilled jargonist creatively combines word and phrase, taking on board insightful strategies, offering packages of innovative and exciting concepts, annually reviewing and updating situations in terms of looking at the relevant material on a year-to-year basis.

The jargonist's greatest powers of invention appear in something that is hardly metaphor, scarcely slang, and not quite cliché. I need a word – something to add to the jargon on jargon. Let me then suggest *metaphrase* – a technique of transmuting simple, sturdy expression into ramshackle verbiage. The police officer who wrote to a national newspaper that 'operational situations requiring a military-style organization and command structure are comparatively few, and mostly confined to public order situations' was earnestly metaphrasing his view that the duties of the police, apart from quelling riots, do not demand that they should be organized and led like an army. The example suggests, however, that metaphrasing may not be entirely a matter of transforming or inflating some basically simple turn of phrase. It is that, but it is something in addition. It is a claim to status. To speak in this way is to assume the guise of the articulate, the secure, the self-assured; the speaker lets the world know that he knows his stuff. 'Military-style organization and command structure' is bold and burly talk; 'having the sort of units and officers that they have in the army' would probably do rather less for one's self-confidence. It is sometimes hard to speak simply without feeling a bit of a simpleton, and that is possibly the worst and saddest thing about show talk: it brings out all our fear of being weighed up and found wanting.

(v)

AND SALES TALK GOES WAY OVER THE TOP

But showing off is not necessarily the most culpable and dangerous effect of jargoning. There are possibly worse consequences. There is sales talk, which pleads acceptance for some kind of product, whether in the form of goods, or ideas, or political policies, and which seeks to control the potential consumer's responses to the product. The competent adman or manifesto-maker looks for language that will preclude free analysis of any proposition; set terms have to be imposed on the buyer, the elector, or the political opponent, and these terms shape whatever follows between the negotiating parties. You do not easily escape the bonds of a huckster's words. When the car salesman has you at his mercy (you only wanted to try the doors on the Volvo) his talk of 'economic fuel consumption' and 'ample five-seater comfort' commits you to the acceptance of 'kind on your pocket' and 'plenty of room for the kiddies in the back', while subtly precluding 'comparatively expensive way of getting around' and 'a bit of a squash for three moderately sized adults'. Beware: every phrase to which you nod assent compels acceptance of some other phrase, farther from your thoughts, nearer to your cheque-book.

A typical and striking example of the directive power of the salesman's jargon is the language of time-share peddling. 'Time-sharing' is a way of paying rent (a lot of rent) in advance, to secure tenancy of a holiday apartment for a short period each year, and incidentally to supply the developer with a return of capital which he can deposit with his friendly bank in some happy tax-free haven. The notion that Mr and Mrs Robinson and their heirs are in any real sense 'owners' of the flat they occupy for two weeks every April is wholly specious. Nor can it properly be said that they buy a share of time. They are going to spend time, certainly, but they do not buy the time they spend; they only buy the right to spend it in a certain place. Common phrases like 'buying time' and 'playing for time' act here like semantic salesmen, promoting the figurative notion of time as a commodity that can be measured out, divided and purchased, so that a phrase like 'time ownership' might appear to make some sort of realistic sense. But the true purpose of the phrase is not to refer to a fact or an idea, which is what we generally and perhaps somewhat naively expect of the phrases people use. It is rather to presuppose, indeed to create, another sort of reality, a realm of Hi-Cockalorum, in the minds of prospective clients and even in the benign fantasies of the salesmen themselves, who must take great comfort from sincere commitment to the perceptions they try to fabricate.

These perceptions require a plausible misunderstanding of the words 'ownership' and 'time', and of the ideas associated with them. The purchaser does not – cannot – 'own' a piece of a place and a slice of a season. He 'owns' no more than the right to reserve a limited tenancy; yet the general discourse of time-sharing encourages and enforces, often with a manner pitched somewhere between the gravity of the lawyer and the evangelical fervour of the theologian, the sense of ownership as having and holding, and the sense of time as for ever and ever. A typical brochure utterance describes time-sharing as 'A concept that is gaining favour with all types of people, in all walks of life, in all parts of the world, to let, to sell, to bequeath . . . Not just for one year, but for each year, every year, forever – in perpetuity. To guarantee you and your family (and your family's family) luxurious holidays from this day forward.'

Whoever composed that extraordinary piece of Old Low Poppycock has raked through recollections of forensic and liturgical solemnities (the echo of the marriage service in 'from this day forward' is particularly fetching) in order to convey the solemn and promissory sense of inalienable possession which the phrases 'time-sharing' and 'time ownership' are meant to imply. Usages of this kind reinforce one of the powerful myths of our culture, the myth of ownership. To be an owner is to be a decent citizen. Owning is infinitely superior, morally, to renting. Ownership is respectable, a duty, almost a sacred commitment; and 'time ownership' is first cousin to 'home ownership', a phrase of some importance in the ideology of British conservatism. Time-share touts and other salespersons have their own derivative ideologies and their compelling phrases which the customer-victim can resist only by some act of robust discourtesy. And since few of us are capable of bawling appropriate denunciations while we knock over the chair and mangle the polystyrene coffee-cup, we put ourselves more or less at the disposal of those phrases that guide us fatefully towards documents and signatures. When this happens in commercial transactions, we have to accept the verdict of *caveat emptor*, let the buyer beware. When the same wheedling power of the phrase appears in the language of politics, that is potentially a much more serious compulsion, to which we should not so readily subscribe. 'Let the buyer beware' is fair warning; 'let the citizen accept' is a proposition that ought to be resisted.

(VI)
A MULTI-COLOURED SWAP-SHOP

Sales talk, political rhetoric, the adman's wheeze, the schoolman's notion, the sportsman's patter, the committeeman's chatter – all of them create and foster some form of jargon, and each of them offers something to the others. Jargon at large is a multi-coloured swap-shop: financiers may talk like field marshals, educationists like stockbrokers, politicians like athletes, fast food vendors like romantic novelists. In general, however, there are three jargoning styles. There are *Jargons of Profession*, there are *Jargons of Production*, and there are *Jargons of Pretension* – corresponding respectively to our 'shop talk', 'sales talk', and 'show talk'. Bookmakers, computer programmers, actors, bankers – etcetera – create Jargons of Profession; mattress manufacturers, restaurateurs, car salesmen, copywriters – among others – devise Jargons of Production; and Jargons of Pretension are generated by – for example – educationists, office administrators and professors of critical theory. Some jargons (generally those recognizable as Jargons of Profession) provide sources from which other jargons borrow, or from which general usage is supplied, so that one might indeed speak of 'source-jargons'. When the stock-marketeer, for example, speaks of a 'dawn raid' – meaning a wholesale purchasing of a particular stock as soon as the market opens and before rivals have had time to waken to the event – his jargon of movements on the exchange has its source in an older jargon of military movements. Scraps of professional phrase, bits of particular shop talk, can enter figuratively into more than one style of jargoning, and the relationship between one jargon and another can be a matter as interesting as the question of how jargon-in-general relates to the language-at-large. Each jargon has its distinctive phraseology, its particular lexicon; we always know what kind of shop is being talked, and we know it without benefit of introductions or headlines – unless some poet or clever parodist is playing with us. On the other hand, there appear to be common features of jargoning, perhaps in the general treatment of language, perhaps at a deeper level, in creative principle; and thus chalk becomes interestingly compatible with cheese.

3

Elements of Jargon

(VII)
HOW TO TALK BEANS AND BRICKLAYING

Now here is a problem for the aspiring jargonist: how should we represent, for the benefit of a prospective consumer, a helping of beans on toast? Of course, the problem needs to be – as they say – contextualized; we have to define our parameters, so to speak. Where do you go for your beans? This wholesome dish is not going to figure on the menu at L'Auberge aux Quat' Petites Grenouilles; and at Jax Snax and All-Nite Eaterie it will be crudely slated as Bean's on Tost; but perhaps at the Tasty Dip-In, or the Happyday Burgerbar and Diner, where they offer a colourful and rhetorically adept bill of fare, we shall find something along these lines: 'Delicious golden beans, steeped in a tangy, featherlight sauce, and served on two crispy portions of lightly browned farmhouse bread for your gourmet pleasure.' This is not a definitive text. 'Steeped' might at a venture be replaced by 'swimming', and 'crispy' could be sacrificed in favour of 'generous', which is a useful all-purpose epithet in burgerspeak. Let us, by way of further example, attempt a menu entry for sausage and mash. We may choose to construct our rhetoric round a few key-words, of which 'generous' could be one: 'Three generous prime pork Wiltshire sausages, seductively nestling on a bed of exquisitely textured creamed potato and brought to you with a mouth-watering gravy made to our chef's own recipe.'

From examples such as these a grammar, or at least a stylistic principle, might be deduced. The apprentice menu-maker must study his adjectives (romantic), his epithets (wholesome), his adverbs (thrilling), his verbs (busy but non-finite), his compounds (romantically, thrillingly, infinitely busy and wholesome). Somewhat different principles will emerge from other styles of jargoning. Let our question now be: How would you describe your TV tutorial course on, say, the Elements of Bricklaying?

What is required of the London-based teacher as he addresses his pupils in Basingstoke, Birmingham, and Berwick-on-Tweed? First of all, you might think, an 'approach', which is to say a methodology (not to be confused with a mere method). But since what he is proposing to teach falls under the heading of a skill, it will have to be 'a skills approach', or, for greater precision, 'a manual skills approach'. (Or even, at a peradventure, a 'hands-on approach'.) Then, since the subject can hardly be taught in one lesson, but will call for painstaking, step-by-step instruction, he must ensure that his approach is 'graduated' – 'a graduated manual skills approach'. Finally, let him consider his students, in their homes up and down the country. They are involved in 'distance learning', and what their instructor devises for them is a course entitled 'Better Bricklaying: A Graduated Manual Skills Approach For Distance Learners'. Those who take this course may find that they progress slowly at first, but then with greater speed as their walls stop falling down or bulging awkwardly. Diligent students will find themselves happily placed on 'a learning curve', which undoubtedly tends towards 'the maximization of achievement potential' (or the achievement of a potential maximum, or the maximum potential achievement – the beauty of it being that the word order makes very little difference). Thus, a graduated manual skills approach will be designed to implement the progress of the distance learner along a curve tending towards the maximization of achievement potential; as a result of which he will presently discover how to erect a brick toolshed.

Or, you might say, he will have had the benefit of a step-by-step, easy-to-follow approach enabling him, the distance learner, to enhance his bricklaying skills and achieve projects like the one in the prospectus: a really workmanlike, do-it-yourself garden utility store in handsome, weatherproof brick, with a pitched roof of traditional red tiles resting on sturdy frames of seasoned timber. If you say that, or anything like it, you are commingling two styles of jargoning, the patter of the advertiser (a Jargon of Production) and the babble of the educationist (a Jargon of Pretension). They can, after all, be mixed and matched; it is possible for one kind of gabble to harmonize with another.

(VIII)
MODE WORDS

A common impulse, whatever the jargon, is towards the use or creation of mode words (or vogue words, or buzz words; some introductory examples are cited on p. 11 above). 'Mode word' can be taken as a pun of sorts, intending *mode* in two senses: (a) 'fashion', and (b) 'manner', 'way of doing'. When the occasion calls for it, the adept slips out of plain English and into the jargoning mode, the state-of-the-art way of amazing your friends while you formulate valid perceptions. This requires a fairly large vocabulary of accredited terms, because every such word may be the necessary nucleus of a jargoning phrase or a nodal point in the jargoning text. Here, for example, is a short list of expressions virtually indispensable to the management of current socio-political jargon: 'aggressive', 'alternative' (as adjective or noun), 'approach', 'area', 'attitude', 'capability' (as in 'weapons capability'), 'character', 'clinical', 'commitment', 'concept', 'concern', 'constraint', 'construct' (noun), 'context', 'credibility' (of various kinds, beginning with 'street credibility', a.k.a. 'street cred'), 'designer' (as in 'designer water', 'designer stubble'), 'development/al', 'dimension', 'discourse', 'distance' (as verb, in 'to distance oneself'), 'dynamic', 'ecological', 'efficiency', 'entrepreneurial', 'environment/al', 'expertise', 'factor', 'flexible', 'formula', 'framework', 'generate', 'growth', 'image', 'implement', 'imperative' (as noun), 'incentive', 'innovative', 'interface', 'issue', 'management' (especially as epithet, e.g. 'management response'), 'market' (also as epithet, e.g. 'market sentiment'), 'model', 'negative', 'organizational', 'pattern', 'parameter', 'perception', 'positive', 'posture', 'potential', 'presentation', 'problem', 'project', 'proposal', 'radical', 'relevant', 'regulate' (whence also 'deregulate'), 'response', 'scenario', 'sector', 'sentiment', 'situation', 'squeeze', 'stance', 'strategy', 'syndrome', 'technology', 'tendency', 'thrust', 'valid', 'vehicle'. Only to read through a list like that is to be primed with the Jargons of Pretension, or at least with the feeling of having browsed through a Sunday newspaper without needing to think too much about its contents.

At first it might seem that this list is no more than a catalogue of everyday words, all innocent of guile and gobbledygook. But with words as with people, much is told by the company they keep. The fact is that these words and others – the aunts, uncles and cousins of their lexical family – keep turning up at various stylistic functions: the political debate, the financial gathering, the educational conference. In some cases they arrive as well-recognized clichés: 'thrust', for example, nearly always brings an 'argument', for no politician would be without 'the thrust of my argument', meaning 'the point of what I am somewhat ineffectually trying to say'. In other instances, words obligingly act as fillers, making up the weight of otherwise flimsy phrases. 'Character' is a good example of this. It means *thinginess* or *whatshisname* in 'the generally positive character of the proposals' (= 'the proposals are goodish, sort of'), and in 'a situation of a somewhat different character' it means 'I am stuck with the wrong construction and should have said *a somewhat different situation* or even *another matter entirely*'.

Most strikingly, mode words turn up in pairs and partnerships. We have 'negative perceptions', we 'implement strategies', we discuss the need for 'flexibility in our approaches', we applaud 'innovative measures', discuss 'market perception', and possibly 'widen the framework of discourse' in 'positive response to the growth scenario outlined in the Chancellor's proposals'. Such constructions are easily made, and our sample word-list will tell us why, prompting us to notice that most of its items fall into one grammatical category: they are nearly all nouns. Of course jargoning includes modish verbs and fashionable adjectives – the adjective is an important category in Jargons of Production – but in socio-political chatter the mode words are most commonly nouns, and the noun becomes the centre, the node, the *head* (as grammarians say) of imposing and potentially expandable phrases. An 'issue', for example, can become an 'environmental issue', which might further grow into a 'radical environmental issue'; or a 'concept' could become a 'concept in design theory', or even a 'funda-mentally new concept in design theory'. To make the phrase, pick a modish noun and qualify it with other mode words, or possibly with expressions that of themselves have no obvious colour of jargoning. There is nothing very modish about the word 'verbal', for example, but if we conjoin it with the noun 'environment', or better still if we then add the innocent adjective 'immediate', to make the phrase 'immediate verbal environment' – if, in other words, 'verbal' and 'immediate' are made to share the immediate verbal environment of 'environment' – then we shall have contrived an almost irresistibly glamorous way of saying what linguists mean by 'construction' or 'collocation', and what people at large mean by 'phrase'.

These nodal nouns, furthermore, are commonly abstract and generic. Concrete and specific expressions are rare, apart from those that can be figuratively transformed (for example, 'framework'). Abstractions are needed for the business of metaphrasing (see above, p. 11); instead of asking what is to stop us from setting up more saucepan factories, we demand to know what factors operate as constraints on the supply of industrial venture capital in the domestic hardware market. A notable consequence of this curious need to speak out ever louder and more inanely is that one word presently comes to outbid another in modishness, so that hierarchies of swanking synonyms are formed. What in the past was regularly called a 'line' ('What's his line?', 'What line of business/of research are you in?') became a 'field' (as in 'field of enquiry'), which then developed into an 'area' ('area of postgraduate study'), which finally burgeoned into a 'dimension' ('current work in the area of computerized texts, a whole new dimension of applied linguistics'). In another sense, 'line' (as in 'what line are you taking on this?') has been superannuated by 'approach' ('I'm using a developmental approach/an audio-visual approach/ a child-centred approach'). Other groupings link 'pattern', 'structure', and 'framework'; 'attitude', 'perception', and 'response'; 'position', 'stance', and 'posture'. The striving is for a kind of theatrical power, not for precision. 'Thrust', for example, in the phrase 'thrust of an argument', supersedes 'tendency' and 'gist', weakling words with no muscular pre-tensions. In their book *The Elements of Style*, William Strunk and E. B. White appropriately describe 'thrust' as 'this showy noun, suggestive of power, hinting of sex'.[2]

(IX)
WORD FORMATION

The general lexicon of jargon is formed and expanded in some readily discernible ways. One is for words to be derived by the addition of a suffix or a prefix, either to a mode word – thus one mode word gives rise to another – or to some word as yet unblemished by the symptoms of jargon. Thus 'problem' (a very common mode word, a veritable Euromode), extends to 'problematize'; 'entry' yields 'entryism', 'active' is the base for 'proactive', 'select' for 'de-select', and 'benefit' for 'disbenefit'. This use of affixes is, of course, not peculiar to the formations we perceive and deplore as jargon; it is reflected in the general growth of English vocabulary, even in the literary vocabulary which supposedly represents jargon-free English. If there are specific symptoms of jargoning they are to be found in the almost manic recurrence of certain word-forming elements, and the absence, very often, of real semantic necessity for the words they form. Some learned affixes appear to have taken command of the current dictionary: '-ate', '-ation', '-ative', 'auto-', 'de-', 'dis-', '-ism', '-ist', '-ive', '-ize', 'para-', 'pre-', and 'pro-'. They help to form squadrons of new words, sometimes beyond all need of invention. Do we really need 'autocondimentation', meaning 'seasoning your own food'? Do our contemporary neuroses require 'autochondriac', signifying one who frets about the state of his car? Oh, give a mark or two for clever frivolity. There ought, after all, to be a little happiness in the dictionary; but what serious need is served by 'proactive', purporting to mean 'active in anticipation of the need for action', 'stimulated to activity?' (Strictly speaking, 'proactive' should be an antonym of 'retroactive'.) Affixing, however, has become a creative principle of jargoning, and affixes are continually being pressed into new or extended service – for instance, 'hyper-', 'mega-', 'macro-', 'micro-', and 'tele-'. The word-forming elements '-led' and '-driven' illustrate shifts of fashion in jargon. The affix '-led', as in 'export-led', 'consumer-led', is the older usage, which is now showing some signs of being overtaken by '-driven', as in 'market-driven', 'savings-driven'. Another recent phenomenon is the rise of 'Euro' as a prefix, in, for instance, 'Eurocrat', 'Eurosceptic', 'Eurofanatic' (abbreviated to 'Eurofan'), 'Eurobooze', 'Eurobabble', 'Eurobore', 'Europhobia', 'Europhoria'. This is a word game in which skittish Eurohacks (or 'journos') have been remarkably proactive.

Jargon of any kind is highly productive of compound words. Orthographically, they take various forms: either of the undivided word, or, more frequently, of the word divided by a hyphen, or, more frequently still, of the phrasal compound, two (or more) words read as a compound but not hyphenated. Thus we have 'bagstuffer' (in sales language, a small promotional item, a 'freebie'), 'baby-boomer' (demographic jargon, meaning someone born between the years 1945 and 1952), and 'loss leader' – in marketing, a product sold at a loss, to encourage subsequent purchases; sometimes erroneously represented as 'lost leader', to the bafflement of Browning scholars. The formative principle for phrasal compounds in jargon is simple: a noun is premodified (preceded) by a noun, which in turn may be preceded by another noun. Wherever possible, stack up your premodifying nouns; do not write 'study of feasibility' when a flexible grammar offers you 'feasibility study'. This may not be an invariable principle, but it is an important one. My dictionary defines 'shoe' as 'one of a pair of matching coverings shaped to fit the foot', but a metaphrase, couched in the Jargon of Pretension, would read 'a pedal extremity protection device'. Or again, to take a *valid* example ('valid' is the mode word to be used when 'authentic' palls), the so-called Gulf War of 1990–1 produced the expression 'human remains pouch', metaphrasing 'body bag', in crude archaic English called a 'shroud'. The example recalls Orwell's observations on the repellent euphemism of some of the phrases used by politicians and generals.

Another kind of compound is the hyphenated phrasal epithet. Shakespeare has given us, most memorably, 'the world-without-end hour'. We have responded with the once-in-a-lifetime opportunity, with the easy-to-assemble cocktail cabinet, with do-it-yourself bathroom tiling, and with the learn-while-you-sleep language course. That kind of construction is most commonly characteristic of the language of advertising, which does not mean that it is denied to jargonists in other domains. One of the most frequent phrasal epithets in current use is 'state of the art' (with or without hyphens), a description applicable to missile systems or astronomical telescopes as well as to CD players and vacuum cleaners.

These methods of word-building and phrase-making are major formal resources for the jargonist, but the vocabulary of jargon can be developed in other ways. Acronymy is rife in all the species of modern shop talk. In general usage, it has given us 'yuppie' (from '*y*oung *u*rban *p*rofessional'), and, fairly recently, 'lombard', meaning 'a young man with more money than sense' (the underlying legend is '*l*oads *o*f *m*oney, *b*ut *a* *r*ight *d*ickhead'). Portmanteau forms occur frequently, e.g. 'boomflation' (inflation caused by high spending), 'whanny' ('*w*e *h*ave a n*anny*'), 'mockney' ('mock cockney', a middle-class resident of London's East End), 'dockney' (a mock cockney with a smart apartment in the Docklands), 'affluenza' ('affluent' + 'influenza', an ailment seemingly confined to the well-to-do). There is also much use of sportive mimicry, re-modelling, punning and abbreviation: 'alcoholic' provides the model not only for 'workaholic', but also for 'chocoholic', 'milkaholic', 'creamaholic', even 'clothesaholic' and 'shopaholic'; 'filofax' (= 'file of facts', a.k.a. 'personal organizer') prompts 'filofiction', fiction designed to be fitted chapter by chapter into one's filofax. 'Agitpop', popular music engaged in a political cause, makes playful reference to 'agitprop', a portmanteau of 'agitation' and 'propaganda', and incidentally a sample of jargon long past its 'sell-by-date'. 'Numerati' and 'glitterati' are based on 'literati'; and 'bezzle' is a charming piece of shop talk created by the American economist J. K. Galbraith, to signify a state of happy entrepreneurial illusion. As long as an embezzler thrives and the embezzled are unaware of their losses, the *bezzle*, according to Galbraith, benignly rules the social roost; it disappears embarrassingly when the crime is discovered. The activities of the late Robert Maxwell provide a brilliant example of the Galbraithian bezzle.

(x)

METAPHOR AND WORD-PLAY

Ingenuity in word formation frequently makes a link between jargoning and something more closely akin to poetic invention, or at least to a touch of wit with a by-taste of poetry. Jargon would be blessed if this were the whole story of it. The ingenious coinage 'frauditor' (a portmanteau of 'fraudulent auditor') was struck by a reader of *The Times* (17 April 1988); from the same source came 'stockbroken' (gone broke on the stock market), and 'sharecropper' (a financial catastrophe, as in 'he came a sharecropper'). There is much ingenious punning and blending, here: on 'stockbroker' and 'heartbroken', on 'buying shares' and 'coming a cropper', resulting in a new and entirely separate significance for an already existent word, a 'sharecropper' in the standard sense being a tenant farmer whose landlord receives as rent a share of the crop. If such inventions, worthy of a Carroll or a Joyce, were to become characteristic of routine shop talk, we should indeed be fortunate. Jargon is by nature anonymous, unattributed, a collective product, though now and then a word might suggest the activity of some creative individual. 'Double-hatting' is such a word, based on the phrase 'to wear two hats', meaning to function in two officially distinct capacities. The originator of 'double-hatting' may possibly be a British politician, Mr Tom King, who was reported as saying, on the subject of defence cuts and the formation of a 'strategic reserve': 'Well, there is going to be quite a lot of double-hatting here, possibly even quadruple-hatting' (see the *Spectator*, 4 August 1990).

Jargoning necessarily involves some use of metaphor, since as one jargon draws on another, or as we make a general usage out of a particular piece of shop talk, there is always a figurative transfer of meaning to be recognized. For example, when political commentators refer to the Lebanon as the 'epicentre' of 'disturbances' in the Middle East, they are obviously borrowing from the shop talk of the geologist. 'Epicentre' is the primary loan, but 'disturbance' then becomes an appropriate extension of the figure: like earthquakes, political tremors disturb the fabric of things. Journalists, the usual practitioners of this kind of jargon, are unluckily prone to figurative fuzziness and mixed metaphor. Take two examples from the same issue of a Sunday newspaper:

Saddam's will be the signature on a quantum leap of violence in Europe . . .

The military is only an arm of the economic squeeze implemented by the UN, not the alternative to it. (*Observer*)

A 'quantum leap', a dictionary will tell us, is 'a sudden jump of an electron, atom, etc., from one energy level to another' (Collins). This certainly lends itself to the development of the sense apparently intended by the journalist – except that his quantum leap bears, or requires, a *signature*. The meaning appears to be that Saddam will be responsible for a sudden increase of violence in Europe. Then there is the matter of the 'economic squeeze' – squeezing being a degree of compulsion between pinching and strangling – which is 'implemented' (a modish slot-filling verb, meaning 'put into effect', 'carried out', or simply 'done'). This pompous phrasing becomes downright ludicrous with the presentation of the 'military' as 'an arm of the squeeze'. The metaphor is presumably echoic of the traditional representation of the policeman as 'the arm of the law', but figurative propriety has gone cruelly adrift here.

(XI)
PACKAGE PHRASES AND HANDY ADJUNCTS

In jargoning, figurative propriety often goes adrift (we commonly speak of mixed metaphor); even more often, the figure of speech settles down to sleep in some routine form of words which is used without any of that feeling of exhilaration that ought to accompany the living metaphor. The result is the catch-phrase – or better, the *package phrase*, which, like the mode word, makes a sturdy wrapper for fragile meanings. Typical package phrases are 'at the end of the day', 'across the board', 'light at the end of the tunnel', 'recovery is just round the corner', 'a big hill to climb', 'everything to play for', 'giving value for money', and 'in real terms' (not to be confused with 'in terms of'). Most of these are standard items in the political lexicon. One of the most common of current packages is the expression 'in place', which can be applied to policies, proposals, schemes, arrangements, provisions, regulations, machinery, facilities, or anything resembling a structure, ordinance, or plan. 'The machinery is already in place for the effective implementation of the new council charge proposals' means 'We have already made arrangements for collecting the new council charge'. 'Adequate provisions are not at present in place for British entry into the ERM' means 'We are not ready to play this game just yet'.

Occasionally a public figure will say something striking enough for journalists to record or for the public at large to seize upon – for example,

George Bush's 'where's the beef?' (an advertising slogan borrowed by Bush and used with insistent satirical reference to his opponents' political policies); or the remark attributed to Margaret Thatcher, that 'there is no such thing as a free lunch' – meaning that everything has to be paid for; or the celebrated reply of Mandy Rice-Davies, from the witness box, when it was put to her that a certain nobleman had denied sleeping with her – 'Well, he would, wouldn't he?' Such phrases have entered the common stock – the cliché-stock – and are brought out in response to a suitable stimulus – the discussion of a political manifesto, an argument about grants and subsidies, the reliability of someone's word. In a few years' time, there may be comparatively few people who will remember the origin of the phrase 'economical with the truth'; but the phrase itself looks like having a permanent place in the repertoire of British jargoning.[3]

Almost as useful as package phrases are package connectives, or handy adjuncts, the linking and qualifying words that get the jargonist off one hook and more or less onto another: 'in that regard', 'having said that', 'such being the case', 'as such', 'such that'. 'Liverpool were unbeatable on the day, but having said that, Portsmouth failed to take their chances' means 'Liverpool won handsomely, although Portsmouth missed several chances to score'. 'The book requires no knowledge of Sogdian, and as such will be welcome to non-linguists' means 'The book requires no knowledge of Sogdian and therefore will be welcome to non-linguists', or 'Because the book requires no knowledge of Sogdian, it will be [all the more] welcome to non-linguists'. But probably the leading product in the fasten-and-forget or link-it-'n-leave-it shop is 'in terms of': 'Are you satisfied with your team's performance in terms of your position in the league?' ('Do you think you ought to be so near the bottom of the table?'); 'What will your policies mean in terms of the housewife's shopping basket?' ('If we elect you, how much is a loaf of bread going to cost?'). I recall, from several years ago, a TV interviewer saying to the owner of a spectacular greyhound, 'You were worried about him in terms of his health'. That eludes the grasp of common phraseology and almost rises into literature. Shall I compare thee to a summer's day, in terms of temperature? Death, where is thy sting, in terms of worms?

4

Building the Repertoire

THE DUBIOUS POWER OF ALLUSION

Journalistic jargon makes occasional use of literary or other cultural references, invoking them as a kind of sanctioning lore, or a benchmark of respectability. Curiously enough, in the broadsheet press it is the sports reporters and sub-editors who often appear to be the wide readers, or at least to be close students of *Brewer's Dictionary of Phrase and Fable*. Some allusions are worked and re-worked into the muddy texture of cliché, the dreariest of recent examples being, beyond a doubt, 'winter of discontent', a quotation from the opening lines of *Richard III*:

> Now is the winter of our discontent
> Made glorious summer by this sun of York.

The point of Richard's words is, of course, that discontent is like a winter, not that it was winter and he was discontented, a conclusion to which Fleet Street has all too eagerly leapt. The phrase 'winter of discontent' was grimly misapplied in the sense 'winter when everyone is unhappy' during some long dark months of 1978–9, when industrial disputes and strikes constantly threatened the economic and social well-being of Britain. It is now lodged in the socio-political lexicon, along with older samples of habitually misapplied quotation, such as 'a sound mind in a healthy body', and 'who will guard the guardians?',[4] and is produced whenever a stock-market tremor or a rumour of industrial recession brings on a fit of speculative gloom. Strange to say, a recovery in the market, a fall in interest rates, an improvement in labour relationships, an adroit Budget performance by the Chancellor of the Exchequer, is never hailed as 'glorious summer', although during Mr Nigel Lawson's Chancellorship one national newspaper (*Daily Telegraph*, 27 August 1988) did carry a headline reading 'Hot and cold summer of Lawsonomics'.

Another Shakespearean phrase in current favour with commentators is 'sea change'. The source is the song in *The Tempest*, in which the invisible Ariel tells Prince Ferdinand:

> Full fathom five thy father lies;
>   Of his bones are coral made:
> Those are pearls that were his eyes:
>   Nothing of him that doth fade,
> But doth suffer a sea-change
> Into something rich and strange.
> Sea-nymphs hourly ring his knell:
>   [*ding-dong*]
> Hark! now I hear them – ding-dong, bell.

It would be interesting to know exactly when the phrase 'sea change' was first taken up into British journalese as a kind of emphatic, with the meaning of 'extensive change', or even 'complete reversal'. 'Sea change', it appears, is related to simple 'change' as 'proactive' is related to 'active'. Political policies, for example, undergo a sea change, or there is a sea change in public attitudes. That Shakespeare is poetically describing a process of transmutation is obvious; but it is a gradual, all-consuming process, the work of the sea which turns mortal remains into 'something rich and strange' – something of another kind and category altogether. 'Sea-change' in the Shakespearean text is a hauntingly mysterious word; in journalistic usage, with the banal sense of 'turnabout', it undergoes its own sad transformation into auto-speak, the dialect of the undead, available on any news-stand, price 40p.

Some allusions are happy, particularly those that serve to augment and illuminate a field of shop talk. An old example in linguistic shop talk is 'portmanteau', meaning a blend-word like 'laundromat', or 'talkathon'. Or 'shambolic' – which, however, has suffered its own sea change. In the 1950s it passed current, at least in academic circles, as a portmanteau of 'sham' and 'symbolic', and was an emphatically dismissive epithet for some pretentious works of art or literature; it is now understood as a combination of 'shambles' and the pseudo-suffix '-olic', meaning 'utterly disorganized', 'in a state of total confusion'. The original reference of 'portmanteau' – as everyone must surely know – is to the scene in *Through the Looking-Glass* when Humpty-Dumpty provides, for Alice's benefit, an exegetical commentary on the poem 'Jabberwocky'. Alice questions him about the meaning of several strange words, among them *slithy*. 'Well,' says Humpty-Dumpty, ' "*slithy*" means "lithe and slimy". "Lithe" is the same as "active". You see it's like a portmanteau – two meanings packed up into one word.' Carroll could not have known that he was providing a useful addition to the lexicon of modern linguistics; we have to thank our scholars for going to such a playful source, and not, for once, ransacking the Graeco-Latin lexicon in search of an appropriately learned term.

A rather more recent example of creative shop talk – an instance of literature in the service of science – is the word 'quark', adopted by the American scientist Murray Gell-Mann as a term for a fundamental particle in atomic structure. Sub-atomic particles, Mann proposed, were combinations of three fundamental particles, or *quarks*. The word came from a fairly unlikely source, Joyce's *Finnegans Wake*; there is a passage in which the dreamer, H. C. Earwhicker, hears the curate (barman) in a Dublin pub shouting *Three quarks for Muster Mark*. Gell-Mann's recollection of words from a fictional dream gave him the memorable term he was looking for. The three types of quark he called 'flavours': they were the 'up quark', the 'down quark', and the 'strange quark'. Subsequently, other scientists have found other quarks, even stranger than those spilling out of Muster Mark's tankard. Joyce, were he alive, might not be wholly displeased to think that his monumental compilation of surreal language had served as a source for physicists seeking a jargon for their own kind of surrealism. I would not expect, however, that the language of *Finnegans Wake* will ever see much service as a source-jargon; that is a function more appropriate to some general fields of shop talk and professional usage – to the language of soldiers and seafarers, to business, to the theatre, to the vocabulary of manual trades, and above all to the muscular, masculine business of sport in all its forms.

(XIII)

ON OWN GOALS AND SHOOTING YOURSELF IN THE FOOT

'*A soldier boy without a heart*' sang the man in the musical '*has two strikes on him from the start*' – his own cardiac installation having been left, we gathered, at the stage-door canteen with a girl named Eileen. (Hardly anyone below the age of 65, going on 72, will remember this event.) In the 1940s, few filmgoers in Britain had any idea what it meant to have two strikes on you; but this did not prevent lugubrious British conscripts in their barracks and hutments from wailing the sad message while they shaved their chins and buffed up their boots. For my own part, I always misheard *strikes* as *stripes*, assuming the burden of the argument to be that a soldier without a heart was immediately eligible for the rank of corporal – a not unreasonable interpretation, under the circumstances. I learned better, as we all did when we became more familiar with the rules and terminology of baseball, and although I have yet to go to a stadium and watch a game in all the instant glory of hotdogs and catcalls, I have been known to use expressions like 'getting to first base', 'throwing a curve', and 'out of left field', for all the world as though I knew my way round Candlestick Park, or could be heard routinely rooting for the Red Sox at the bottom of the ninth with the scores tied. What is more I am fairly certain, not only of what I am talking about, but also – a more important assurance – of how to use what I am talking about to talk about other things. I know, for example, that you get to first base (or do not) with a lovely woman, or a plea, or a sales pitch. This idiomatic familiarity, divorced from the originating substance of the idiom, is, I suppose, a result of American cultural dominance, which sends language off on one-way errands. The inhabitants of New Jersey and Pasadena seemingly do not import British words and phrases. I have not noticed in American speech any disposition to use cricketing talk like 'being on a sticky wicket', or 'playing a straight bat', much less 'sending down a yorker', or 'coming in from deep fine leg'. Americans are never clean bowled, seldom stumped, and do not make last-wicket stands. They sometimes strike out, which is bad, and have been known to do it when the bases are loaded, which is worse. At all events, they do things differently, and their sporting jargon tells us to listen and do likewise.

(XIV)
TALKING SPORT ISN'T JUST A GAME

Most Britons over the age of 60 – not yet to be described with complete accuracy as 'wrinklies' or 'crumblies', but people most certainly in the late afternoon or tea-interval of experience – have been to some extent educated by Hollywood, and through films have acquired the shop talk of American sports and pastimes. Our understanding of these exotic expressions may be a little vague, but in our youth we learned at least to grasp their general intention. When the pin-striped, wide-brimmed gangster, pale with fury beneath his five o'clock shadow, snarled 'Lissn, wise guy, *I* call the plays, OK? Ya get me? Yunnerstand English, or do I gotta draw it for ya?' we understood that 'calling the plays' had something to do with giving the orders that prescribed a course of action. And when the victim of some social mischance, the patsy, stooge, or fall guy in some nefarious venture, complained of having 'wound up behind the eight ball', we knew just where he was. (Usually in jail, with no apparent chance of getting out; 'snookered', as the British might say, or as my father, an old-fashioned card-player, would have put it, 'euchred'.) These people were talking sport, but it was hardly a game. It was a horse from a whole new ballpark.

The jargon of sport, whether American or British, has the peculiar property of acquiring serious credentials in non-sporting applications. Its occurrences in general discourse seldom signal the intention 'I am speaking in fun'; rather, they announce 'I am speaking in earnest, and with emphasis'. Take, for example, two expressions now so well established in the common tongue that we hardly recall their origins in sporting shop talk: 'to take something in one's stride' and 'to give someone his head'. (The latter may become an endangered, or contaminated expression, since the phrase 'giving head' has other, much less respectable connotations.) They are both derived from the language of riding and the race-course, and both are regularly, indeed predominantly used to express notions that have no more than a tenuous figurative connection with steeplechasing. We might say, for instance, 'Just give the youngster his head and you'll see, he'll take all these fences in his stride', in which case the likelihood of the youngster being a thoroughbred steeplechaser would be small, and the probability of his being a gifted but wayward young fellow with a number of problems in prospect would be quite high. Furthermore, the idiom would present the message with appropriately serious emphasis. 'Let the lad do things in his own way and he'll get over all these problems' commits itself to an opinion much less emphatically than 'Just give the youngster his head and he'll take all these fences in his stride'. There is often in jargon a voucher of emphasis, comparable to that offered by metaphor and slang.

Sporting jargon issues its 'vouchers of emphasis' to the language of personal relationships, of controversy, of competitive endeavour, of social interaction and negotiation in all its forms; and different sports characteristically promote different images of discourse. The language of boxing, for example, allows us to conceive of worldly affairs as conflict, but as conflict between evenly matched opponents, fighting under rules. In our general dealings with others, to act in a way not provided for in the rules of procedure or in the unwritten convention is to invite the accusation of 'hitting below the belt' or striking 'a low blow', or (in American usage) taking 'a cheap shot'. When both parties abandon the rules, 'the gloves are off'. The rule-bound conflict is read as developing in phases, or 'rounds'; the first round in an electoral fight may go to the Big-Endians, but at length the Little-Endians may 'win by a knock-out', or 'strike a knock-out blow', or at the very least inflict a 'body blow'. To be rescued from a critical situation by the closure of the period allotted to the contest is to be 'saved by the bell'. Arguing without taking the defensive precaution of 'keeping one's guard up' may be called 'leading with one's chin'. Replying effectively to assertive or accusatory argument is 'counterpunching', and a debater or conversational wit who specializes in the retort or annihilating follow-up is a 'counterpuncher'. An experienced, well-informed, or otherwise formidable contestant is a 'heavyweight'; if less well-equipped to compete in serious affairs, a 'lightweight'. In many ways the terminology of boxing assumes the figurative character once supplied by the language and imagery of fencing (e.g. the 'cut and thrust of debate', 'striking home', 'parrying') in representing the exchanges of vigorous argument. It is, of course, not the only way of talking about altercation of any kind, but it is at least an element in the jargoning repertoire that can be frequently observed in the pages of the daily press.

Cricket, the prime example of sport as morality, requiring strict observation of rules in letter and spirit – whence the condemnatory judgement 'it's not cricket' – provides a strain of language generally devoted to notions of stubborn defensiveness ('stonewalling'), or patient, self-denying collaboration ('keeping your end up'), or long experience ('a good innings'), or humorous cunning ('yorker', 'googly', 'chinaman'), or occasional bafflement ('stumped'), and only in a few instances of vainglorious triumph ('knocked for six'; a notable example of this expression in figurative usage was General Montgomery's prediction, during his victorious North African campaign in 1942–3, that the British 8th Army would 'knock the enemy for six out of Africa'). If boxing jargon offers metaphors of competition and debate, the language of cricket projects a kind of noble defensiveness, flawless self-possession, an unselfish allegiance of the individual talent to the collective identity of the team. This perception of the moral values of cricket persists, even though the modern game is often played in a rather different spirit. In the British public school culture that developed during the nineteenth century, cricket above all other pastimes embodied the thesis that games were good for the character – a proposition assiduously sustained by characters who were good at games. This is the thesis that embarrassingly informs one of the most celebrated of all cricketing poems, Sir Henry Newbolt's '*Vitai Lampada*':

> There's a breathless hush in the Close to-night
>> Ten to make and the match to win –
> A bumping pitch and a blinding light,
>> An hour to play and the last man in.
> And it's not for the sake of a ribboned coat,
>> Or the selfish hope of a season's fame,
> But his Captain's hand on his shoulder smote –
>> 'Play up! play up! and play the game!'

The grammar of the last four lines is a little odd, but no matter; they present the moral *motif* of the poem, 'play up! and play the game!'. The recital goes on to place the anonymous young hero as a subaltern in a foreign field, engaged in desperate battle against barbarian hordes, fighting for his side though all seems lost:

> The sand of the desert is sodden red, –
>> Red with the wreck of a square that broke; –
> The Gatling's jammed and the Colonel dead,
>> And the regiment blind with dust and smoke,
> The river of death has brimmed his banks,
>> And England's far, and Honour a name,
> But the voice of a schoolboy rallies the ranks:
>> 'Play up! play up! and play the game!'

Newbolt's poem enjoyed a very long season of popularity, as an anthology piece and as verse for memorizing and reciting; and no one appears to have questioned the propriety of the analogy it proposes – that fighting the Mahdists or the Fuzzy-Wuzzies is a 'game', just like a school cricket match. (The 'broken square', we presume, being somewhat like a disastrous collapse of the middle-order batsmen.) But are we allowed to ask what 'play up! and play the game!' really signifies? No doubt it suggests 'do your best', 'try to win', or even 'go down fighting', but these are things that hardly need to be said to anyone in the desperate situation evoked by the poem. It is hardly plausible that the 'schoolboy' would rally the 'ranks' with an exhortation to 'play the game' ('come along, you chaps, no slacking!'); and even if that were so, it is more than likely that the hard-pressed rankers would receive the message with pardonably foul-mouthed bewilderment. In a context such as this, 'play the game' is an absurdity, we might think, a meaningless phrase. And yet in the sense Newbolt intended, it is packed with meaning.[5] It has what our modern sages would call *ideological implications* – as well as *epistemological presuppositions*. It means all the assumptions that inform the behaviour of a class or caste. An officer and a gentleman faces the bowling, resolutely playing forward, moving to the pitch of the ball, killing the spin – no craven flinching from the bouncers, none of your wild cowshots, getting a thick edge and giving a dolly to first slip, or worse still, going for the quick single and running your captain out, just because you want to get away from that grimacing demon with the big cheek-bones. Play up!, play up! and play the game! A man's gotta do what a man's gotta do, and if 'twere done, when 'tis done 'tis commonly in the sanctifying language of sport, because sport – any sport – enshrines for its keenest practitioners a sacred significance transcending the actions on the field of play. The late Bill Shankly (known and revered throughout the civilized world as the manager of Liverpool Football Club) put the matter admirably: 'Football isn't a matter of life and death', he said. 'It's more important than that.'

(XV)
SOURCE-JARGONS: THE GAMES OF PEACE AND WAR

Managers in all guises, not least political managers, understand the tran-scendent importance of sport as the source of potent parables, strong symbols, motivating metaphors. At the beginning of the baseball season, Presidents pose on the pitcher's mound; in cricket's motherland it will be a luckless photographer who cannot find an ambitious politician willing, for the sake of a photo opportunity and a sound bite, to don pads and demonstrate an elegant on-drive. Richard Nixon, a supporter of the Washington Redskins, once sent in a 'play' which the team coach, in view of the distinction of the sender, felt obliged to use – an extraordinary piece of presidential behaviour, tantamount to having Her Majesty the Queen signify to the manager of the Arsenal football team her royal pleasure in playing a flat back four and pushing up to spring the offside trap. (Nixon's play was by all accounts a disastrous failure, resulting in a score for the opposing side; but his intentions were good, or at least well-calculated.) More recently, a debate in the House of Commons has raged round the symbolic issue of 'broken cricket bats', and a British prime minister has returned from stern negotiations at a conference of European statesfolk (Maastricht, December 1991), claiming a diplomatic victory 'game, set and match'.[6] This was perhaps a little immodest; it appeared to many that the umpire had merely called deuce. The principle, however, is clear: when the talk is political, say it in sport.

In the discussion of political and social matters, or of what are sometimes called 'questions of the day' – also known as 'issues' – sporting analogies abound. They often turn up in the introduction to a theme, where they serve like the *captatio benevolentiae* in ancient rhetoric, as a hook to catch the interest and good will of the audience. Here, for instance, is the opening of an editorial in a national newspaper:

The playing field remains level, but there is no longer any doubt about where the referee's heart lies. (*Independent*)

The 'level playing field', meaning conditions under which adversaries may fairly compete, is a current favourite in socio-political jargon; it goes along with 'moving the goalposts' (changing the supposed objective of the competition) and 'kicking into touch' (putting something beyond the bounds of argument, at least for the time being). The editorialist has characteristically extended the 'playing field' metaphor, and brought in a 'referee', a supposedly neutral arbiter. The sentence tells us, however (taken in paraphrase), that although the conditions are fair, the arbiter is biased. The sporting jargon thus has a sub-text; it says that you can hardly expect fair play when the referee is one of the players.

The 'referee' was Mr Kenneth Clarke, then Secretary of State for Health, and the 'playing field' refers to the chance offered to hospital managements to choose between so-called 'health authority control' (in effect, a direction of finances by local government officials) and 'trust status' (a system of budgeting controlled by the hospitals themselves). Mr Clarke was inclined to the latter, not surprisingly, since he more or less invented it. The newspaper editorial goes on to make his preference quite explicit:

Speaking to officials from NHS 'units' which are considering their future under the second stage of the health service reforms, Kenneth Clarke, the Secretary of State for Health, yesterday expressed his apparently confident expectation that 'trust status would become the model of choice'.

The sporting jargon of the preceding sentence has served its purpose and has been dropped; we have no more figurative extensions, with disputants perhaps 'going for the bye-line', or 'getting their crosses into the box', or 'pointing to the penalty spot'. Instead, the ground of jargon changes, and now it is Mr Clarke himself who is the jargonist, with his 'trust status would become the model of choice'. Translate: 'hospitals would prefer trust status', or more plainly 'would prefer to look after their own money'; *model* and *choice* are mode words, 'model' being derived from academic jargon in various disciplines, while 'choice' is an essential item in the vocabulary of governmental cant, going along with 'freedom' and 'the tax-payers' money'. The sporting source-jargon at the beginning of the editorial is invoked with telling, rather than lasting effect; it is used for temporary emphasis, to give an impetus that may catch the reader's fancy.

For manly emphasis, scribes and speakers will also draw on that other great source-jargon, the shop talk of armies and navies and men grimly at war. Politicians are cosily belligerent, particularly when an election is in the offing ('in the offing', as we have all conveniently forgotten, is by origin a grand old specimen of shiver-me-timbers navalese). Thus we find the Liberal Democratic Party resolutely preparing for the fray:

'When we leave conference on Thursday, it will be to go to our battle stations in the constituencies.' (Ian Wrigglesworth)

Or a Conservative, with the elate and combative resolve of some beleaguered veteran of Agincourt:

'Show me where the fight is thickest and put me there.' (Michael Heseltine)

On the very day when Mr Wrigglesworth sent Liberal troops off to dig their trenches (17 September 1990) a TV commentator mused:

'... can they turn that high moral ground into a credible battle position for the next election?'

'High moral ground' derives from the military strategist's injunction to 'take the high ground', that is, take positions from which the enemy can be overlooked and rendered powerless. In military language, 'high ground' implies a tactical advantage, and 'high' has a purely topographical sense. But in political commentator's jargon, when 'high ground' becomes 'high *moral* ground', the sense of 'high' slips into that of 'admirable', 'noble', 'lofty'. Hence the necessity for *credible* ('credible' and 'credibility' are currently important mode words). The sub-text reads: it is all very well having lofty purposes and Simon-pure professions, but being high-minded never won an election. You have to be 'credible', meaning, in this context, capable of mounting a campaign which will crush your foes and comfort your friends. It is in fact the same 'credibility' that appears in 'street cred'. You are credible if you can kick the bully in the groin; if you confine yourself to deploring his actions, you are merely moral.

Soldierly talk has become so common in political contexts that expressions like 'strategy', 'sector', 'campaign', 'front', 'flank', 'reserves', 'position', 'command' have virtually lost the power that makes for vital metaphors, and have become husk-words, automatic usages. Consider some examples, culled in January 1992, as a new season of electioneering began:

> 'We have a more disciplined campaign, and we have a better strategy.' (Des Wilson, Liberal Democrat)

> '. . . if the campaign is as late as May 7, we will be well in place.' (Jeffrey Archer, Conservative)

> 'We mustn't imagine that's the only front on which we're fighting' (i.e. the assault on the Labour party leader, Neil Kinnock). (Jeffrey Archer)

> 'You are the vanguard of the effort, and I know you can be relied upon to help secure the prize.' (Christopher Patten, Conservative)

These were all noted in the course of television broadcasts, either as direct quotations (Wilson, Archer), or as reported remarks (Patten). What was remarkable was the ease – glibness would be too harsh a word – with which the speakers appeared to take on this combative strain of vocabulary, and their readiness to use it emptily or fuzzily, simply as a type of verbal gesture appropriate to the occasion. Mr Archer *could* have said 'We mustn't imagine that's the only thing we have to do'; and if Mr Patten had given himself time to reflect on his words, it might have occurred to him that he was encouraging worthy members of Conservative Associations up and down This Great Country Of Ours to regard themselves as storm troopers or boarding parties, sweatily bent on glittering conquests.

But in political discourse, this military source-jargon, like sporting shop talk, is a provider of emphasis, or colour, rather than a variety of language that genuinely illuminates a topic with instructive analogies and interesting parallels, carefully drawn. It might be noted in passing that the Roman rhetoricians had two words denoting the function of metaphor: *lumen*, 'light' – or possibly 'eye', a way of seeing – and *color*, 'colour', 'decoration'. Jargon, you could say, brings colour but does not shed a great deal of light. Political commentary freely mingles the talk of the battlefield with other varieties of jargoning, as in the following passage:

> For all this, spending and taxation remain Labour's most vulnerable point. And the Tories know that. Hence the 35p-in-the-pound ramp with which the Government has opened the election new year. To turn that flank – as Mr Kinnock will try to do today, with a programme for economic recovery – Labour has to establish its credentials as the party of economic growth, and

hang the recession round the neck of the Government's monetary and fiscal stewardship. (*Independent*)

The centrally emphatic figure here is military – to 'turn a flank', meaning to come round the enemy's line of battle; hence an attacking manoeuvre, though Mr Kinnock's predicament, as described here, would appear to be defensive. But the strict propriety of the metaphor is neither here nor there; it is only one taste of jargon in a dish of mixed figures. To turn a flank, Labour has to 'establish its credentials' ('credential' is first cousin to *credibility*) as the party of 'economic growth'. ('Growth', 'recovery' and 'recession' are standard items of politico-economic shop talk.) Presently, however, the 'recession' is grotesquely 'hung round the neck of the Government's monetary and fiscal stewardship' (meaning 'blamed on the Government's economic policies'). Apparently the jargonist is now playing the allusion game – but alluding to what? To the millstone hung round the neck of the sinner (St Luke, 17: 2)? Or to the albatross round the Mariner's neck? Or perhaps to any burden hung round any neck, outcrop, or prominent feature conveniently stuck out for stylistic purposes? There is the further possibility that 'stewardship' is also an allusion, however distant and distorted, to another passage in St Luke (16: 1–2) describing the predicament of the unjust steward:

> ...There was a certain rich man, which had a steward; and the same was accused unto him that he had wasted his goods.
>
> And he called him, and said unto him, How is it that I hear this of thee? give an account of thy stewardship; for thou mayest be no longer steward.

What with necks and stewardships, there is much ado here to find a convincing figure. That this has happened in making the sentence that also includes 'turn that flank' by no means testifies to a daring, poetic collation of diverse images – from the battlefield to the Bible in one illuminating movement; it merely illustrates the *olla podrida* or hot-pot principle of jargoning, which allows you to toss in the ingredients as they come. This short passage has three main constituents: the shop talk ('growth', 'recovery', etc.) which one would expect to find; the dip into a source-jargon ('turn that flank') which makes the conventional representation of political conflict as a species of warfare; and the allusions, not very clearly resolved but none the less evident ('hang round the neck', 'stewardship') which sound a note of Biblical morality. Collectively, these jargoning devices supply this short text with its substance (what it is 'about'), its scenario (the image or metaphor round which it principally turns), and its seasoning (the accompanying flavour of judgement or evaluation).

(XVI)
VERSIONS AND INVERSIONS

But what do source-jargons do when they are not lending expressions to others? Consider again the language of sport, or, in the examples which follow, of sports reporting. Every sport or game, obviously, has its own shop talk, sometimes so dense as to repel all but the initiate. I am qualified by old enthusiasm to understand the language in which some sports – for example, cricket or rugby – are discussed; in other cases I am a purblind outsider and might as well be trying to decode a paper on astro-physics or trace the ramifications of the New York stock market. Here is a piece I can understand without the benefit of a primer:

> With Felton finding ample bowling that he could tuck away off his legs and Fordham revelling in the room he was given outside the off-stump, there was no margin for error. The openers raced to three figures in only 26 overs and Martin, the raw young fast bowler from Accrington, was roughly handled whenever he overpitched.
>
> Hughes gave the attack variety with his left-arm stuff, though he could do nothing more menacing than drift the ball gently in to the right-hander. He broke through when Felton played an impetuous stroke and was caught at the second attempt by De Freitas at mid-wicket. (*Observer*)

Now here is an exercise: attempt to paraphrase, translate, render or rewrite the above passage, with full explanatory glosses on 'bowling', 'fast bowler', 'off-stump', 'opener', 'over', 'overpitch', 'left-arm stuff', 'right-hander', 'mid-wicket'. In addition, try to describe the scene pictured in the expressions 'bowling that he could tuck away off his legs', 'the room he was given outside the off-stump', 'drift the ball gently in to the right-hander', and 'played an impetuous stroke'. Then study your paraphrase and commentary, and try to make sense of the mess you will certainly have made, because the original is couched in the purest, most exclusive kind of professional jargon, an idiom that borrows nothing and makes no concessions. It can only be fully understood by those who already understand.

The same might consequently be said of another report, from the same newspaper, on a different kind of athletic contest:

> Despite a four carved from the sand at the long third, Nick Faldo was out in a calamitous 40. A mere yard off the fairway at the fourth, he could only hack out from the clinging Bermuda rough, three putts adding up to a six. Much the same happened at the par-five sixth for another six.
>
> Then, at the seventh, he was bunkered, his recovery cannoning obliquely off an overhanging branch into the trees. Another bogey and the prelude to three putts at the par-three eighth. The course had got to him and a macabre triple bogey at the tenth opened the homeward half for the golfer even the Americans have been hailing as the best in the world.

This invites similar treatment. What is a 'third', and why is it 'long'? Who, or what, is 'the Bermuda rough'? Are 'bogeys' macabre only if they are 'triple'? If Faldo was 'out', where was he? How could the course have 'got to him' – surely he had already got to the course? What is a 'par-five sixth', and where are you when you are 'bunkered'? If you cannot answer, give up. The talk is of golf, and golf has its secrets which only golfers know. A little further on in the same report, however, comes this:

> The inconsistency of the greens has been arousing sentiments akin to those of a batsman who does not know whether he is about to receive a bouncer or a shooter. A basket-ball hop with one shot, a plugged dart with the next. Even the determinedly patient figure that Faldo cuts in a major championship found it too much, confessing to losing his rag.

To understand this we need no longer be golfers (though it helps); what we do need is some acquaintance with cricket, basketball, and darts. The 'inconsistency of the greens' cannot be conveyed (it seems) in the idiom proper to golf, or even in general terms; the talk and common notions of other sports must be called upon, and thus the languages of cricket, etc., become source-jargons temporarily supplementing the dialect of the golfer.

From the same newspaper comes this further example, in which the writer's jargoning draws consistently on a non-sporting source:

> It is only fair to mention that Olver had a good tour and that Ryan also survived his initiation. It is also true to point out that, by and large, the forwards paid their way but the backs were rarely solvent. Half a dozen were in credit at the end – including Carling, Oti and Heslop – but the creditors were outnumbered by the debtors as English back play came close to bankruptcy. That does not mean England are heading for a recession.

The sport is rugby, but the idiom, consciously cultivated by the writer, is the general shop talk of finance. Do source-jargons find sources in other jargons? The answer suggested by this passage is, yes. Here the task of assessing the performances of a team of rugby players is not entrusted to the language customarily used by coaches and managers, but to the currently fashionable idiom of commerce. At a time when the phrase 'value for money' has so much prominence in public debate, it is almost a matter of stylistic orthodoxy to have the grunting ogres of the pack 'paying their way' rather than 'giving out for the full eighty minutes', and nimble backs being 'in credit', as opposed to 'deserving full marks for one-hundred-and-ten per cent effort'.

Jargons of Profession all tend to borrow and innovate, though some borrow more than others. What is borrowed may be shop talk, or it may be something rather less specific than shop talk; it may be something in the general way of slang, or a cliché, or a well-travelled metaphor, or some phrase which happens to be in current fashion. The consequence of rubbing two tired phrases together is nearly always to awaken and enliven the sense of jargoning. Here is a short extract from an article on the apprehensions of the business community:

> The only thing we can be sure of in the year ahead is that uncertainty abounds. But that in itself is an important piece of information with predictable consequences. Corporate decision makers, already anxious, are likely to respond by battening down the hatches and preparing for stormy weather. (*Independent*)

It would seem that sailor-language is the illuminating source-jargon on which the final sentence of this piece of commercial prophecy draws. But is it after all so illuminating? This is one of those instances in which a figurative source matters rather less than a handy cliché. 'Batten down the hatches' has been pattering around in general usage for quite a long time (like 'leeway', 'on a different tack', etc.), and has weathered into folk-metaphor or package-phraseology; if you batten down the hatches you are of course preparing for 'stormy weather', be it in the form of typhoons, revolutions, domestic disputes, high interest rates, a downturn in growth, or a shortage in the oil supply. Thus, of the two pieces of jargon perceivable in this sentence, one – 'corporate decision makers' – is a clear instance of current commercial shop talk; the other, 'batten down the hatches', is faded shop talk that has become a stock idiom. The purport of this plug-in phrase is purely emphatic, stressing the energetic activity of the decision makers and the enormity of the crisis they face. The writer does not tell us that 'corporate decision makers will do all they can to prepare for serious troubles in the year ahead'; he may mean simply that, but jargoning gives his meaning a bolder and more lurid colour.

Professional jargons vary in their readiness to borrow or innovate from other sources. The impression given by current commercial jargon, for example, is that to some extent it feeds on its own substance, creating a lexicon of the market definable only by reference to the marketeer's lexicon. Outsiders are left to struggle with their ignorance, which their understanding of the world at large will not dispel; the financial sections of the daily press are dense with expressions not readily illuminated from another source. Political jargon, by contrast – or, to insist for once on the distinction, political *jargoning* – is a prolific borrower. Politics has its own professional jargon, seen in the language of parliamentary life; we talk of 'divisions', of 'votes of no confidence', of 'guillotines', of 'ayes and noes', of 'early-day motions' ('laid before the House'), of 'going to the country', of 'three-line whips', and so on, but one interesting fact about this quite rich vein of shop talk is that it is rarely if ever worked by other people for other purposes. The jargon of political practice offers little scope as a source-jargon. On the other hand, when politicians come out of their parliamentary workshop and begin to address each other and the general public, with the intent to persuade, to rebut, to bombard and bamboozle – in short, when they assume a style of address, a *jargoning* – then they are your only clothes-stealers and bower-birds, ready to rifle any resource, take up anyone's line of talk. They become salesmen of a sort, and political rhetoric begins to resemble a Jargon of Production; but that brings in another topic.

5

Jargons of Production

A long time ago, when a used car was only a used car and not a serious commercial enterprise, I would regularly scan the small ad columns of my local evening paper, in the hope of finding a bargain in the Vehicles section. The vendors (local garages and agencies) offered their second-hand wares in a language confined to a few short but pregnantly significant phrases: 'a specimen'; 'a snip'; 'a good runner'; 'must be seen'; 'full service record'; 'a host of extras'; 'needs some attention'; 'one careful lady owner'; 'very clean'. Decoding these phrases was an important matter for any would-be purchaser with a healthy respect for the old principle of *caveat emptor*. A shopper's guide to the lingo might have read like this:

specimen, a: a very large, very, very shiny, long-nosed motor car with leather seats.

must be seen: a fairly large, shiny car with a host of extras; alt., a rather peculiar foreign model that you might hesitate to buy because of the rumours you have heard.

host of extras: (usu. in conn. with must be seen), A sun-roof, stereo speakers, badge bar, and a horn that plays the opening strains of 'Dixie'.

one careful lady owner: boringly sedate and reliable; unscratched, over-hoovered, taken through the car-wash once a week; called Belinda.

full service record: (in conn. with the prec.), garage bills inadvertently left in the glove compartment by the careful lady owner.

snip, a: a vehicle priced at £50–£100 below the sum the vendor originally thought of, because the reading on the mileometer is suspect, because the alternator is *in articulo mortis* (called, in the trade, 'dead dodgy') and because he needs to get this car off his forecourt in order to make room for a **specimen.**

good runner, a: a vehicle which has not had the benefit of **one careful lady owner.** It will do you no credit at the Country Club, but will trundle you round the houses well enough. Sometimes abbreviated to **a runner,** in which case it may not be good enough to trundle you all the way round *all* the houses, because it **needs some attention.**

needs some attention: (usu. in conn. with **runner**), needs a new gearbox, clutch, offside rear wing panel, windscreen wiper motor, doorlock and window crank on driver's side; otherwise, in A1 condition.

very clean: a specialist's motor; once a **runner,** now well past the stage of **needing some attention;** bodywork a miracle of rust and filler-paste; rear seats long since removed, by medical students, to create a spacious, estate-type loading platform/sleeping berth; overheats at traffic intersections; balks at second gear, sticks in third, but can be got directly into fourth with sympathetic handling; suitable for ambitious paupers and younger sons.

The decodings here are perhaps a little playful, in the fond light of memory; but the words and phrases they gloss were in regular and attestable use. Collectively, they amounted to a sales jargon, systematically used by our local car-dealers, and well understood by knowledgeable readers shopping around for a personal vehicle ('must be seen'), or maybe a runabout for the wife ('one careful lady owner'), or perhaps a set of wheels to keep young Jacky quiet ('a good runner'). This neighbourhood code was one of the many varieties of sales talk that make up Jargons of Production. Such jargons create styles of talking about a product – be it an automobile or a bottle of wine or a package holiday – and of presenting it to potential consumers in ways intended to control their responses.

The main features of a Jargon of Production are (a) an *encoding*, or naming of the product, (b) a device of *involving* the consumer through some form of direct personal appeal, and (c) a way of *appraising* the product through language that goes beyond the call of strictly descriptive necessity. Encoding can be quite plain (e.g. 'vanilla ice cream'), but is much more likely to be twopence coloured and periphrastic (e.g. 'Angel's Dream Coupe'). The commonest way of involving the potential customer is to draw him or her into the treacherous tangle of 'you' and 'we', 'your' and 'our'; but there are other ways – for instance by specifying a social grouping or civil status ('Fun and games for *all the family*'; '*Senior citizens* will love our romantic Golden Twilight Ballroom Evenings'). The usual instrument of appraisal is the hyperbolic or supersensuous adjective ('unbeatable', 'fantastic', 'melting', 'downy', 'luxurious'), though the adjectives are often supported by suitable nouns ('romantic seclusion', 'succulent relish'), and verbs also play some part in promoting illusions of Sardanapalian excess ('You'll *thrill* to the rhythm of Joe Tonks and his Moonlight Samba Band'; 'High speed lifts *whirl* you aloft to our intimate Nightowl Bar on the twenty-second floor').

One of the jargons we all know well is hotel language – the brochure-talk that enthusiastically commends the Fine Old Coaching Inn (log fires, arch serving-men in Sam Weller waistcoats, frantic hammering in the water-pipes, distressed Americans, murky little bedrooms over the kitchen area) or the Hacienda Style Motor Home (clean towels, all smiles, Spanish decor, snooker, derelict swimming-pool). Which of us has not, at some time or other, reading some pamphlet or other, been cajoled with something – or other – like this?:

> '*You'll enjoy mouth-watering roasts from our friendly Carvery*'

Or this?:

> '*Relax in the elegant tranquillity of our Foxhunter Lounge*'

One of these might refer to the nightly appearance of a little grinning fellow who dresses up like a chef and serves out portions of reasonably palatable if slightly lukewarm meat; the other might conceal the identity of a morose and fusty chamber with little to offer by way of entertainment and relaxation beyond a large oil painting of an ugly horse and some superannuated and coffee-stained numbers of *Country Life*. Each, however, is true to the principles of the jargon – never mind how disgruntled customers, cynical from long experience, might choose to interpret them. Each *encodes*, with a name – 'Carvery', 'Foxhunter Lounge'; each *involves*, whether with pronouns ('you', 'our') or with the imaginary imperative, the on-the-spot directive to the person who is not yet on the spot ('relax'), or, indeed, with the future tense that might be called the 'promissory and commanding future' ('you *will*'); and each *appraises*, with words that tell customers how to feel their way towards feeling good ('mouth-watering', 'friendly', 'elegant', 'tranquillity').

(XVIII)
THE RIGHT PACKAGE FOR THE RIGHT PRODUCT

These are primary characteristics of the jargon, but they are not equally apparent in every specimen of sales talk. There are horses for courses – as the sporting source-jargon puts it – or, shall we say, packages for products. The right package for promoting a cruise liner includes quite a lot of appraising, some involving, and just a little encoding:

> The moment you step aboard the 'Noordam', you'll sense that you are in a very special place.
> Undeniably so. For she and her sister ship, the MS Nieuw Amsterdam, are easily today's best samples of what luxury liners used to be like.
> For here is a ship conceived and built within the context of a unique

seafaring tradition. A tradition which has its roots in the heroic saga of the bold Dutch explorers – and reflects the timeless standards of cruising's golden age.

Touches of class are everywhere. In the polished railings and extravagant teak decks. In the grand arrangements of fresh-cut flowers that adorn the lobby, lounges, and restaurants. And in a million dollar art collection casually presented as part of the living environment.

Room after elegant room invite you to days of lighthearted diversion. From elegant restaurants like the Amsterdam Dining Room to the casual atmosphere of the Lido, where you may dine indoors or out. From inviting settings like the Explorer's Lounge, the perfect place for after-dinner espresso and chamber music – to the high-energy Horn Pipe Club, where the action goes on till the wee hours. (*Holland-America Line Brochure*)

This is larger in scope than the promotion of the Carvery or the Foxhunter Lounge, but the method is much the same. The encodings come in the final paragraph, where the reader is invited to imagine sub-texts colourfully appropriate to 'The Amsterdam Dining Room', the 'Lido', the 'Explorer's Lounge', and the 'high-energy Horn Pipe Club'. In a few places the reader is involved – as 'you' – in a tour of the vessel: 'you step aboard', 'you are in a very special place', 'room after elegant room invite [*sic*] you', 'you may dine indoors or out'. The predominant feature, however, is the vocabulary of appraisal. The place is 'special', the ship represents a 'unique seafaring tradition' rooted in a 'heroic saga' and culminating in the 'timeless standards' of a 'golden age'. The decks, being made of teak, are 'extravagant', the railings are 'polished' (not like the rotting boards and rusting stanchions of less well-conceived vessels); the rooms and restaurants are 'elegant', the settings in general are 'inviting'. Some of these appraising epithets might be moved around or cross-matched; the settings could be elegant, the restaurants inviting, the tradition timeless, the flower arrangements extravagant. It is less important to make the description appropriate to the noun than to find an expression generally applicable to the package.

The text has its moments of jargon-in-general, that is, of devices that could occur in almost any jargoning style. There are familiar turns of well-worn phrase – 'the living environment', 'touch of class' – but the most notable instance of general jargon is the first sentence of the second paragraph: 'For here is a ship conceived and built within the context of a unique seafaring tradition'. 'Context' is a mode word (first cousin to 'area'), and 'within the context of' is a modish phrase (stable-mate to 'within the parameters of'). But the most striking usage is 'conceived'. Abraham Lincoln told his audience at Gettysburg: 'Four score and seven years ago our fathers brought forth upon this continent a new nation, conceived in liberty and dedicated to the proposition that all men are created equal.' The copywriter for the shipping line tells prospective travellers, 'here is a ship conceived in the context of a unique seafaring tradition'. Somehow the conceptions are different – or is it that there is a difference between a conception and a 'concept'? (Copywriters love concepts.) A child or a new nation may be conceived, and be conceived in liberty – towards the end of the speech Lincoln proclaims 'a new *birth of liberty*' – but for a ship to be conceived in a context is a puzzling thing. The writer seems to mean something like this: 'The Dutch have always been a seafaring people, and are proud of it; and this passenger liner is an expression of that pride.' However, *context* is one of the words that no modern writer with pretensions to fluency in any of the branches of jargoning can afford to omit, and a concept in a context must be doubly valuable.

The mixture of encoding, involving and appraising is a little different in the following extract from an advertisement proclaiming the efficiency of a new system of language-learning, 'based on Nobel Prize winning research':

Some people learn best by listening, others by seeing, others through 'hands on' experience. **Accelerated Learning** commands all three, so the course is guaranteed to be right for you.

You **hear** your new language in a series of 12 entertaining radio plays, in short easy-to-absorb sentences. You follow the script with the vocabulary **pictorialised** in unique 'Memory Maps'. The stories and these pictures build vivid mental images that make recalling the language easy and natural.

Then you **experience** the language through a series of enjoyable games and activities. These include the Name Game, which enables you to understand literally hundreds of words from the very first day.

The combination ensures that **Accelerated Learning** activates the learning power of your whole brain. Not just your analytical left brain – but your more imaginative, visual and faster working right brain. (advertisement in *Observer Magazine*)

The ruling device here is involvement, the appeal to the consumer; the second person pronoun figures in almost every sentence – 'the course is guaranteed to be right for you', 'you hear your new language', 'you follow the script', 'you **experience** the language', 'the Name Game ... enables you to understand', this marvellous method 'activates the learning power of your whole brain', 'not just your analytical left brain – but your more imaginative ... right brain'. There is some vocabulary of appraisal, but it is not particularly colourful: the course is 'right', the radio plays are 'entertaining', the sentences are short and 'easy-to-absorb', the Memory Maps are 'unique', games and activities are 'enjoyable', this way of learning 'activates' the learning power of your whole brain (as opposed to other systems which merely set you thinking).

Evidently it is the promise of attainment that rules this piece, rather than the appeal to cruder sensational appetites. But that is doubtless because it is by implication – like a 'biological' washing powder, or a seven-day-trial slimming girdle – *scientific*. This raises the status and the power of a series of encodings, beginning with the master code-phrase, **Accelerated Learning**, continuing with Memory Maps and the Name Game and boldly going into bold type for **pictorialise** (which seems to mean drawing pictures, doubtless in a scientific, experimentally proven way), as well as for **experience** (no, not meaning the way you stand struggling for words while Manuel rapidly insists on his ambitious taxi fare, and no, not meaning the way your French teacher used to rap you over the head with the board-duster every time you forgot that *genou, hibou, joujou* and *pou* form their plurals in -*x*; not that kind of haphazard happening; we are talking about **experience**, conceived in a Nobel Prize winning context and embodied scientifically in the form of **Accelerated Learning**. That kind of experience).

The jargoning does its job fairly well, half-convincing the reader that he or she has been badly taught, in some old-fashioned, irregular, uninspiring way, and that there lies at hand a new method of teaching languages, systematic, conceptually unassailable, rooted in an informed perception of what goes on in the convolutions of Broca and other mystical bits of the mid-brain. A shrewd move is executed in the short opening paragraph. The first sentence reads 'Some people learn best by listening, others by seeing, others through "hands on" experience'. Here is a common mark of salesmanship, the contrivance of something *given*. The salesman proposes, as a matter of indisputable fact, beyond the reasoning of the ignorant, and therefore to be amiably accepted by his victim, something like a *pons asinorum*, an axiom full of holes. What do we know, we dupes? We can only know as a matter of anecdote what *some* people learn *best* by. We can guess that learning involves the concerted use of all the faculties. We might also suppose that the predominance of one way of learning over others will depend on what you are trying to learn: that if you are learning to swim, for example, you may learn *best* by 'hands-on' (or 'bottoms-in') experience. We further know, and have known for a long time – and no one has yet won a Nobel Prize for saying so – that languages are learned by listening, reading, writing and speaking, to do which learners must needs hear, see, flex their fingers and wag their tongues. This is so obvious that even a person with a low-grade analytical left brain could work it out; yet it is presented as a precious insight for the happy few.

There ought to be a trade term for this device. It recalls the practice of certain entrepreneurial gentlemen on the streets of London in the 1950s, who would entice passing innocents with a large gemstone, a glittering artifice known in the fraternity as a 'jargoon'. The jargoon would be said to be worth a hundred pounds in any jeweller's shop, but because of some personal crisis – a bereavement in the family – a sick child with no toys – the collapse of a promising small business – the want of a ticket to Australia to bring comfort to Mum – this kindly pitchman in the camel-hair coat would be prepared to let the heirloom go for a tenner. The proposition or promise that brings in the salesman's routine is like a jargoon; take the jargoon on trust, and you take the stories that follow. The salesman in this instance immediately goes on to claim that '**Accelerated**

Learning commands all three' (ways of learning), 'so the course is guaranteed to be right for you'. Note, *commands*; not 'includes', or 'makes use of', but *commands*, as in 'controls', 'directs', 'summons' and 'disposes'. This method affords you, nay, commands on your behalf, the chance to listen, to speak, to read and to write, like no other method before it. Any system that can do that is naturally *guaranteed* to be *right* for *you*. Indeed. Some are born to speak, some achieve fluency, and some have **Accelerated Learning** thrust upon them.

The example teaches something very important about Jargons of Production: that passages of sales talk are often preceded by something that softens punters' resistance, favourably conditions their responses, and predisposes them to accept and properly interpret the jargon that follows. It may be, as above, some form of jargoon-proposition; or it may be more ingenious, as in an advertisement for one of the *Minolta* range of cameras. The advertisement fills a whole page of a magazine supplement. In the top left-hand corner of the page is a charming close-up of a baby's face – the eyes large, gloss-black, enquiring, focused; in the bottom right-hand corner is a picture of the new Minolta Dynax 3xi – looking at you with its large, shiny lens. What we are meant to infer from this juxtaposition is quite clear: two little marvels, a state-of-the-art infant and a living, breathing, new-born camera.

A great wedge of copy, printed in half-inch capitals, fills the mid-page between these two images. It reads: FOR ONE SO SMALL AND NEW TO THE WORLD, ITS LEVELS OF INTELLIGENCE, INNATE EXPERTISE, SENSORY SOPHIS-TICATION AND SPEED OF REACTION ARE LITTLE SHORT OF A MIRACLE. The arrangement of the text suggests at first glance that it applies to the baby; then the reader perceives that it can apply alike to the baby and the camera; then it begins to appear that the camera is the prime object, and that expressions like 'innate expertise' and 'sensory sophistication', apparently the shop talk of human neurology and physiology, are more properly akin to the language of computing or artificial intelligence.

This impression is confirmed by a longer piece of copy, crammed into a much smaller space, at the bottom left of the page. This is the true sales pitch, to which the rest has been a most effective prelude. (The baby's eyes glisten like jargoons.) The text reads:

A child is born with a remarkable array of instincts, senses and behaviour patterns. So too is Minolta's new Dynax 3xi, the world's smallest, lightest autofocus SLR with built-in flash. Using state of the art electronics and remarkable fuzzy logic computer technology, its automated systems replicate the precise reactions, instincts and creativity of a great photographer. So that, however new to the world of photography, anyone can now be one of the world's greatest photographers. The new Minolta Dynax 3xi. From around £299 with a 35–80 power zoom. *Nothing matches Minolta.* (advertisement in the *Observer Magazine*)

The opening sentence confirms the connection projected by the pictures of the baby and the camera. This sentence is, indeed, an assertion of 'given' assumptions, a verbal jargoon. (Compare 'A child is born with a remarkable array of instincts, senses and behaviour patterns' with 'Some people learn best by listening, others by seeing, others through "hands on" experience'.) It tells us what we well know, as well as what we do not altogether know – i.e. whether a child can be said to be born with behaviour patterns. We have to accept it if we are to swallow the ensuing yarn, in the course of which the image of the baby, new to the world, is replaced by the figure of the adult learner, 'new to the world of photography', who may in time become a great photographer, with 'precise reactions, instincts and creativity' which are 'replicated' by the 'automated systems' of the camera. Baby will grow into Bailey, we are led to presume. But finally this advertisement copy rejects the analogy it exploits, between human intelligence and electronic sophistication. *Nothing matches Minolta*, it declares at last. The machine is the true marvel. It uses 'state of the art electronics' and 'remark able fuzzy logic computer technology'. 'Electronics' we know as a good word, a buzz word, and 'state of the art' as a five-star epithet, but I dare say that very few people, if asked, could say exactly what 'fuzzy logic' is. Jonathon Green defines it as 'a form of logic in which the variables may assume a continuum of values between 0 and 1'.[7] (Thus, not 'either it's so or it ain't', but 'it could be', 'just about', 'we-e-ell', and 'not altogether'.) Green goes on to say: 'This branch of logic is especially suitable for the representation of knowledge and human reasoning in terms useful for computer processing. Fuzzy logic is applicable to expert systems, knowledge engineering and artificial intelligence.' In a long entry under 'expert system', Green defines 'a computer system which reflects the decision-making processes of a human specialist. The system embodies organised knowledge of a defined area of expertise . . .' These definitions interestingly bring us back to our advertisement, with its talk of 'levels of intelligence' and 'innate expertise'. A phrase like the latter blends two strains of shop talk. 'Innate' belongs to the psychology of learning – Noam Chomsky, for example, has taught us that human beings have an 'innate competence' for language; but 'expertise', we now see – with Jonathon Green's help – is closely connected with the 'expert systems' of artificial intelligence. Thus in the detail of its language this advertisement persistently urges the broad comparison on which it is constructed, of neural sophistication in the human being with electronic sophistication in the camera. It is a clever piece of sales talk, most clever in that it dictates our reading of what it encodes. It tells us how to read the riddle. There is little room here for those playful or satirical decodings that can give an irascible enjoyment to the reading of other sorts of advertisement. Accelerated learning may be fair game, but fuzzy logic demands to be taken solemnly.

(XIX)
OF WHEELS AND WINE

There is talk used for selling things; and there is talk used for talking about things that are sold. The styles in which some products are reviewed are special instances of Jargons of Production. One such product is the automobile, regularly brought to judgement, along with ski holidays, French restaurants, personal equity plans, health farms, second homes, designs for the smaller garden, etc., in our Sunday newspapers. Here, under a picture captioned 'Claimed to be as hot as a Vindaloo curry: Ford's Fiesta RS Turbo', the reviewer gets down to some strenuous technical detail:

> ... the turbocharger is a Garrett T2, smaller than the T3 more usually used. That may restrict the ultimate power potential, but the smaller turbo is more responsive, and that means more shove lower down the rev range. So if peak power arrives unfashionably early, at 5,000 rpm (many a modern 16-valve engine peaks 1,500 rpm later), a flood of torque (135 lb/ft of it) washes in at 2,400 rpm. This means that you do not have to wring the engine to make it work, and it is easier to hear the stereo.

This reassurance, that the engine is mechanically efficient, is followed in due course by an estimate of what it feels like to ride in this turbocharged, torque-flooded vehicle:

> The seats convey the message best. You are in for quite a ride. Not of the Concorde sort, all grace and technology, but the roller-coaster, hang-on-tight, here-we-go kind that is exhilarating but a bit wearing.
>   The steering is heavy, the engine sounds as coarse as it does when fitted to a builder's van, and the ride makes you realise a further benefit of seat-belts. But it is damn quick. The turbo stokes the coals swiftly, and, if you are not careful, wheels will be spinning in first gear. Second, too, if a glistening sheen coats the road.
>   Unlike some hyperactive hatches, the Fiesta does not snake uncontrollably in these circumstances – the wheel just writhes enough to let you know that you are going a bit, mate. There is no shortage of grip through corners, anyway. (*Independent*)

The style in these two passages is an extraordinary blend of technical terms, the patois of the motor trade, some picturesque metaphors, and a roistering way with words that involves the reader (you, *mate*) in a tense, fast-moving action yarn. A solemn exercise, perhaps, but a revealing one, would be to separate the technical and the rhetorical in the carman's code:

Technical

technical terms, stock	'turbocharger', 'T2', 'T3', 'torque'
phrases and descriptive	'power potential', 'peak power', 'responsive'
conventions:	'the steering is heavy', 'the engine is coarse'
'clip words' and slang:	'rev range', 'shove', 'hatch', 'grip'

Rhetorical
phrasal epithets: 'roller-coaster, hang-on-tight, here-we-go'
tropes: 'peak power arrives unfashionably early', 'flood
                            of torque washes in', 'wring the engine', 'the
                            seats convey the message', 'the Concorde sort',
                            'the turbo stokes the coals swiftly', 'a glistening
                            sheen coats the road', 'hyperactive hatches',
                            'snake uncontrollably', 'wheel just writhes
                            enough', 'no shortage of grip'

In the text, the technical and the rhetorical are not strictly separated; rather, they are mingled to make up a style of hi-there jargoning for sophisticates and city slickers. Thus 'peak power' (a stock technical phrase) 'arrives unfashionably early' (like some rebel against a stuffy social code). 'Torque' (the purest of technical terms) metaphorically 'washes in', in a 'flood'; for which reason it is not necessary to 'wring' the engine. The 'turbo[charger]' (technical) 'stokes the coals' (tropical). 'Hatches' (= 'hatchbacks', a manufacturer's trade term), are 'hyperactive' (commonly applied to disturbed patients, a therapist's trade term). As for 'grip' (shop talk, meaning what used to be called 'road holding'), there is 'no shortage of it' (shopkeeper talk, in reference to necessary or desirable commodities).

Is this no more than a naive mixing of metaphors? Or does it have claims as a purposeful stylistic medley, creating a discursive genre, the Driving Experience? Two impressions persist. One is that cars are animate – they are hyperactive, they snake, they writhe, they let you know about things, just like your dog or your toddler or your spouse. The second, even more powerful, is of the reviewer's relationship with the car. It is not the vehicle, but the idea of 'me driving this vehicle' that is promoted; and that extends to the reader – you, mate – who is invited to go along for a fictional drive. The eventual product is a state of mind, an invitation to invest in a good feeling; what the reader is coaxed into asking is not 'do I want to buy that car?', but 'would I like to buy that sensation and play that role?'

And so from Us Driving to Me Drinking. Wine-writing, like car-testing, produces a jargon for the benefit of readers who like to know what it is like to be in the know, and who have a taste for talking about tastes. The genre is a little intense; it has, as its practitioners might say, a fruity, full-bodied attack. Some samples:

Chablis has three qualities occurring together which make it unique; an immediate green hardfruit freshness; softness and the aromatic freshness, very subtly, of decaying hay, and – throughout all this – a metallic quality which, in the *grands crus* becomes like some mysterious mineral, and in the *petit* Chablis takes the form of a more kitchen utensil sharpness. (*Weekend Guardian*)

It has a lovely nose with varietal characteristics of spice and vanilla, and is creamy, buttery and smooth in the mouth with good, refreshing acid and a punchy finish.

. . . smells interestingly of flowers and curiously of bath salts, but has tropical fruit on the palate, with rough sauvignon blanc edges absent, except perhaps on the finish.

This is a refreshing red, particularly nice lightly chilled. Its green cedar wood nose gives way to sweet raspberry fruit, with slight attractive tannins. Bright and snappy with a long finish; terrific with cold meats. (*Observer*)

. . . the 1969 Negru de Pulkar (£7.74) has a creamy, blackcurranty nose and a fresh mintiness on the palate.

They have done a deal with a winery in Odessa to bring in two sparkling wines, the Grand Duchess, rather doughy and rich but an appetising wine made by the same methods used in Champagne, and Saint Petersburg, an unremarkable, fruity but rather rich and blowsy wine made by a patent Russian method. (*Independent*)

This is a lovely wine – one of the tasters claimed to find bananas and cream in it, but I will stick to thyme and marjoram in hot climate fruit.

. . . it really is a honey of a wine; beautiful gold colour, slightly one-dimensional smell of oak and honey ripening into peaches and banana skins on the palate.

Without any of the metallic improprieties of so many heavier Italian wines, this Barbaresco presents a cheesy violets smell, and its rich, sweet, heavy attack is finished with a good sting. It goes well with tomato and garlic and strong cheese or pizza.

Chateau Bertin, a Moueix property on the Montagne St Emilion, has produced a soft wine with a good, rich, sewery smell, remarkably forward for a four-year-old. It is feminine, young, yet ripe enough, a bourgeois young lady, I would say . . . (*Spectator*)

There are enough stylistic similarities between these passages from the columns of various periodicals to suggest that wine writing is a genre with distinct stylistic conventions and ambitions. Like car-writing, the style mingles the technical and the rhetorical. Technicalities are the names of chateaux, of wine-growing regions, of species of grape ('pinot noir', 'cabernet sauvignon', 'chardonnay', 'merlot'), of designations of quality, usually in French (*grand cru, appellation controlée*). These namings create a code, or sacred language, for insiders. The product is further described in terms which are technical in the sense that they occur regularly in the language of wine tasting. 'Nose', 'attack', 'finish' correspond to the stages of judicious drinking: if your wine has 'a good nose', it smells nice; the 'attack' is the first impression on the palate; and if it has a lingering aftertaste it may be said to have 'a long finish'.

These are technicalities which are then wedded to an extraordinary rhetoric of appraisal, generally illustrated by the passages quoted above. Wines can be 'brilliant' or 'unremarkable', like people; 'fresh' or 'rich'; 'bright' and 'snappy', or 'blowsy' and 'doughy'; also 'remarkably forward' and 'feminine'. (The old parodic joke used to have the taster describing 'an amusing little wine' but adding 'one has to admire its presumption'.) Most astonishing and amusing, though – so amusing and astonishing that one suspects some competition among wine-writers to produce increasingly absurd descriptions – are the words and phrases used to record the successive impressions of 'nose', 'attack', and 'finish'. References are commonly to flowers, plants and trees, to fruit, or to other kinds of comestible (cream, cheese, honey), but not infrequently to quite unflowery objects: to kitchen utensils, bath salts and sewers (see the examples above), or to saddle leather, or rubber. One well-known wine-writer describes the taste of Pouilly Fumé as sometimes having 'a tomcat element'; the same writer speaks of 'the ratty taste of young merlot'. The outsider – the fellow who occasionally takes his wife out to dinner at the local three-star hostelry and diffidently orders a carafe of the house red from some unsmiling, dolichocephalic devil of a self-styled *sommelier* – is naturally bewildered by these wayward strains. Can it be that these people are possessed of palates so sensitive that their responses go far beyond the ordinary judgement of 'sweet' and 'tart' and 'rough' and 'smooth', into domains of discrimination that identify the nuances of cedarwood, bath salts, honey, banana skins, tomcats, and the municipal sewer? The outsider can never know the answer to this, until he becomes an insider, for wine talk – like some styles of literary criticism – is a privileged dialect, the Babylonian babble of a priesthood, designed to make insiders feel happy about being on the inside, and in command of mysteries divulged only to the lucky and deserving few. It is not a jargon that invites borrowing or imitation. It is happily exclusive, and even parody cannot altogether catch it. Most parodies of wine talk give themselves away by their restraint.

(xx)
FOODIES AND FASHIONFOLK

The language of the gourmet, or 'foodie', is comparable in some ways with that of the wine enthusiast. It has its encoding names – famous restaurants, distinguished chefs, master dishes – and its own fulsome, farced vocabulary of appraisal. The approved lip-smacking idiom is well illustrated in this short extract from a reviewer's sensational account of supper at a London restaurant:

His breast of chicken with tarragon and girolles goes back to the classic French repertoire: the skin of the fowl crisped to gold, odoriferously swathed in a thick, creamy sauce, golden also, piled with fleshy mushrooms, fried in butter until they take on the gleam of varnished wood.

End with a chocolate marquise, a thick slab of palate-cloaking chocolate, drizzled with an unctuous coffee-caramel sauce, or, better still, a mound of tiny wild strawberries on a slick of jersey cream, thick and yellowed with artery-clogging richness. (*Spectator*)

Made, in short, to our chef's own recipe, for your gourmet pleasure, just like the bangers and mash down at the Golden Egg; a sure-fire prescription for obesity, cholecystitis, angina pectoris, and getting up in the night to go to the bathroom. Note, however, two features essential to 'authentic' food-writing. One is, very simply, the introduction of the word *classic* – which is also a standard word in wine talk. 'Classic' goes with *cuisine*, usually 'French cuisine', although it might be Cajun gumbo or Lancashire Hot Pot, or guid Scots neeps and champit tatties; 'classic' is a type of the sanctifying word which Jargons of Production often seem to require (compare 'genuine', 'authentic', 'traditional', 'guaranteed'). This word has an important place in the general history of ideas; it can mean so many things, in so many contexts and ongoing scenarios, that it calls for redefinition almost whenever it occurs. Put it together with some equally elusive and culturally loaded expression – for instance, 'concept' – and you are treading in deep semantic trouble; you might say you have a classic problem. In the world of pots and pans, however, 'classic cuisine' means 'the best, in the good old style – and therefore safe', whereas *nouvelle cuisine* means 'the style for adventurous modern people to adopt'. To appreciate the *nouvelle* one must of course be acquainted with the classic. All Jargons of Production regularly suggest the importance of links with the past, with continuity, with tradition, with time-honoured practices, while with equal regularity they stress modernity, innovation, discovery. 'Classic' and 'innovative' are key words, descriptive partners in the language of promotions and sales. You can have a classic wine, a classic line (in clothes), a classic dish, a classic car; and you may buy innovative furniture, an innovative CD system, some innovative leisure-wear – all doubtless conceived in a context of respect for traditional (or classic) values.

The other essential feature of the piece from which the above extract is taken is stylistic: its larding of descriptive adjectives, spiked with piquant adverbs and served up with succulent verbs. We learn in the course of the article that 'classical cuisine' is 'nostalgically buttery', but that in the restaurant under review it is 'tempered by the less frilly *nouvelle* innovations and spiky seasonings of the orient'. A plain white portion of steamed cod is said to be 'marvellously offset by the tequila-sunrise colours' of the sauce in which it is served. The quoted extract informs us that the skin of the chicken is 'odoriferously swathed' in a 'thick creamy sauce', that the mushrooms are 'fleshy', that they have 'the gleam of varnished wood', that chocolate is 'palate-cloaking', that a coffee-caramel sauce is 'unctuous', that jersey cream is 'yellowed', its richness 'artery-clogging'. Food is 'crisped', 'swathed', 'piled', and 'drizzled' – and if that suggests the texture of a Jackson Pollock or some other specimen of excited action painting, the suggestion is not altogether impertinent. It is possible to describe cooking in language that recalls the technique of painting: impasto for pasta, the palette knife as palate knife. What is a little odd about the vocabulary of this extract, so dense in its references to sensuous experience, to colour, to texture, to constituency of materials, is that taken one by one the words are potentially repellent: 'odoriferously', 'fleshy', 'palate-cloaking', 'drizzled', 'unctuous', 'slick', 'yellowed', 'artery-clogging'. Can we really feel tempted to eat this smelly, messy, oily, slimy, jaundiced, perilously thrombotic repast? Wash it down with a beaker full of the true, the blushful bath salts, or a Chablis *grand cru* with the aromatic freshness of decaying hay, and you are ready to hie you home to the bicarbonate of soda as fast as your taxi-driver can get you up the front steps. But perhaps things are not as distressing as that. Perhaps the food-writers, like the wine enthusiasts, only mean to develop an exclusive style of jargoning, one that puts in a claim for their own astonishingly wide-ranging sensitivity to the appearance and flavour and feel of comestibles. Jargons of Production offer you, reader, vicarious glimpses of sensations routinely enjoyed by others: of driving expertly and confidently in a smart car, of drinking wine that comes from faraway places with strange-sounding names, of eating meals so rich that fantasy could scarcely devise them. You never enjoy the world aright until you have tasted a chocolate marquise drizzled with an unctuous coffee-caramel sauce.

And even then perhaps not until – given the appropriate gender – you have swathed yourself, odoriferously or otherwise, in one of the alluring confections of an Italian clothes designer:

> Gianni Versace put on such a display of confidence in his own belief that the effect was fairly uplifting – whether or not you would wear his clothes and whatever opinion you might have of the women that do. From the short lime, pink, mauve and emerald macs to the trapeze coats in violent clashing prints and the outrageous beaded cut-away baby-doll dresses, the effect was dazzling. (*Observer*)

Another sample from the same source:

> MaxMara has reached a perfect compromise between two strains of Italian fashion, laying the gentleness of Romeo Gigli's aesthetic over what was once the hardness of power dressing, resulting in covetable shawl-collared coats and foster suits that reassure a woman in her femininity while still maintaining her executive confidence.

These extracts suggest points of resemblance with the language of winefolk and foodpersons, the most obvious likeness being the intense cultivation of a vocabulary of appraisal. This appears in the strings of premodifiers (adjectives and epithets 'stacked up' in front of a noun): 'the outrageous beaded cut-away baby-doll dresses'. The adjectives denote colour ('the short lime, pink, mauve and emerald macs') or shape ('the trapeze coats'), or the possible effect on an observer ('violent clashing prints'). All this is by way of descriptive business; fashion-writing, like wine-writing and restaurant-puffing, has its conventions of appraisal. What is slightly different about fashion-talk, at least in the article quoted here, is a strain of political appeal, a suggestion that fashion and its jargon may be an element in the polemics of gender: 'whatever opinion you might have of the women that do', 'the hardness of power dressing', 'that reassure a woman in her femininity while still maintaining her executive confidence'. The phrases suggest a style of social commentary and debate, going beyond shop talk about fabrics, colours, lengths, and 'lines'; a political style that begets a jargon in expressions such as 'power dressing' and 'executive confidence'. 'Power dressing' is an interesting example. It has a recognizable mark of jargoning in its phrase-form, dramatically compressing into two words a fairly elaborate underlying notion. Power dressing means wearing the right kind of suit for the money market, or the outfit that will establish you as a serious contender in the boardroom battle. The expression may seem a little pretentious, but is actually quite useful. It can at least lay claim to a meaning not easily expressed in any other way, and that is something that cannot always be said for phrases that ornament the Jargons of Pretension.

6

'Emerging Blankness'

FROM THE VERNACULAR TO THE SPECTACULAR WITHOUT MAKING SENSE

Pretension is something you can fall into out of sheer idleness. It is often much harder to be plain and direct; you have to struggle to cast off your own misbegotten assumptions before you can achieve a lucid and unassuming word. This sports writer clearly supposes that circumlocution rules:

> The goal did at least succeed in adding even more of a competitive edge to the proceedings and Arsenal's determination was even more obvious in the second half, though the skill factor available to them did not unfortunately match up to their commitment. (*Observer*)

He means that Arsenal's players were more willing than skilful. 'Commitment' (like 'dedication') is a commonplace in sporting jargon; the soccer player shows his commitment by giving one hundred and ten per cent effort for the full ninety minutes and making every ball a fifty-fifty ball. The 'skill factor available' to soccer players is their talent. 'Adding a competitive edge' means making them try a bit harder, and the 'proceedings' are, of course, the game. In simple terms, the passage might have read:

> The goal at least had the effect of making the teams try harder, and Arsenal's determination was obvious during the second half, although their players were more willing than skilful.

That makes for briefer and possibly duller reading, but it is not pretentious. Why did the journalist need to talk of 'the skill factor available to them'?

To fill up a column inch? Because he liked the important sound of 'factor', that muddy migrant from the sociology seminar and the PhD thesis? Or simply because he was unaware of writing pretentiously, and supposed that this was a classy style of self-expression?

Innocent pretentiousness is a possibility pardonable in sports writers, who occasionally stumble into the pitfalls of producing picturesque copy and producing it fast. Other professionals, academics with more leisure to reflect on questions of language and style, are more often and more deeply guilty. The question is, whether they can help it. We need to distinguish, if possible, between what is legitimate as shop talk – however wordy and obscure an outsider may find it – and what seems to be jargon in a bad sense, the tawdry, show-talking sense. Perhaps this entry from a Dictionary of Sociology will pass muster as a specimen of intelligible, pardonable shop talk:

> There have been two major debates within the sociology of gender. The first has addressed the issue of whether gender is a separate and independent dimension of social stratification and of the social division of labour. The second debate concerns the appropriateness of general theoretical perspectives for the analysis of gender differences and divisions in society. For example, one aspect of the debate is whether feminism is compatible with Marxism.[8]

This may be a little ponderous, and it certainly draws on some standard items from the jargonist's lexicon of good words – 'issue', 'dimension', 'perspective', 'analysis', 'aspect', fluently fitted into concordant phrases – 'addressed the issue', 'separate and independent dimension', 'appropriateness of general theoretical perspectives', 'analysis of gender differences', 'aspect of the debate'. But this jargoning is not altogether opaque, and is not a smoke-screen for a non-existent fire. There are real 'issues' in sociology, represented by words like 'gender' and 'stratification', words that in other contexts might promptly raise polemic hackles. Sociologists are commonly vilified as breeders of jargon, but it must sometimes be said in their defence that they are honest folk talking their peculiarly productive shop. It is less easy to feel charitably disposed towards academic culture-babble of this sort:

> Feminine texts know no boundaries, no beginnings and endings, instead reaching towards the *non-encore-là* of infinite desire and inconclusion. Like the feminine sexuality from which it originates, *l'écriture feminine* (over)flows in endless expulsions of blood, milk, child, and orgasms. The erotic writing floods and explodes the Logos with exuberant texts of multiplicity, simultaneity, ruptures, and wetness that defy phallogocentric notions of coherence and meaning.[9]

There's gender for you. Somehow it seems to fill my head with ideas, as Alice would say, though I don't know exactly what they are. I recognize a lot of the words, but the writing (over)flows from the vernacular to the spectacular, apparently without eddying into sense. That is possibly an unfair comment, because there is a small measure of not very impressive meaning in those lines. It attaches to that Humpty-Dumpty of a word, 'phallogocentric', a portmanteau, or veritable valise, of 'phallus' and 'logocentric', which is in turn a blend of *logos* and *centrum*. This coinage, French in origin, pays tribute to the teaching of the psychoanalyst and structuralist Jacques Lacan, who has argued that a society's culture is dominated by the symbol of the phallus. The domination, some feminists claim, extends to the *logos*, to language and the way words are put together. Syntax is a male construction, or erection; coherence is a patriarchal imposition, a manipulative stratagem to be resisted by all sisterly libertarians. To write well, defy your dad and write wildly; maximum comprehension is finally achieved via the scenic route, travelling through luxuriant thickets of the almost totally incomprehensible. And if that seems excessive, then at least adopt a stance of rejection; say that saying things clearly is not saying what you mean. The passage quoted above may be clear in nothing else, but it is certainly clear in its implication that the letter killeth. The writer's own prose, consequently, is a challenge to that masculine *logos* which dictates rules of 'agreement' and 'collocation' – rules decreeing that some types of X do not consort regularly with all types of Y. The patriarchy may well be puzzled by, for example, 'endless expulsions of child' and 'exuberant texts of rupture and wetness'; such expressions suggest that whatever meaning they are travelling towards, the result is not so much a matter of *non-encore-là* as of *c'est-magnifique-mais-ce-n'est-pas-la-gare*.

(XXII)
AN ABSTRACT NOUN WILL BRING YOU DOWN

Bad jargoning becomes possible because abstraction is always possible and occasionally necessary. 'Phallogocentrism' is an extreme example of what H. W. Fowler called *abstractitis*, a condition most commonly observed in nouns. Other writers have warned against the noun as a linguistic disease-carrier. Sir Ernest Gowers, for example, cites G. M. Young: 'an excessive reliance on nouns ... will, in the end, detach the mind from the realities of here and now ... and insensibly induce the habit of abstraction, generalization and vagueness'.[10] This raises comic visions of young writers tripping out on the *OED*, but what Young meant, I take it, was that it is often easier to summon up an abstract noun, or, if need be, to invent one, than it is to struggle with the precise expression of details.

That is undoubtedly so, and a regrettable consequence of the ease with which most of us fall into abstractions is that we lose faith in them.

They begin to look like half-lies and empty promises, and the commonest words fall suspect. An example is the word 'society', currently memorable because of a saying of Margaret Thatcher's, still the subject of indignant or approving quotation, to the effect that there is no such thing as society, but only individuals and their families. Among Mrs Thatcher's opponents this remark enjoyed gleeful notoriety, because it seemed to them that she was at her customary game of crying up the benefits of individualism and crying down the reality of organizations and institutions through which we express our common obligations to respect and care for one another, as citizens. But Mrs Thatcher may only have been saying that 'society' is a specious abstraction, a buzz word or a bogey word with which to coax or hector a submissive audience. A caring society is a good notion, but a caring mother is a better fact. A crime against society is deplorable, but a crime against Uncle Bert is a measurable wickedness. Mrs Thatcher, an astute politician, perceived and shared the instinctive judgement of her electorate, that the concrete is closer to home than the abstract.

Compare her instinctive response to the word 'society', as a treacherous abstraction, with the painstaking definitions proposed by Talcott Parsons, one of the eminent names of modern sociology:

> A society is a type of social system, in any universe of social systems, which attains the highest level of self-sufficiency as a system in relation to its environments.
>
> This definition refers to an abstracted system, of which the other, similarly abstracted sub-systems of action are the primary environments. This view contrasts sharply with our common-sense notion of society as being composed of concrete human individuals. Organisms and the personalities of members of society would then be internal to society, not part of its environment. We cannot argue the merits of these two views of societies here. But the reader must be clear about the usage in this book.[11]

Whatever usage the reader must be clear about, it is fairly certain what Mrs Thatcher would think about this. Hers would assuredly be 'the common-sense notion of society as being composed of concrete human individuals' – that is, if she were willing to grant the existence of society. Parsons himself prefers to see it as an abstraction of abstractions, and that is good for a sociological theorist, but not so handy for the citizen in the polling-booth. It creates an insider's term deeply suspect to outsiders, who can cope with Mum and Gran and baby Sharon and that mannerless madam in the Post Office, but will make nothing of 'an abstracted system of which the other, similarly abstracted sub-systems of action are the primary environments'. Nobody is going to vote on that ticket. Depend upon it: if you want to go up, an abstract noun will bring you down.

(XXIII)
THE AWFUL EASE OF EDUCATIONESE

That is often forgotten by educationists, who are obliged to do quite a lot of abstracting to maintain the honour of their mystery and to establish its claims to consideration as a social study. Education, meaning teaching, is a skill looking for a framework and generating frequent abstractions by the way. Theory is the name of the pedagogic game. The word 'approach', so common in educationese that the tombstones of disappointed professors might bear the legend 'his approach was counter-productive', is a typical example. When Tom asks Dick, who teaches maths to backward students, 'How do you go about it? How do you tackle it? I mean what line do you take?', Dick needs a noun that will make his line something more than a line, something more like an area, more global, more multi-dimensional. 'Method' did the trick once upon a time, yielding the still useful 'methodology', but 'method' has been overtaken by 'approach'. Dick's answer to Tom is, 'I am using an audio-visual approach to reinforce basic spatial concepts in geometry' (meaning 'I chalk and talk until the beggars can tell a rhombus from a triangle').

Here is a short extract from a paper on the subject of continuous assessment. The paper deals with something called 'a CRT approach' (CRT = *criterion-referenced testing*), and after some discussion on the usefulness of this method, goes on to observe:

> Having said this there is no doubt that the approach will appeal much more to some course teams than to others. Thus within the faculties the approach is most likely to appeal to course teams which see concepts and skills within their subject areas as building very much on one another, and as such the approach is likely to be of greater interest to course teams in the science, mathematics and technology faculties.[12]

A piece of writing like that reinforces G. M. Young's warning about the narcoleptic perils of abstract nouns. The phrase 'the approach' occurs three times in two sentences, and in its fuzzy generality of reference, or as Young might have put it, its detachment of the mind from the realities of here and now, it might as well be 'the marmalade', or 'the joy of sex'. (Try replacing 'the approach' with those phrases.) Then we have 'concepts' and 'skills', 'building very much on one another' within 'subject areas'. The abstract nouns in all their loose familiarity begin to infect the whole text with laxity; a symptom is the botched use of 'as such', raising the question 'as what?', and apparently meaning 'for that reason'. It is not very good writing because it is not very thoughtful writing; thought has almost fallen asleep. The long second sentence, beginning 'Thus within the faculties', will appear on close examination to be idly repetitious. It says (in very broad paraphrase) that the 'approach' will appeal to scientists, and for that reason will have a scientific appeal.

An extract from another paper, on 'self-help in distance learning', displays some more of the words educationists like:

> With this conceptual shift in mind, and the assumption that all self-help involves an implicit stance toward the wider context of institutions and knowledge, some factors in self-help might be identified as particularly relevant to distance learning. As a system of variable distance from the most long range to the direct face-to-face, the Open University produces a remarkably wide spectrum of learning patterns amongst its students and − one would expect − many permutations in its patterns of self-help.[13]

The symptomatic items are 'conceptual', 'stance', 'context', 'factors', 'relevant', 'system', 'spectrum', 'patterns', 'learning patterns', and 'distance learning'. Some of these snap promptly, like verbal Lego bricks, into phrase-construction: 'implicit stance', 'wider context', 'relevant to distance learning', 'a system of variable distance', 'remarkably wide spectrum of learning patterns'. There is an impression of something done automatically, a rote procedure, as though coloured words and phrases had been drawn out of a shaken receptacle in the mind. We play a game of metaphrasing. Bingo! Where it says on our card, 'a lot of different ways of learning', we overlay the text with 'a remarkably wide spectrum of learning patterns'. It sounds impressive, almost scientific, and it is quite easy; oh, the awful ease of educationese.

If it were only articles and learned papers that are composed in this dialect − but that is not enough; it gets into departmental documents and memoranda circulated among colleagues who are capable, in their better hours, of speaking like ordinary, comfortable beings. This, for instance:

> The questionnaire itself is unacceptable both in terms of the agreement and in terms of its technical standard. It is not a technically acceptable approach to attempt to assess different forms of teaching by using a single instrument. The first requirement is that the Department commences a discussion on the goals, aims, and organisational opportunities and constraints of its various forms of teaching. It needs to ask what it is attempting to do in providing its various courses − stimulate, guide, inform, substitute for reading, provide opinions. From this it might be possible to generate useful statements which could then be assessed by the students.

This is a product of academic politics. It had been decided to undertake a review of the courses offered by a certain university department, and in keeping with the democratic temper of the times to ask the students to respond to a questionnaire seeking their judgement of what they were being taught. An expert from another department was asked to comment on the value of the questionnaire, and the above text was his reply (or part of it). He might have written something simpler:

> The questionnaire will not do. It is not what you were asked to provide, and it is badly designed. You cannot use one method alone to assess different forms of teaching. Your first task is decide for yourselves how best to organise your various forms of teaching, what you expect to achieve in each case, and what drawbacks you foresee. You must then ask yourselves about the purpose of your teaching. Is it to stimulate? To guide and inform? To save students the labour of reading? To provide them with opinions? From your answers to these questions you might be able to deduce statements to which your students could helpfully respond.

But he did not write that. It takes quite a long time to write that, sentence by sentence, thinking about every phrase, its meaning, its place in the argument. And why take all that time over one matter among many when you have at your disposal your trade's guaranteed stock of good new and used parts?: 'in terms of', 'acceptable approach', 'organisational opportunities and constraints', 'to generate useful statements'. Grammarians of the transformational school talk about 'generating sentences', but that is 'authentic' shop talk, whereas 'generate useful statements' (for 'say something sensible') is mere pomposity. These things certainly do not grace the English language; but then, alas, there may be worse offences.

(XXIV)
TALK, KEEP TALKING HAPPY TALK

There may be, for instance, a way of talking about art and literature that serves only to obscure the artist and promote the talker. If the talk is dense enough, if its contrivances can only be followed by a coterie of initiates, who understand that words and meanings come and go like the Cheshire Cat's grin, the uninitiated tend to conclude, grumpily, that there is nothing there to be talked about. Giles Auty, the *Spectator*'s art critic, voices this suspicion about 'modernism': 'Once a veneer of rhetorical language is stripped away from a lot of recent art, its bare bones show through.' He continues:

> As in no other discipline I can think of, the use of language in modern art has become almost entirely rhetorical, i.e. language designed simply to persuade or impress. Rhetorical language finds its principal outlet in politics and advertising. Apologists for modernism have learned from both sources in making inflated, rhetorical claims for the art they support. Modernism surrounds itself in a comforting cocoon of self-congratulatory language and, all evidence to the contrary, believes in its continuing right to the moral high ground. But here and there, not least in its chronic incapacity to deliver, late modernism reminds me of nothing so much as Marxism in its final stages.[14]

This critic believes that 'the modernist pays no heed to ordinary perceptual realities', and thoroughly detests 'galleries full of imageless and often incomprehensible art'. It follows for him that the language used to describe and advocate the imageless and incomprehensible must in itself be empty of meaning, 'designed to persuade or impress', 'self-congratulatory', a language of bankrupt politics. Evidently Mr Auty has his own political axe – of conservative manufacture – to grind. Nevertheless, he makes an interesting point. There are indeed connections between the language of criticism and the expression of social or political beliefs. Words like 'progressive', 'traditional', 'development', 'experimental' lie handy for the politician and the art critic alike. As for Auty's hint that the language of the modernist critics has some affinity with Jargons of Production, that, too, is an interesting point. The implication seems to be that critics, like wine-writers, try to keep their privileged clientele happy in the relish of exclusive activities: 'happy talk, keep talking happy talk', as the lady sang in the musical (*South Pacific*); 'talk about things you like to do'.

(XXV)
TALK ABOUT DECONSTRUCTING THE DONKEY

Talking about literature is something many of us quite like to do, and talking the hind leg off a donkey is another pleasant fancy, but when those two things unite in the mind of the professional literary critic, new style, the product may do poor Neddy a real injury, so strenuous is the talk:

> But I have not paused over the confrontation between J. H. Miller and M. H. Abrams to grow nostalgic over the lost battles of the sixties. To do so would ascribe to the discursive practices of the time a theoretical and practical sophistication they sorely lacked. Nor have I lingered over this scene to deconstruct the later Miller in terms provided by the earlier. To do so would only neutralize and co-opt the power of Miller's turn to deconstruction and abjectly corroborate his interpretive strategy by helplessly miming it. I can begin to discern some of the power Miller has invested in the transfiguration when I acknowledge his reappearance in his response to Abrams on another scene, as an instance of transfiguration at work. This 'other scene' was not, however, subject to the uncanny logic of Derrida's 'double scene' with its 'supplemental' ability to disrupt the security of settled referents by signifying in excess of the captivating power of referentiality. Instead, as has been mentioned, it derived its power from an affiliation with an already established practice – deconstructive criticism – at an established academic institution, Yale.[15]

This is of course not directly about literature. It is about two literary critics, erstwhile comrades in the craft, sundered by a doctrine. The name of the doctrine is 'deconstruction', and we need to know at least a little of what that word implies before we can properly understand the passage in all its detail – before we can grasp, for example, the import of 'Nor have I lingered over this scene to deconstruct the later Miller in terms provided by the earlier'. We must likewise understand 'transfiguration', 'scene', 'supplemental', as carrying meanings not accessible in the dictionary, but available only through an intensive course of reading in other writings of this kind. It is thus easier to catch the general drift of this passage than it is to paraphrase it sentence by sentence. For instance, how is the uninitiated reader to interpret the ability 'to disrupt the security of settled referents by signifying in excess of the captivating power of referentiality'? The sense of it seems to be that ordinary words with dictionary credentials ('settled referents') can be asked to mean rather more ('in excess of the captivating power of referentiality') than such words can readily say (or 'signify'). If this is the sense, it is only what every lover knows. 'Seems to be', however, is properly cautious, because one of the most unmannerly, upstart things you can do with this kind of critical prose is to attempt paraphrase, summary, reduction. That would be to revert to the discursive practices of sorely unsophisticated times. But it does seem to be carrying more words than it needs; a case of referentiality in excess of captivating power, perhaps. For a further example, try this taste of designer bewilderment:

> As has been suggested in our discussion of genre in Chapter 2, the categories of periodization employed in such readings – troublesome indeed if we take them as exercises in linear diachrony where they seem to generate the usual unanswerable questions about the chronological establishments of this or that 'break', this or that 'emergence' – are meaningful only on condition we understand that they draw on a linear fiction or diachronic construct solely for the purpose of constructing a synchronic model of coexistence, non-synchronous development, temporal overlay, the simultaneous presence within a concrete textual structure of what Raymond Williams calls 'residual' and 'emergent' or anticipatory discourses.[16]

That passage will emerge into a hazy outline of sense after the third or fourth reading, once the reader has shaken off the depression engendered by a sentence 104 words long. It contains a parenthesis of 33 words wedged between the subject ('the categories of periodization employed in such readings') and the verb ('are') of its main clause. Its complement (everything following 'are') is 49 words in length. It is a syntactic monster; but willing readers will manage to find their way round the construction. They have then only to discover, or recollect, the meanings of 'categories of periodization', 'linear diachrony', 'diachronic construct', 'temporal overlay', expressions which are not readily open to paraphrase. Is 'linear diachrony', for instance, only a learned way of expressing what the King of Hearts tells the White Rabbit: 'Begin at the beginning . . . and go on till you come to the end: then stop'?

Deciding what the vocabulary means, at the occasional whim of the writer, or with reference to other parts of the text, or in allusion to other vocabularies in other critical texts, is one of the obligations put upon the reader of modern literary philosophy. Another task is to make sense of a figurative frenzy that can border on the grotesque. The knowledgeable word here is 'trope', and tropes are such stuff as screams are made on. Here a learned critic meditates on a Nietzschean metaphor:

> The metaphor, 'the tender, shuddering skin of the sea,' revises the words 'a man who was suffering continually,' which, for Nietzsche, is itself a metaphor that appears to be purely literal, a 'dead' metaphor which we have forgotten. The result of the resurrection of this metaphor as metaphor, and its continued life in the grand tomb of 'the tender, shuddering skin of the sea,' is not a dialectical sublation of antithesis, but an emerging blankness, a spectral smile haunting the most serious work of transfiguration. Such spots of apparent and momentary indeterminacy, such 'intervals and interstices' whose 'void forever craves fresh food,' draw out a writer's revisionary tendencies and define the scope and master-figures of interpretation he would impose upon that void. This is why Derrida, like Nietzsche and Joyce, attempts to disrupt this process repeatedly, to keep it going, to keep flushing out the hollows of the text with figures of his own that parody the revisionary impulse of the act as it were. If the irony of revisionism can be compared (as Harold Bloom has compared it) to Milton's Satan copulating with his own offspring, Sin, to produce the horrible giant, Death, then Derrida's Nietzschean or Joycean deconstructive project – the irony of irony as it were – can be likened to a simulated coitus interruptus, after repeated artificial stimulation of an eccentric kind.[17]

This invites a simplifying paraphrase, but the reader is forbidden any such undertaking by abstractions that sonorously warn, 'professional personnel only, no public right of way': *dialectical sublation, emerging blankness, transfiguration, momentary indeterminacy, irony of revisionism.* There is also the obstacle of the grotesque trope with which the passage triumphantly concludes. The close of the final sentence (which may be a joke – one never knows) reminds me mischievously of those grubby cards that used to appear in the windows of corner-shop newsagents in the backstreets of London NW1, advertising 'Discipline and French Lessons'. What is this all about? Is there no other way of putting it? If we say that when critics attempt the interpretation of literary language, which is essentially figurative, they often do so figuratively, and thus ironically create successive problems of interpretation, one after the other, seemingly without end: if we say that, are we so very wide of the mark? Well, no, a deconstructionist might admit, but 'if we say' is a mark of revision, or 'supplementation', a deconstructionist process. But then is this process – amusing, bemusing, a decent distraction after all – to be compared in all seriousness to the effect of corrective treatment plus relief massage from Mademoiselle Sylvie (Qualified Therapist)? Now there, indeed, is a source-jargon: critical illumination from the red light quarter.

It is easy to laugh – to laugh in irritation and bafflement – at this kind of critical show-talk, even when something is being said that could be worth deciphering, if one had time and belonged to the club. There is no doubting the seriousness of the writers. They struggle, they wrestle, they fight for breath, they have things to get off their chests, and these things are heavy – or as the old hippy sages used to say, with deep inhalations of hash, 'heav-ee'. They would not think of themselves as jargonists, or their compositions as samples of headlong jargoning, show cases of show-talking shop talk, specimens of a Jargon of Pretension that has some of the characteristics of a Jargon of Production. (Deconstructionists 'sell' their showroom product, deconstruction, as assiduously as motoring correspondents promote cars, and with as much reckless rhetoric; the important difference being that the critics sell their stuff to each other and have no intention of letting the public in on the transaction.) Yet they do jargon, they do indeed jargon, and they 'do jargon' as others 'do drugs'. There is a vocabulary which the 'ephebe' (the adept, convert, conscript or promising research student) must learn, and which contains resonant abstractions like 'logocentrism', 'univocality', 'referentiality', 'reflexivity', 'problematization', 'supplementation', 'textuality', as well as large numbers of words familiar from general jargoning but taking on a particular colour in their critical contexts (e.g. 'structure', 'strategy', 'paradigm', 'stance'). There are verbs to learn, like 'signify' (to create signs, or images) or 'captivate' (to grasp, retain, make captive, or even capture) and adjectives like 'abysmal' (deeper than deep in the mind). When ephebes have done their homework and learned to signify, they can produce (or rather, 'generate'), abysmal sentences like this:

> 'To get a better understanding of the disymmetrical and supplementary nature of the non-reflexive folding of the textual instance, it may be useful to circle back to the figure of the hymen, which may have appeared as nothing but a theme in Derrida's reading of Mallarmé.'[18]

To get a better understanding. Just so. Quite. Here the hind leg falls off the donkey, and there goes the tail, and the ears, leaving – bless thee, Bottom, bless thee! thou art translated – not much more than the bray.

7

Jargon and Literary Creativity

Common responses (among those who are not ephebes or veterans) are impatience, scorn, even anger. We make resentful protests on behalf of literature and clarity. I tell myself that were it not for a want of brain I would be eager to understand the language of cosmology or quantum mechanics (always assuming that mathematical discourse is not haunted by self-reflexive rhetorics); but I am not going to spend too much time with the deconstructors. Don't get mad, I say, get out – and yet I get mad, and not for literature's sake or for the honour of my mother tongue; I get mad for me. I get mad because I cannot get in – and therefore have no hope of getting out. 'Impenetrability! That's what *I* say!', cries Humpty-Dumpty, whose views qualify him as a primitive deconstructionist ('When *I* use a word . . . it means just what I choose it to mean – neither more nor less'). Critical jargon is often both arbitrary and, to the outsider, impenetrable. This is what sets us sulking, though perhaps the critics' language is no more impenetrable than the lexicon of the stock exchange. It has the peculiar property of being almost impossible to parody. Many jargons can be spoofed and ragtimed, because they are not too difficult to understand, or because definitions and explanations are reasonably accessible. Understand them and you begin to feel some little affection for them; feel affection, and you are able to imitate. But critical jargon defies imitators to do their vulgar, philistine, no-account, outsiders' worst.

The question of 'intelligibility' or 'clarity' arises. All right-thinking, taxpaying citizens like to understand fully what they hear or read, and if a speech or a text appears to be arrant nonsense at the first encounter, they will struggle to make sense of it. 'Maybe I'm stupid' – the usual preliminary to a confession of non-comprehension – conceals a full admission of what the speaker fearfully suspects, *I am as thick as two short planks.* We are vulnerable. We want the world and its words to be intelligible. There was once a comedian, called Stanley Unwin, whose ingenious act involved an improvised language, a farrago of Joycean phonetics and made-up words (I can only recall 'essensuabubble' and 'fundymoly') that *almost* made sense. His audiences would strain their necks and their nerves, eagerly, achingly, trying to follow the drift of his monologues. He would ring up stores and enquire about supplies of this or that from assistants who would ride the Finnegan tide of rubbish with superb courtesy and helpfulness. They would pretend to understand, and, in pretending, understood. They would even offer to order things for him. At the end of the act, everybody laughed and applauded – clever, wasn't it? – brilliant, really, because nothing was at stake for the audience. They were not obliged to trudge home thinking, well, maybe I'm stupid – in fact I *know* I'm stupid – but I couldn't make head or tail of that; and so to bed, and then to wake up in the morning worrying rather sullenly about not being able to understand Stanley Unwin's act. They were spared that embarrassment. With the critical act, however, it is a little different.

The critics themselves are seldom moved by accusations of obscurity. On the whole they welcome them, as assurances that they are doing their office properly. *Procul o procul este profani* is their line, get down you dirty rascals, either learn the mystery or leave us alone. That attitude is in itself not unsympathetic; professional defensiveness, whether in gas fitters or philosophers, can be understood and sometimes even commended. What raises the hackles of the profane is the combative readiness to argue that unintelligibility is a virtue, or possibly a manifestation of divine grace, like speaking in tongues. Some feminist writers would have us believe that old-fashioned clarity is a swindle devised by father to subjugate mother. Academic Marxists often write as though an uncluttered sentence were a token of abject surrender to capitalist ideology. What some people praise as 'lucidity' becomes suspect to others, as an historic declaration of political will, the will of the middle class to entrench itself in its privileges, and beat the dirty rascals down with grammar, with correctness, with a hatred of nasty hybrids and a firm resolve to avoid any suggestion of mixed metaphor.

There are no doubt concessions to be made on these matters, and certainly the exegetes do not always deserve to be pilloried as language-breakers. But they are at their least amiable when they make their commonest pitch, claiming that obscure and tortuous language is necessary because the subject is so difficult, desperately riddled with insinuations of thought that can only be expressed in a desperate, riddling way. 'Difficulty is, as we know, an ideological notion', writes Colin McCabe.[19] 'As we know' begs a very large question, and Professor McCabe's assertion has a lot in common with the 'jargoon' or 'come-on' sentences used in advertisement copy (see p. 44). 'As we know' lives in the same street as 'Laboratory tests have shown'. One might expect him at any moment to invite his readers to ring the Freephone number for the brochure, or details of this month's bargain offer. But he goes on to say:

> No matter how great the commitment to clarity, no matter how intense the desire to communicate, when we are trying ourselves to differentiate the practices and objects which are crucial to understanding our own functioning and for which we as yet lack an adequate vocabulary, there will be difficulty.

I can accept that it may be hard to frame today's perceptions in yesterday's words, and that new terms have to be invented from time to time. I find it harder to accept that the long tradition of Anglo-American literacy, in philosophy, in science, in the work of historians and essayists, in poetry, in those very fictions to the explication of which critics so painfully address themselves, as yet lacks 'an adequate vocabulary' for the modern seer. If Stephen Hawking can find an adequate vocabulary to discuss the boundless boundaries of the universe, there must surely be words, and styles, to accommodate lesser, sublunary themes. If Stephen Jay Gould can manage to communicate his perception of the intricate designs of nature in its smallest forms, there ought to be a reasonably clear way for critics to communicate their perceptions of literature and creativity. If – but this is a profitless and self-indulgent game. Jargonists come and go, protesting their pure intentions, and the jargoning goes on and on.

(XXVII)
OF EAGLES, GULLS, PISTOLS AND FLASH KIDDIES

It has been going on for a long time, and writers through the ages have enjoyed its comic possibilities. I am thinking in the first place of Geoffrey Chaucer and his poem *The House of Fame*, with its immortal Eagle, a literate, learned, irrepressibly pedagogic bird, truly a feathered Derrida of the fourteenth-century airways, who comes to carry the terrified Geoffrey to the House of Fame, and by way of in-flight entertainment reads his passenger a lecture on cosmological acoustics (which is in fact an academic account of how rumours get about). His discourse is highly technical in content, but, as he considers, jargon-free in delivery:

> Telle me this now feythfully,
> Have y not preved thus symply,
> Withoute any subtilite
> Of speche, or gret prolixite
> Of termes of philosophie,
> Of figures of poetrie,
> Or colours of rhetorike?

> Pardee, hit oughte the to lyke!
> For hard langage and hard matere
> Ys encombrous for to here
> Attones, wost thou not wel this?
> And y answered and seyde, 'Yis'.

('Now be honest – tell me – haven't I demonstrated it quite simply, without any subtlety of speech, or great prolixity of philosophical terms, or poetical figures or rhetorical tropes? By God, you should be pleased! Because hard words on top of hard meanings make cumbersome listening, know what I mean?' And I answered and said, 'Yes'.)

Modern 'yes' almost misses the fun of medieval 'yis', the frightened squeak of the traveller gripped in the Eagle's talons. This homely monosyllable is all that Geoffrey can manage in response to the Eagle's grand parade of out-of-town words – 'subtlety', 'prolixity', 'philosophy', 'rhetoric', 'cumbersome'. The straight-talking avian is delighted:

> 'A ha!' quod he, 'lo, so I can
> Lewedly to a lewed man
> Speke, and shewe hym swyche skiles
> That he may shake hem be the biles,
> So palpable they shulden be.'

('Aha!' he said, 'you see, I can speak to a layman in layman's language, and show him arguments so cogent, he could have 'em all by the beaks.')

Part of the linguistic comedy of the Eagle is his unselfconscious blending of the don and Jack the lad. We see it in the lines just quoted, in the juxtaposition of 'shake hem be the biles' and 'palpable'. 'Palpable skiles' – cogent arguments – we can make shift to translate. 'Shake hem be the biles' – literally 'shake them by the bills (i.e. beaks)' – is more difficult; perhaps the nearest piece of modern vulgarity would be 'have them by the short hairs'.

I cannot think of an earlier instance in English literature of a writer conceiving a major comic character as an example of linguistic dissonance – which is my own jargoning way of describing a startling blend of high shop talk and common colloquy. The Eagle represents in his own discourse the contrast expressed in the medieval phrase 'lered and lewed', learned and lay. He does not complain of the lack of an adequate vocabulary, or put his passenger/auditor at a disadvantage by declaring that difficulty is an ideological matter; far from it. He takes pride in reducing difficulty to what he considers the simplest possible terms. He can explain all this tricky stuff, he says, even to ignorant chaps like Geoffrey Chaucer. He is old England's first would-be popularizer.

This is not the only place in his writings where Chaucer makes ironic fun of academic language and its pretensions. In *The Canterbury Tales*, when the Clerk of Oxenford is about to tell his story, the Host nervously warns him off all that scholarly jargon – those figures of rhetoric, those tropes, those technical terms; keep them for writing to kings, says the Host, and speak plainly now, so that we can understand what you say. The Clerk promises to obey the Host, *within reason*. (The text says, 'As fer as resoun axeth', as far as reason requires.) A noteworthy feature of this exchange is the Host's distinction between speaking and 'enditing', i.e. writing: 'Keepe hem in stoor til so be that ye endite / Heigh style, as whan that men to kynges write. / Speketh so pleyn at this tyme, we yow preye, / That we may understonde what ye seye.' If there is to be a jargon, let it be kept for writing; speech should be straightforward. This view of jargon as essentially a documentary disease has persisted down to the present day.

Elsewhere in the *Tales*, and particularly in the *General Prologue*, Chaucer uses jargon as a playful device of characterization, wryly turning his characters' shop talk against them. Some lines from the portrait of the Merchant illustrate this trick:

> Wel koude he in eschaunge sheeldes sell.
> This worthy man ful wel his wit bisette:
> Ther wiste no wight that he was in dette,
> So estatly was he of his governaunce
> With his bargaynes and with his chevyssaunce.
> For sothe he was a worthy man with alle,
> But, sooth to seyn, I noot how men hym calle.

(He knew all about selling *ecus* [i.e. he was an expert in currency exchange]. This excellent man had his wits about him. No one knew that he was in debt – he put such a dignified face on his deals and his borrowing. Really, he was a splendid man in every way, but to tell you the truth I don't know his name.)

The vocabulary in which Chaucer admiringly describes the wheeling and dealing of this medieval Maxwell is enough to give the game away to an audience familiar with the jargon. It was an offence for a trader to conceal debt, but the Merchant balanced the books through profitable and illicit deals in foreign currency. These 'bargaynes' and his 'chevyssaunce' (ostensibly straightforward borrowing and lending) involved the proscribed practice of usury (i.e. putting out money at a high rate of interest). The Chaucerian audience would be as familiar with the implications of these words as we are with 'insider dealing'. The terms label the worthy Merchant a commercial crook; no wonder the poet either cannot or would rather not recall his name.

The *General Prologue* is the beginning of a long tradition of turning jargon to literary account, in so-called 'humours' writing, in the comedy of manners, frequently in the rapid delineation of minor characters, generally

in any passage or scene in which language is the master-key to the comedy
of a character or a relationship. Some professions are repeatedly exposed
to literary mimicry: the law, medicine, even religion if it is of the non-
conformist sort. (In *Bartholomew Fayre*, Ben Jonson mocks Puritan cant
as embodied in the person of Zeal-of-the-land-Busy; the name reminds us
that we owe at least one word, the word 'zeal', to the Puritan jargon of the
seventeenth century – 'tender-heartedness' and 'soul-searching' are further
examples.)[20]

Social climbers, aspirants to upward mobility and good marriages, have
also had their jargons, happily ridiculed by poets. If you are impoverished,
down-at-heel, gullible, provincial, slim, into singing and dancing, value
compatibility and would like to meet a well-preserved, well-endowed (own
house and income) lady, with a view to marriage, how do you find the
right words? Andrew Aguecheek, in *Twelfth Night*, marvels at a rival's
fluency:

Enter **Olivia** *and* **Maria**

Viola:	Most excellent accomplished lady, the heavens rain odours on you!
Sir Andrew:	That youth's a rare courtier. 'Rain odours!' Well.
Viola:	My matter hath no voice, lady, but to your own most pregnant and vouchsafed ear.
Sir Andrew:	'Odours', 'pregnant', and 'vouchsafed'. I'll get 'em all three all ready.
Olivia:	Let the garden door be shut, and leave me to my hearing.

Here is Sir Andrew, our skinny song-and-dance man, ludicrously taking
tips from Viola on how to talk to a high-class lady and get through the
garden door. 'Ludicrously', because Viola herself is a fake, a lost lamb in
wolf's clothing, who is obliged to make her own guess at the language of
the romantic lover, and produces a kind of parody, a mimicry of the
'aureate' style much satirized by Renaissance writers and scholars. We all
know that the garden door is going to stay shut in Sir Andrew's long face,
even if he does master 'pregnant' and 'vouchsafed', but still there is a
transient pathos in his jargoning ambitions and his want of self-knowledge.
The words he uses tell much about him; the words he would like to use tell
more. His is an incidental case of linguistic envy, one of the most durable
motives of jargoning. Poor devil, he only wants to 'talk posh' and be
socially acceptable.

The comedy of manners is a fertile source of information about fashions
in social jargoning. A play like Sheridan's *The Rivals*, for instance,
is a succession of scenes exhibiting different social styles – of lovers
speaking, fathers speaking, friends speaking, even of servants speaking. It
is a demonstration of language, and includes one triumphant linguistic

invention, a character whose name has given a word to the language, Mrs Malaprop. A minor but none the less interesting element in this stylistic mix is the language of the code of duelling. It is used with a delicate touch when Sir Lucius O'Trigger instructs Bob Acres in the art of writing a challenge:

Acres:	I must be in a passion, Sir Lucius – I must be in a rage – Dear Sir Lucius, let me be in a rage if you love me. Come, here's pen and paper. – *(Sits down to write)*. I would the ink were red! – Indite, I say, indite! – How shall I begin? Odds bullets and blades! I'll write a good bold hand, however.
Sir Lucius (Sitting on table):	Pray compose yourself.
Acres:	Come – now, shall I begin with an oath? Do, Sir Lucius, let me begin with a damme.
Sir Lucius:	Pho! pho! do the thing decently, and like a Christian. Begin now – *Sir* –
Acres:	That's too civil by half.
Sir Lucius (Pacing slowly up and down):	*To prevent the confusion that might arise –*
Acres:	Well –
Sir Lucius:	*From our both addressing the same lady –*
Acres:	Ay, there's the reason – *same lady* – well –
Sir Lucius:	*I shall expect the honour of your company –*
Acres:	Zounds! I'm not asking him to dinner.
Sir Lucius:	Pray be easy.
Acres:	Well then, *honour of your company* –
Sir Lucius:	*To settle our pretensions –*
Acres:	Well –
Sir Lucius:	Let me see, ay, King's-Mead-Fields will do. – *in King's-Mead-Fields.*
Acres:	So, that's done – Well, I'll fold it up presently; my own crest – a hand and a dagger shall be the seal.
Sir Lucius:	You see now this little explanation will put a stop at once to all confusion or misunderstanding that might arise between you.
Acres:	Ay, we fight to prevent any misunderstanding.
Sir Lucius:	Now, I'll leave you to fix your own time. Take my advice, and you'll decide it this evening if you can; then let the worst come of it, 'twill be off your mind to-morrow.

Acres:	Very true.
Sir Lucius:	So I shall see nothing more of you, unless it be by letter, till the evening. – (*Shaking hands*) I would do myself the honour to carry your message; but, to tell you a secret, I believe I shall have just such another affair on my own hands. There is a gay captain here, who put a jest on me lately, at the expense of my country, and I only want to fall in with the gentleman, to call him out.
Acres:	By my valour, I should like to see you fight first! Odds life! I should like to see you kill him, if it was only to get a little lesson.
Sir Lucius:	I shall be very proud of instructing you – Well, for the present – (*They bow*) but remember now, when you meet your antagonist, do everything in a mild and agreeable manner. – Let your courage be as keen, but at the same time as polished, as your sword.

The comedy arises from Sir Lucius' professions of mildness, decency, polish, Christian composure: kill or be killed, but observe the gentlemanly forms appropriate to an 'affair' of 'honour'. Words like 'confusion', 'misunderstanding', 'explanation' are authentic examples of the duellist's code, which included such expressions as 'adjusting difficulties', 'accommodating matters' (the character of Falkland actually uses that expression: 'Sir Lucius shall explain himself and I dare say matters may be accommodated'). In the etiquette of measured manslaughter, seconds are asked to 'do an office', or even 'a kind office' for a friend. It is all deucedly civil and sickeningly euphemistic. As the ninny Acres remarks in one of his lucid moments, 'we fight to prevent any misunderstanding'.[21]

Sheridan's mockery of duelling jargon makes a joke in itself, but it is only one kind of joke in a comedy which at other levels ridicules other forms of duelling, confrontations more pacific but none the less absurd: the chronic quarrelling of the two Absolutes, father and son, the gloomy courtship manoeuvres of the intolerably capricious Falkland and his Julia, the brisker exchanges of Anthony Absolute and Lydia Languish – much of the play is a matter of 'explanations' and 'accommodating matters'. The duelling jargon takes on a peculiar significance, as a joke worth enjoying in its own right, but also as representing ironically the general action of a play in which everyone is struggling to come to an 'understanding' or an 'accommodation' with someone else.

There are many possibilities in literature for jargon as irony, whether the jargon is shop talk or show talk – or low talk, as in some lines from the eleventh canto of Byron's *Don Juan*. The canto describes Juan's arrival in England, and how he descends from his carriage at the summit of

Shooter's Hill, to look down upon the great city of London and muse upon the moral grandeur of the English people and their institutions – when he is held up by a gang of footpads, one of whom he incontinently shoots in the belly. It is an unlucky beginning to his visit, for it appears that he has killed a likely lad:

> Poor Tom was once a kiddy upon town,
> A thorough varmint, and a *real* swell,
> Full flash, all fancy, until fairly diddled . . .

'Byron comments on the fatal misunderstanding and the demise of a hero:

> He from the world had cut off a great man,
> Who in his time had made heroic bustle.
> Who in a row like Tom could lead the van,
> Booze in the ken, or at the spellken hustle?
> Who queer a flat? Who (spite of Bow-street's ban)
> On the high toby-spice so flash the muzzle?
> Who on a lark, with black-eyed Sal (his blowing),
> So prime, so swell, so nutty, and so knowing?

The language is thieves' cant, the jargon of pickpockets, highway robbers, street-wise mendicants, con men, and 'varmints' generally. Some of its elements go back a long way: Shakespeare probably knew what a 'ken' was (a house, a 'boozing ken' being a tavern), but would not have come across 'spellken' (a theatre, a *spieler*, in the early nineteenth century a good place for the operations, or 'hustle', of pickpockets). 'Queering a flat' meant working a swindle on some gullible victim; 'the spice' was the trade of robbery, the 'high toby' was the highway, and so 'the high toby-spice' signified highway robbery, with the added nuance that practitioners in that branch of the profession were mounted, and equipped to 'flash the muzzle', to point a pistol. Tom's 'blowing' (or 'blowen') is his loving consort Sal, who accompanies him in his role of 'kiddy upon town', when they are out together on a 'lark' (a pleasurable, possibly mischievous excursion). Several of the words in Byron's description of Tom and his activities have come down to us with generally the same meanings. 'Row' meant then what it does now – except that it is now respectable and was then 'low'. 'Booze' is another obvious instance (and an old one – Herrick used it in a poem; 'rum booze' meant good, or potent drink, whence 'rum'). 'Flash', which now has a pejorative sense of 'vulgarly showy', a sense which it could also carry in Byron's time, probably denotes something a little different with reference to Tom, namely a proficiency in the art of boxing; especially since it is coupled with 'fancy', a word with similar connotations (boxing itself was 'the fancy', or 'fancy-lay'). 'Diddled' meant 'swindled' – as it still does – but also *killed*, so that in poor Tom's case it has an ironic double meaning: Tom, the master diddler, is at last diddled. 'Swell', as adjective and noun, is almost archaic in British English, but has had quite a long run in America (e.g. in song lyrics: 'Gee, I like to see you looking swell, baby'; 'We're a couple of swells, We dine at the best hotels'). 'Prime' needs no gloss; 'knowing' has the sense of 'stylish' (Eric Partridge cites *Tom Brown's Schooldays*, 'Tom thought his cap a very knowing affair');[22] and 'nutty' betokens 'amorous' (and in that sense lives on in such passionate declarations as 'He's nuts about her').

Byron, foreseeing that his audience might need a little help with this passage, provided a note, but a mischievous note, such a note as might be described by the ancient tag *ignotum per ignotius*, the little known rendered by the less known. He perversely withholds explanation. Instead of glossing the jargon word by word, he gives his readers even more to puzzle over:

> The advance of science and of language has rendered it unnecessary to translate the above true and good English, spoken in its purity by the select mobility and their patrons. The following is a stanza of a song which was very popular, at least in my very early days; –
>
> > 'On the high toby-spice flash the muzzle,
> > In spite of each gallows old scout;
> > If you at the spellken can't hustle,
> > You'll be hobbled in making a Clout.
> >
> > Then your Blowing will wax gallows haughty,
> > When she hears of your scaly mistake,
> > She'll surely turn snitch for the forty –
> > That her Jack may be regular weight.'
>
> If there be any gemman so ignorant as to require a traduction, I refer him to my old friend and corporeal pastor and master, John Jackson Esq., Professor of Pugilism; who, I trust, still retains the strength and symmetry of his model of a form, together with his good humour and athletic as well as mental accomplishments.

Of course the gemman would need a traduction, and Byron surely knew it. The keys to this new puzzle are that 'gallows' is an intensifier, like 'very' or 'extremely', that a 'scout' was a watchman, 'hobbled' meant arrested, and 'making a clout' signified stealing a handkerchief. (Large silk kerchiefs were preferred objects of theft; Fagin put his boys to stealing them.) 'Turn snitch for the forty' and 'regular weight' demand a little more unravelling. To 'weigh forty' denoted the importance of a criminal; it meant that his capture carried a reward of forty pounds. A 'snitch' was (as still in modern American usage) an informant. The 'blowing', the girlfriend, does not want her man to figure in the humiliating role of an incompetent and petty malefactor, so she perversely turns him in for a forty-pound crime, as befits his 'regular weight', i.e. his true professional standing. In translation the piece reads: 'Smartly bring off your highway robbery, never mind all those decrepit watchmen; if you can't work fast in the theatre crowd, you'll be arrested as you try to steal a handkerchief. Then your lady love will grow quite high and mighty when she hears of your ridiculous mishap; she'll turn you in for a forty-pound job, just to make sure her Jack is prized at his real value.'[23]

Byron's 'note', which does not tell the enquiring 'gemman' a great deal about the 'good and true English' of the *Don Juan* text, at least tells him that Byron was a patron and amateur devotee of 'the fancy' (pugilism). It was an enthusiasm shared by other members of the gentry, and this fashion for boxing, and for being on terms of patronage with the 'professors' of the art, may have done some good in diverting the thoughts of bold young bucks from the murderous practice of duelling. When Byron speaks facetiously of the 'select mobility', he means the superior representatives of the common people (the masses, the 'mob'), the flash kiddies who might tap your claret but would never run you through – the boxing fraternity.[24] Clearly it is their jargon that Byron supposes himself to be aping, although boxing talk was only one element in low-life talk generally. Pugilism was a privileged domain, allowing gentlefolk to come as close as they were ever likely to get to the criminal and semi-criminal underworld out of which the fist-fighters emerged. Social history conveys the crude impression that, as every Elizabethan gallant had his actor, so every Regency buck had his boxer. Byron certainly had, and he boxed too; you may see his gloves at Newstead Abbey, along with his Missolonghi helmet, a telling conjunction.

But after all this work on the text, we are entitled to ask why, at that point in his narrative, Byron abandoned Standard English in favour of a brief, intensive course of underworld jargon? At no other point in his long poem does he go in for this Corinthian slang. If it was for fun, well and good – fun it certainly is. But it is arguably more than fun. These deliberately obscure lines are placed with considerable ironic force, directed firstly at complacent notions of Englishness, and secondly at the epic convention of speaking a hero's praises. The jargon and low language have a debunking power; they strike postures in order to make a mockery of posturing. We have only to read the account of Juan's musings as he looks down on the great capital to recognize the tone and rhetoric of empty political oratory:

> 'And here,' he cried, 'is Freedom's chosen station;
>   Here peals the people's voice, nor can entomb it
> Racks, prisons, inquisitions; resurrection
> Awaits it, each new meeting or election.
>
> . . . .
>
> Here laws are all inviolate; none lay
>   Traps for the traveller; every highway's clear –'

But at this point in Juan's eulogy of This Great Country Of Ours, the 'people's voice', speaking 'good and true English', 'peals': – 'Damn your eyes! your money or your life!' The varmints have arrived.

What follows is knockabout comedy with a black border. Juan, having despatched the leading footpad, regrets his hasty action. He has come to 'Freedom's chosen station' after many wanderings, and the first thing he does is to shoot one of the welcoming committee – who has his own rhetoric, a most mystifying and passionate dialect. This character is evidently quite unlike the freeborn Englishmen he – Juan – has hoped to meet. The poet-narrator, however, treats English Tom as a representative hero in the best of native traditions, and bids him an epic farewell, couched in the East End Doric. And so at length – 'Heroes must die', says Byron, resuming the standard tongue, 'and by God's blessing 'tis / Not long before the most of them go home.' He is sceptical of heroes, and of patriotic posturing (being, as he tells us 'half English . . . to my misfortune'), and hence makes the provocative suggestion that if there is a type of English hero, poor Tom the footpad, a thorough varmint and a *real* swell, will serve as well as any other. Now, to convey all this, the jargon is necessary. Without the jargon, the curious, mocking ambiguity of Byron's narrative would not trouble the reader. It helps the poet to declare a political posture and at the same time reserve the right to stand neutral. It says 'I don't care for crooks, of course, but some crooks are more sympathetic than others – aren't they, gentlemen?' It says 'Don't talk about the people until you know who 'the people' are.' It says 'Think about your values and your virtues and ask yourself if they are more real, more solid, more praiseworthy than those of your average footpad.' But having teased his reader with these insinuations, Byron returns to his tale of fashionable life as securely as an affluent patron of the fancy might return to his London lodgings after witnessing a 'gruelling' bout. Such are the uses of jargon when a poet commands them.

8

Movers and Shakers

But jargon is not made in the first place for the creative convenience of poets and playwrights. It is made for and by people living their present lives, defending their current interests, spreading the contemporary gospel. To read carefully through a single copy of a daily broadsheet newspaper is to be forcibly struck by two observations. One is that there is hardly a page without some form of jargon, new or old, shop talk or show talk – indeed, that the language as we now know and use it seems to require a general, supporting fabric of jargon. The other is that many pages are devoted to special interests and exhibit varieties of usage all but impenetrable to the non-specialist. Our brothers and sisters are talking in ways that relegate us to the ranks of the educationally disadvantaged. The business pages, for instance, may appear to be particularly devoted to the breakdown of common English, but a reader of the arts and entertainments section will discover quickly enough that here, too, be aliens. I am getting old, and even with my bifocals, my hearing aid, and a reasonable complement of faculties I find it difficult to keep up with the young when they talk thus:

> Ragga gets its head on 'Roots' and 'Slackness', and there's even a fairly straight house-soul cut, 'Fantasy', featuring Kenyatta as guest vocalist.
> Most satisfying of all, though, are the dub 'Into U' and especially 'Tribute', a house-funk-dub instrumental which mixes a whirl of backward tapes, jazz piano, riffing horns and rhythm guitar.

Or thus:

> *Closet Classics* collects together a bunch of house tracks from Boy George's More Protein label opening at a pitch it can't possibly sustain with MC

Kinky and E-Zee Possee's glorious part-ragga, part-house, partb-bhangra anthem 'Everything Starts With An E', and including three tracks from George's own Jesus Loves You outfit.

Or thus:

Otherwise, it's a series of dutiful punky thrashes and reggae lopes, with copycat vocals in places, and revisionism of the most backward kind by a group called Mass. (*Independent*)

Tom has given up being a flash kiddy hustling at the spellken; instead, he rocks at the gig, or cuts a track with his band, The High Toby, cheekily sampling guitar riffs from someone else's album. Rock jargon has come along as the new lingo for the knowing set, although it has not yet made great inroads into general usage. It makes some claim on Standard English with terms referring to the recording of music on disc. 'Cut', 'track' and 'album' now require additional sub-entries in the general dictionary. 'Sampling' (taking extracts from one recording and introducing them into another – a kind of unmarked quotation) possibly deserves an entry of its own. Words for different kinds of musical episode – 'riffs', 'thrashes', 'lopes' – take us a little deeper into the language of the mystery until we reach the core-jargon, the words – always changing, always challenging – denoting the varieties of style in rock: 'reggae', 'ragga', 'heavy metal', 'thrash metal', 'speed metal', 'punk', 'soul', 'house', 'bhangra'. At another level of this arcane vocabulary, there are words to denote the activities of a performer – e.g. a disc jockey – improvising an accompaniment to the music: 'dubbing', 'scratching', 'toasting', 'rapping'.

This strange and fetching language characterizes a subculture certainly not made for the elderly, for the established, or for the curators of European tradition in music and the arts. Citizens much above the age of 40 – apart from people directly concerned with the promotion and marketing of music – risk making fools of themselves if they try to talk rock, because rock is restless and the talk is always outdated. Ministers of Government, Heads of Houses and Chairpersons of the Women's Institute may own up to a fancy for Puccini or Andrew Lloyd Webber, or even Diana Ross, but they are on riskier ground if they declare a taste for The High Toby funk, or the reggae beat of Spellken Hustle, because they cannot know what sans-culottish, street-wise, Afro-Caribbean allegiances they are proclaiming. Rock is youthful, subversive, demotic, and its language consequently tends to express a determination not to conform to greybeard tradition.

A typical example is the word 'punk'. This has a long history of pejorative use in English. In Dryden's time, it signified a harlot, or possibly what we would now call a 'bimbo'. In American underworld usage (film underworld) of the early twentieth century it meant 'young hoodlum', 'criminal of low degree'. ('Lissna me, punk, ya gotta learn respect'.) In mid-twentieth-century British English it was used with reference to a self-defining class of young people, not necessarily criminal or hooligan, though the police and the public at large eyed them uneasily, but antagonistic to received conventions and *mores*. They identified themselves with some startlingly original modes of dress, and hairstyles sufficiently bizarre to unnerve the timid. For respectable taxpaying citizens, the word 'punk' kept its pejorative implications; for the punks themselves it defiantly expressed aspirations to liberty and decent disorder. Their defiance was expressed in their musical preferences as well as in their dress and cosmetic flair, so that 'punk rock', which the unconverted might consider an orgy of pointless noise, could be said to have an underlying social and political significance.

Rock jargon, like the criminal and sporting argot of Regency times, is a 'closed' code, spoken by insiders and their patrons, revealed not taught, its meanings learned in practice, not inferred in theory. It makes new words, but its way of making them is mimetic and impressionistic. 'Thrash' and 'riff' are like the onomatopoeic 'zoing' and 'kapow' of the comic strips; if you cannot understand the word in connection with the event, it will not help you to analyse it. In this respect rock jargon is markedly different from techspeak, the language of technology and science. Technical jargon is 'open' at least in this, that its formations can be understood and imitated, even when its references are unfamiliar: you can understand *how* the words signify, without always understanding *what* they signify. The technologist's vocabulary generally conforms to the laws, the patterns, the conventions of English word formation and usage, so that in many cases you may comprehend the outward form of the word without having much understanding of its content.

Take the example of a now familiar word, 'laser'. This is a classic instance of an acronymic formation, derived from the phrase '*l*ight *a*mplification by *s*timulated *e*mission of *r*adiation'. This way of creating a word is widely recognized. You do not have to be a technologist to build a vocabulary by such means; every time someone starts a club, or a movement, or launches a product, the chances are that the resultant name will be an acronym. So 'laser' can be *explained*, can seem comfortably intelligible as a formation, can seem *usable*, though the stranger to science is ignorant of what precisely is involved in laser technology. Furthermore, the word can then enter into the common patterns of grammar. It can furnish an adjective, 'lasable', a verb, 'to lase', a participial modifier, 'lasing', as in 'lasing material', or compounds such as 'laser-guided' and 'laser-heated'; and of course it has given us the compound noun 'laser beam', which we all know and use as freely as if we fully understood the scientific foundations of the thing.[25] ('You need a laser beam to open this can'; 'She had a skin cancer, but they zapped it with a laser beam'.)

Techspeak can be playful, but its playfulness is seldom an arbitrary game of any old name; it is a principled frivolity that creates its words and phrases according to the rules and conventions of the language at large. It is, for example, rich in blend-words – there are piles of portmanteaux, enough to knock Humpty-Dumpty off his wall – but the blends follow familiar and intelligible patterns. A 'transceiver' is a piece of apparatus serving both as a *trans*mitter and a re*ceiver*. There the pattern is – fairly obviously – a blend of initial and final elements. A 'transponder' is a *trans*ceiver that res*ponds* (to certain kinds of incoming signal). A 'pulsar' is a pulsating radiostar, a 'quasar' is a quasi-stellar object, and a 'collapsar' is a collapsed star. It is often possible to guess at the meaning of these blends, from familiarity with the word-forming principle, and from recognition of analogies. (Once you know 'pulsar', you can see the family resemblance of 'collapsar'.) Initial–final blends occur quite often in the naming and marketing of 'technical' products – 'camcorder' is an example; some Jargons of Production, in fact, readily use or imitate technological language. In another kind of word-forming, initial elements are blended, as in 'maglev', *mag*netic *lev*itation, and 'mascons', *mass* *con*centrations (of high gravity on the moon). A few formations of this kind are now so familiar as to suggest a thoroughly domesticated technology: 'hi-fi' (for *hi*gh *fi*delity), 'telex' (*tele*typewriter *ex*change).

Perhaps the most striking feature of techspeak is its ready creation of premodified noun phrases. The pattern for these in 'ordinary' language may be illustrated by a somewhat less than ordinary example: 'the very first British-patented home-assembled fibreglass sailing dinghy'. A detailed grammatical and semantic analysis of that would demonstrate that the premodifiers (everything before 'dinghy') are not freely ordered, but follow rules of sequence, designed to narrow progressively the scope of reference. (The rules exclude, for example, 'the very first fibreglass British-patented sailing home-assembled dinghy'.) The example may seem contrived – which it is – and perhaps too elaborate for common usage. In technological language, however, noun phrases no less elaborate and as regularly ordered are quite common: a scientist might readily refer to 'a 100-megawatt prototype pressure tube heavy water reactor'. The obvious and serious purpose of such phrases is to limit systematically and comprehensively the definition of some object or general concept, in this example represented by the word *reactor*. It is a matter of social significance, however, that this process of methodical definition has become, increasingly, an object of solemn imitation as well as parodic humour. Wits may describe a blackboard as 'a calcium carbonate trace display system', or a pair of spectacles as 'a user-installable, collapsible, free-standing cranially positioned pre-corneal refractive binocular visible-spectrum optical compensator array'.

Edward Tenner, the inventor of those jocund monstrosities, records how a physician treating Ronald Reagan in 1982 reported that the President's sight and hearing were satisfactory, or, to be exact, that 'previously documented decrement(s) in auditory acuity and visual refractive error corrected with contact lenses were evaluated and found to be stable'.

The good doctor obviously felt the need to adjust his language to the rank of his patient. This ascent of jargon into high places is an interesting theme. Tenner prefaces his book, *TechSpeak, or How to Talk High Tech*, with a brief, highly instructive calendar of technical jargon, called 'A Tech-Speak Chronology'. Here are the entries covering the decade 1970–80:

1971 John B. Connally calls controls 'parameters'; first attested official use.

1972 The Nixon Administration decrees that all presidential orders and agency rules are to be written in 'laymen's terms'.

1974 The *Federal Register* (according to *Newsweek*) announces a new position in the State Department to 'review existing mechanisms of consumer input, thruput and output.'

1975 R. Buckminster Fuller, with E. J. Applewhite, publishes *Synergetics*, the *Ulysses* of Tech Speak.

1977 The Carter Administration orders department and agency heads to use 'plain English' in official announcements.

1979 A U.S. Labor Department press release calls truck drivers 'transport equipment operatives'.

1980 President Carter describes plans to 'strengthen linkages among macro-economic, sectoral place-oriented economies.'[26]

Tenner's implicit point is that techspeak is an 'open' jargon, a pattern for word-and-phrase making in domains other than technology, not least in the language of politics and government. The language-breakers, the specialists for whom 'ordinary' English will not do, become language-brokers, passing on their method to others. So the working practice of engineers and physicists, designed to wrestle the intractable generality of words into precisely limiting constructions, is adapted by governors and administrators, whose designs on the public are unlimited and anything but precise. Techspeak, thus transformed into officialese, constructs a highroad to pomposity and bamboozlement. What is produced in this way is not a youthful jargon, the sportive product of high spirits, nor is it demotic, an expression of popular perceptions; least of all is it subversive, a weapon for wrecking the complacent. It is not entirely 'closed', or reserved for initiates; it takes ground in the standard idiom, and grows there. Politicians, copywriters, people unschooled in the sciences, can freely invent it. This neo-techspeak is upwardly mobile, a code available to smooth, ambitious folk; rockspeak by contrast remains a cryptic, defensive dialect. You cannot talk yourself into any kind of power or status by talking rock. Rock language does no harm; I am not going to fret for the future of English if I am unable to find out exactly what 'house-funk-dub' means. But I am going to worry just a little when I learn that presidential advisers call a loss of hearing a decrement in auditory acuity. Come back, Osric, my dear fellow, Hamlet prefers you.

(XXIX)
THE ROAD OUT OF JONATHAN SWIFT...

But what Hamlet prefers, or thinks he prefers, is a long story. It is the story of opinions about 'good' English, and it rambles through many a chapter on simplicity, clarity, plainness, the sins of woolly thinking and fuzzy writing, the undesirability of talking shop, the misuse of learned words, the perils of abstraction, the sacredness of native tradition, the general notion that everything characterized as jargon is necessarily imprecise and vulgar, and therefore that only vulgar, ill-educated people use jargon. The paths and byways of it lead all the way back to Hamlet and beyond, but its modern development begins in the eighteenth century, in the Age of Correctness; this is the road out of Jonathan Swift, and we follow it even now.

Much of Swift's writing is concerned with matters of language. He has a playful way with words, he enjoys puns, he invents baby-talk (in his *Journal to Stella*), he devises strange names and scraps of outlandish speech as he sends his Gulliver off on each new round of shipwrecks and marvels; and hardly a page is without its example of his standard device, the irony that enables him to demolish a position completely by assuming it in the most affable and ostensibly sincere terms. When he comments directly on language and popular usage, it is with an almost pathological vehemence; there are things he *hates*, not once, but again and again and again.

His general view of the best and worst in speech or writing was that popular idiom – the fashionable currency of the coffee-houses, the theatres, the drawing rooms, the assemblies – tended to corrupt linguistic form and meaning, while on the other hand, a show of learning and pedantry in language would defeat its primary object, to communicate. Somewhere between the extremes of Mrs Featherbrain and Dr Dryasdust we might hope to find a few sensible gentlemen (though perhaps not as many ladies) who would never speak fatuously for speaking's sake, but would value clear thought and consequently value its expression in clear language.

Swift's loathing of popular talk is vivaciously expressed in the series of dialogues commonly known as *Polite Conversation*. (The full title is *A Complete Collection of Genteel and Ingenious Conversation, according to the Most Polite Mode and Method now used at Court, and in the Best Companies of England*.) Three things particularly offend him. One is fashionable slang, or 'cant' as he would probably have put it – words like 'bamboozle', or 'bite', meaning to trick, to cheat.[27] Another is the clipping of words, in his eyes a crime almost as treasonous as the clipping of the currency. He feels passionately that language is devalued by abbreviation. Here he is in full ironic flight, in a well-known extract from the Introduction to *Polite Conversation*:

The Reader cannot but observe what Pains I have been at in polishing the Style of my Book to the greatest Exactness: Nor, have I been less diligent in refining the Orthography, by spelling the Words in the very same Manner that they are pronounced by the Chief Patterns of Politeness, at Court, at Levees, at Assemblies, at Playhouses, at the prime Visiting-Places, by young Templers, and by Gentlemen-Commoners of both Universities, who have lived at least a Twelvemonth in Town, and kept the best Company. Of these Spellings the Publick will meet with many Examples in the following Book. For instance, *can't, han't, shan't, didn't, coodn't, woodn't, isn't, e'n't,* with many more; besides several Words which Scholars pretend are derived from *Greek* and *Latin,* but pared into a polite Sound by Ladies, Officers of the Army, Courtiers and Templers, such as *Jommetry* for *Geometry, Verdi* for *Verdict, Lierd* for *Lord, Larnen* for *Learning;* together with some Abbreviations exquisitely refined; as, *Pozz* for *Positive; Mobb* for *Mobile; Phizz* for *Physiognomy; Rep* for *Reputation; Plenipo* for *Plenipotentiary; Incog* for *Incognito; Hypps,* or *Hippo,* for *Hypochondriacks; Bam* for *Bamboozle;* and *Bamboozle* for *God knows what;* whereby much Time is saved, and the high Road to Conversation cut short by many a Mile.

Luckily for Swift, he did not have to live with 'fax', 'synch', 'des. res.', 'brill', 'def', 'max', 'a.s.a.p.', and many others that make our modern high Road to Conversation the merest Hop-Skip-and-a-Jump.

The third and most persistently derided object of his scorn is everyday small talk. We do not think so badly of it now. Vapid and meaningless though it may sometimes seem, it serves an important social purpose, having the function of what Malinowski called 'phatic communion', verbal behaviour by which we seek to associate reassuringly with our fellows. Swift, of course, could not see it in quite that way. The very notion would probably have struck him as a piece of egregious cant; the invitation to 'have a nice day' would certainly have brought on a fit of exquisite irony, along with 'take care', and 'don't be a stranger, now'.

His parodies of polite conversation (by 'polite' he means 'polished', 'sophisticated') are anthologies of common sayings, similes and proverbial expressions of the kind that usually serve as the gap-fillers and emphatics of social talk. In Swift's representation they are more than gap-fillers; they are the very substance of conversation as the characters gossip and banter:

Lady Smart:	Pray, Madam, when did you see Sir Peter Muckworm?
Lady Answerall:	Not this Fortnight; I hear, he's laid up with the Gout.
Lady Smart:	What does he do for it?
Lady Answ.:	Why, I hear he's weary of doctoring it, and now makes Use of nothing but Patience and Flannel.
Miss:	Pray, how does He and my Lady agree?

Lady Answ.:	You know, he loves her as the Devil loves Holy Water.
Miss:	They say, she plays deep with Sharpers, that cheat her of her Money.
Lady Answ.:	Upon my word, they must rise early that would cheat her of her Money; Sharp's the Word with her; Diamonds cut Diamonds.
Miss:	Well, but I was assur'd from a good Hand, that she lost at one Sitting to the Tune of a hundred Guineas; make Money of that.
Lady Smart:	Well, but do you hear, that Mrs Plump is brought to bed at last?
Miss:	And, pray, what has God sent her?
Lady Smart:	Why, guess if you can.
Miss:	A Boy, I suppose.
Lady Smart:	No, you are out; guess again.
Miss:	A Girl then.
Lady Smart:	You have hit it; I believe you are a Witch.
Miss:	O Madam; the Gentlemen say, all fine Ladies are Witches; but I pretend to no such thing.
Lady Answ.:	Well, she had good Luck to draw Tom Plump into Wedlock; she ris' with her A – upwards.
Miss:	Fie, Madam! what do you mean?
Lady Smart:	O Miss; 'tis nothing what we say among ourselves.
Miss:	Ay, Madam; but they say, Hedges have Eyes, and Walls Have Ears.
Lady Answ.:	Well, Miss, I can't help it; you know, I am old Tell-Truth; I love to call a Spade a Spade.

Some of the phrases recorded here have had a long life; some have changed a little in wording; and some are now lost to us. We still 'call a Spade a Spade', and 'make Money of that' is near enough to 'make what you can of that'; but the sarcastic 'I believe you are a Witch' has become 'you must be psychic', and 'Hedges have Eyes and Walls have Ears' is now only half a proverb.[28] It is not clear whether 'I was assured from a good Hand' is a stereotyped phrase, like our 'I have it from a reliable source', 'I have it on good authority'; and 'she ris' with her A(rse) upwards' has, surprisingly, no adequate equivalent in the rude speech of our own time; the lady, it seems, rose up by lying down.

Swift solemnly refers to such pieces of parlour-prattle as 'apopthegms', declaring that 'unto them we owe the Continuance of our Language, for at least an hundred years'. He sardonically praises their 'Smartness of Wit', their 'Fineness of Raillery' and 'Propriety and Energy of Expression'. Their long life is guaranteed, he says, because 'they never can be changed but to Disadvantage, except in the Circumstance of using Abbreviations; which, however, I do not despair, in due Time, to see introduced, having already met them at some of the Choice Companies in Town'. The habit of speaking in clichés is thus ironically linked with the habit of abbreviating everything; Swift perceived in both a vitiation of language, a reduction of speech to social babble, to empty jargoning. This linguistic corruption he attributed to the bad influence of the Court and the Town in 'the last age', meaning the decades following the Restoration.

But if Swift is hard on the polite, he is almost as severe on the pedantic, whose faults he reproves in the course of his *A Letter to a Young Gentleman Lately Enter'd into Holy Orders*. Since his immediate subject is preaching, Swift here chooses to attack the pedantry of theologians. Their language, he finds, is often too pretentious for any clergyman whose first business is the care and instruction of his flock:

> ... I observe several Clergymen otherwise little fond of obscure Terms, yet in their Sermons very liberal of all those which they find in Ecclesiastical Writers, as if it were our Duty to understand them; which I am sure it is not. And I defy the greatest Divine to produce any Law either of God or Man which obliges me to comprehend the meaning of *Omniscience, Omnipresence, Ubiquity, Attribute, Beatifick Vision*, with a thousand others so frequent in Pulpits, any more than that of *Excentrick, Idiosyncratic, Entity*, and the like. I believe I may venture to insist further, that many Terms used in holy Writ, particularly by St. Paul, might with more Discretion be changed into plainer Speech, except where they are introduced as part of a Quotation.

That plea for plain English recalls the controversy among scholars and writers in Tudor times, over 'inkhorn' or 'aureate' terms – learned words adapted from Latin or Greek. It also touches on the question of 'terms of art' – shop talk – which the eighteenth-century mandarins of style considered improper to general literary usage; either because such 'terms' suggested familiarity with horny-handed tradesmen, or, at the other extreme, because they could only be understood by that most 'impolite' of races, the fusty tribe of professors. Conversation and literature, it was felt, should take humane views and consider matters at large, examining (as Johnson was to put it in his *Rasselas*) 'not the individual but the species'.

Swift's plea for plain English is one that has been heard again and again, although the path to plain English is not always as plain as its advocates plainly suppose. Swift's supposition was that if a man would only think clearly, the most suitable words in which to express his thoughts would naturally occur to him. This would lead to the formation of a forthright, unpretentious style, the plainness and clarity of which could be tested by a very simple expedient – try it on the servants:

> I believe the Method observed by the famous Lord Falkland in some of his Writings would not be an ill one ... I was assured by an old Person of Quality who knew him well, that when he doubted whether a Word

were perfectly intelligible or no, he used to consult one of his Lady's
Chambermaids (not the Waiting-woman, because it was possible she might
be conversant in Romances) and by her Judgment was guided whether to
receive or to reject it.

That sounds at first like excellent advice, although the immediate impression
does not easily survive an attempt to picture the scene. What is a cham-
bermaid to say, to keep the gentleman in a pleasant frame of mind? Surely
a lass with her wits about her will watch her master's face, and nod when
his wrinkles say so? But this servant, innocent of sophistication and
pedantry alike, cuts a purposeful figure in the Swiftian mythology of 'pure'
English, which puts so many things in so many words and is not touched
by the corrupt argot of the levee and the gaming room, or by the poly-
syllabic opacities of the learned. 'A common Farmer', he writes, 'shall
make you to understand in three Words, that *his Foot is out of Joint, or
his Collar-bone broken*, wherein a Surgeon, after a hundred terms of Art,
if you are not a Scholar, shall leave you to seek' (i.e. leave you none the
wiser). He adds: 'It is frequently the same case in Law, Physick, and even
many of the meaner Arts.'
    Swift's view of 'good' language as something to be rescued from
scholars and technocrats on the one hand, and from an upwardly mobile
middle class on the other, is echoed by those who come after him. Lord
Chesterfield observes:

> The common people of every country speak their own language very ill; the
> people of fashion (as they are called) speak it better, but not always correctly,
> because they are not people of letters. Those who speak their own language
> the most accurately are those who have learning and are at the same time in
> the polite world; at least their language will be reckoned the standard of the
> language of that country.[29]

Chesterfield means that the proper arbiters of usage are people like
Chesterfield. Two very important words in that description are 'standard'
and 'accurately'. We are told that the linguistic standard is produced and
maintained by a quite limited – not to say privileged – class of people,
literate and genteel; and we also note that the principal claim of the
standard is accuracy, meaning precision, consistency, and logical use.
    Thus usage, including whatever we now call jargon, begins to have an
ideology. Chesterfield's ideological position is generally shared by Samuel
Johnson, even though some of Johnson's contemporaries questioned his
standing as an authority on language. (Noah Webster challenges Johnson's
judgement in presenting as good current English expressions a host of
words including specimens like 'ariolation', 'clancular', 'deuteroscopy',
'discubitory'; and Lord Monboddo declared the great lexicographer
'neither a scholar nor a man of taste'.) Johnson's concern for accuracy led

him into occasional outbursts of spleen. Like Swift, he despised the popular way of conversing in tags and folk-sayings:

> ... for, in the first place, the common people do not accurately adapt their words to their thoughts: they do not mean to lie; but, taking no pains to be exact, they give you very false accounts. A great part of their language is proverbial. If anything rocks at all, they say *it rocks like a cradle*; and in this way they go on.[30]

The need to be exact – not to *lie* – is his motive for irascible assaults on words and phrases in apparently respectable use. The expression 'to make money', for example, irritated him greatly. Boswell, who used it himself, recalls a magisterial ticking-off:

> 'Don't you see (said he) the impropriety of it?. To *make* money is to *coin* it: you should say *get* money.' The phrase, however, is, I think, pretty current. But Johnson was at all times jealous of infractions upon the genuine English language, and prompt to suppress colloquial barbarisms; such as, *pledging myself*, for *undertaking*; *line*, for *department*, or *branch*, as, the *civil line*, the *banking line*. He was particularly indignant against the almost universal use of the word *idea* in the sense of *notion* or *opinion*, when it is clear that *idea* can only signify something of which an image can be formed in the mind. We may have an *idea* or *image* of a mountain, a tree, a building; but we cannot surely have an *idea* or *image* of an *argument* or *proposition*. Yet we hear the sages of the law 'delivering their *ideas* upon the question under consideration;' and the first speakers in parliament 'entirely coinciding in the *idea* which has been ably stated by an honourable member;' – or 'reprobating an *idea* unconstitutional, and fraught with the most dangerous consequences to a great and free country'. Johnson called this 'modern cant'.[31]

By 'cant' in that example, Johnson meant 'lingo' or 'parlance'. In another passage from Boswell we see him using the word in a sense nearer to its present connotation of 'humbug', 'hypocritical affectation':

> 'My dear friend, clear your *mind* of cant. You may *talk* as other people do: you may say to a man, "Sir, I am your most humble servant." You are *not* his most humble servant. You may say, "these are sad times; it is a melancholy thing to be reserved to such times." You don't mind the times. You tell a man, "I am sorry you had such bad weather the last day of your journey, and were so much wet." You don't care six-pence whether he was wet or dry. You may *talk* in this manner; it is a mode of talking in Society: but don't *think* foolishly.'[32]

Here, if we were to seek it, is Johnson's verdict on 'have a nice day', 'freedom of choice', 'the security of the family', 'peace of mind in your retirement', and all the lexical apparatus of euphemism and empty benevolence. The two passages I have quoted suggest that if Johnson were with us now and were asked to render the modern sense of 'jargon', his definition would build on two constituent features, namely (a) particular words and expressions, inaccurately used, or objectionable as 'terms of art', and (b) empty phraseology, ready-cut scraps of language having no function other than that of supplying verbal gestures in commonplace social exchanges. His view of the latter is a little different, apparently, from that of Swift. Swift despises the kind of social talk illustrated in *Polite Conversation* because he supposes that corrupted language takes a hold on corruptible minds. I do not know of any place in his writings where he puts that supposition in so many words, but wherever he talks about language there is always the implication that your way of speaking is your way of thinking and hence your way of life. Your language invades your soul. Johnson puts it differently. 'Clear your *mind* of cant', he says. The emphasis, usually omitted when this sentence is quoted, is important. 'Cant' exists, and is not to be abolished; it is even useful, for going about your daily business. Very well – you may use this social jargon quite freely, just as long as you remember that it has no real meaning (that is, no 'propositional' meaning), and do not allow yourself to be taken in by it. This raises for us a very important question about the psychology of some kinds of jargon. Are we to suppose, with Swift, that if you let them into your own usage they will inevitably cloud and corrupt your thinking? Or do we take the sturdy Johnsonian view that you can always control your jargon, using it, but never allowing it to take charge of your mind?

Johnson, who seems at a two-hundred-year distance to be a wholly secure, intimidating, hugely respected authority on usage, was – as I have said – not without his critics in his own time. In contrast with Swift, he could even be attacked as a maker of jargon. Thus Archibald Campbell, 'a Scotch purser in the navy' as Boswell dismissively calls him, shrewdly picks out one or two of Johnson's favourite expressions, beginning with *powers*. In this passage from his lampoon called *Lexiphanes*, Campbell imitates that scene in Ben Jonson's *Poetaster*, when Crispinus (a mask for the poet Marston) is made to vomit up his 'windy words'.[33] Campbell has physicians administering purges to Lexiphanes-Johnson:

> Come, throw up *powers*, that villainous word *powers*, a word never used by any good writer, but now applied by our modern fribbles to every possible thing, to every thing relating to men or beast, or to things inanimate. We hear of nothing but *powers* of *ridicule, mental powers, intellectual powers, patron powers of literature, powers of dolorous declamation*. Instead of saying, as people did formerly, such a one is a person of talents, parts, or abilities, the word now is, he has great *powers*, and those *powers* are, according to the wares he deals in, either *theatrical, comical, tragical, poetical,* or *paradoxical*. The modern Roscius cannot step upon the stage, but in the next newspapers, our ears are stunned with the *amazing theatrical powers* of our inimitable Garrick; nor M[urph]y *exhibit* a new piece (another of their cant-words, seldom proper but in the mind of a puppet-man, which,

however, they are sure to *exhibit* on every ordinary occasion)...but we have a discussion in the next *Review* on his *comick* or *tragick powers*...[34]

'This malicious drollery.... it may easily be supposed,' says Boswell, 'could do no harm to its illustrious object.' Most certainly not; but the purpose of the 'malicious drollery' was to charge Johnson with the 'affected use' of words – that is, with *jargoning* – and this passage from *Lexiphanes* scores at least one point. Devotees of Johnson will recognize 'powers' as one of the master's favourite words. Whether his use of it is 'affected' is another question, but Campbell's observation interestingly suggests that great writers may contribute to the formation of a jargon by creating their own mode words, which those around them readily adopt. Consider this quite striking passage from Boswell:

> I remember once to have heard Johnson say, 'Sir a thousand years may elapse before there shall appear another man with the power of versification equal to that of Pope.' That power must undoubtedly be allowed its due share in enhancing the value of his captivating composition.
>
> Johnson, who had done liberal justice to Warburton in his edition of *Shakespeare*, which was published during the life of that powerful writer, with still greater liberality took an opportunity, in the *Life of Pope*, of paying tribute to him when he was no longer in 'high place,' but numbered with the dead.[35]

So impressionable is Boswell, so ready to echo his hero's characteristic turns of speech, that having reported a Johnsonian use of 'power' (in 'power of versification') he goes on in the next two sentences to use the same word (or a derivative: 'power', 'powerful') twice on his own account. It is a small example, but it supports Campbell's point. Johnson was as capable as anyone else of becoming a jargon-maker. He was irritated by the general use of the word 'idea', as 'modern cant', as a *façon de parler*; but was as guilty in Campbell's eyes – though he can hardly have been able to acknowledge it himself – of promoting his own specimens of parlance.

Campbell rightly points to the theatre and the press as sources of contemporary jargon. *Exhibit*, which Campbell finds almost as deplorable as *power*, is most probably a piece of eighteenth-century theatrical shop talk. Boswell recalls how, towards the end of his life, Johnson was honoured by a visit from the great Sarah Siddons. 'Mrs Siddons and I talked of plays', Johnson said, 'and she told me her intention of exhibiting this winter the characters of Constance, Catherine, and Isabella in Shakespeare.'[36] Writers like the younger Campbell – not necessarily scholars, and hardly ever Persons of Quality – seem to have been well enough aware of links between the national life and the national language. Another minor writer, Richard Owen Cambridge, comments on the ascendancy of Puritan cant during the period of the Civil War and the

Commonwealth, followed by the fashionable talk of Restoration wits, followed by the naval and military shop talk of the wars under King William and the Duke of Marlborough. And after that:

> The peace taught us the language of the secretary's office. Our country squires made *treaties* about their game, and ladies *negotiated* the meeting of their lap-dogs. Parliamentary language has been used without doors. We drink claret or port according to the state of our *finances*. To spend a week in the country or town is a *measure*; if we dislike the *measure*, we put a *negative* upon it.[37]

'Parliamentary language has been used without doors' is a splendidly concise account of the rise of jargon, a particular metaphor for the general process. At this point on the road out of Jonathan Swift, the native speaker or common cultivator of the language appears to be increasingly aware of his own practices; and increasingly curious; and perhaps just a little uneasy.

(xxx)
. . . AND ON, PAST H. W. AND F. G. FOWLER . . .

The uneasiness comes from confronting awkward questions: am I socially acceptable? do my habits betray me? am I *well-bred*? In nineteenth-century pronouncements on common usage, the object is more and more the definition of respectability and only by the way a concern with scholarship and polite learning, according to Chesterfield's notions of good English (see p. 86 above). The shadowy standard of 'the best authors', always to be glimpsed in Johnsonian pronouncements on language, almost insensibly gives place to the veiled ideal of 'the best people'. Nineteenth-century critics of usage are generally not writers of stature turning from their major works to make some observations on accuracy and taste; there are no magisterial voices like those of Johnson or Swift. The Victorian instructors come from cathedral close or schoolroom, middle-class men of incidental letters, a good deal worried by the rise of science and technology, the flourishing of journalese, the untoward and growing pretensions of the masses. 'Good English' was something to be rescued from these destructive influences – ostensibly as a matter of scholarship, or stylistic precept, or linguistic principle, but essentially as a question of *values*.

Consequently, pronouncements on usage commonly implied what modern jargon would call 'a hidden agenda', but made no consistent appeal to a constructive theory. Rulings were negative, preferring thou shalt not to thou shalt, using arbitrary pronouncements to separate the washed from the unwashed, and sniping at particular words and phrases, to the chagrin of philologists like FitzEdward Hall, who deplored the lack of scholarly integrity and well-founded theory in the polemics and skirmishings of linguistic amateurs. In an essay splendidly untypical of the prescriptive spirit of his age, Hall convincingly rebuts the authoritarian pretensions of what he calls the 'dogmatiser in the province of philology', who, 'instead of intelligent convictions', has 'scarcely more than tenacious partialities'. One such 'dogmatiser' was a contributor to the *Edinburgh Review*, who ridiculed the use of *supplement* as a verb. '*Supplement* is, by its form, the "thing added or supplied", not "the act of supplying it"', this critic declared, adding, 'you might just as well say, that, instead of appending another page to your book, you intend to *appendix* it'.

Hall comes down on this with an incisive demonstration that the form of a word is no impediment to its having more than one function, an argument leading to this conclusion:

> *Supplement*, as a verb, and meaning what it does, is, consequently, not a shade more irregular, viewed etymologically or in any other way, than *augment, ornament, torment*, or the Scotch *implement*, or the obsolete *detriment*, 'injure'. Again, the adduction of the verb *appendix*, with intent to discredit the verb *supplement*, is peculiarly unfortunate. We have often seen the phrase 'to *climax* an argument;' and who, after having heard a few times 'to *appendix* a book,' would revolt against it, any more than against 'to *index* it', or against 'to *catalogue* a library'?[38]

Hall's message, as befits one involved in the preparation of the *Oxford English Dictionary*, is descriptivist rather than prescriptivist: observe, record, describe, try to discern the principles that govern the development of usage, think twice and three times before you venture to condemn.

That is nowadays a respectably orthodox, indeed mandatory stance, at least among professional linguists, but it could not have been generally typical of Hall's contemporaries. More representative of the prevalent habit of dogmatizing was Henry Alford, Dean of Canterbury and author of *The Queen's English* (1864, repr. 1889), a book in which he displays some of his own 'tenacious partialities', with anecdotal comments. (He tells us, for instance, that Coleridge greatly disliked the forms *gifted* and *monied*, observing of the latter: 'I imagine other participles being formed by this analogy, and men being said to be pennied, shillinged or pounded.') But the real importance of *The Queen's English* is its position as the model and titular forerunner of *The King's English*, that godfather text of modern works on usage, published in 1896 by the brothers H. W. and F. G. Fowler.

The Fowlers' manual has many great merits, notably that of ample citation from current journals and literary works, and some demerits, which on the whole are taints of the time. They frequently convey the impression that good English is a middle-class prerogative, going with good breeding, good manners, and good taste. They are severely critical of whatever strikes them as ungentlemanly or unaesthetic, and they adroitly transmute their dislikes into quasi-rational denunciations of particular words – 'reliable', 'banality', 'bureaucracy', 'femininity', 'distinguished', 'amoral', and many others. The arguments with which they support their instinctive positions are of the kind that FitzEdward Hall had rebutted in his commentary on the *Edinburgh Review*'s vehement objections to *supplement* as a verb. Of the latter, the reviewer observed:

> *Supplement* is, by its form, the 'thing added or supplied', not 'the act of supplying it'. You might just as well say, that, instead of appending another page to your book, you intend to *appendix* it.

The Fowlers take a strikingly similar stance in their opposition to *reliable*:

> The objection to it is obvious: you do not rely a thing; therefore the thing cannot be reliable; it should be rely-on-able (like *come-at-able*).[39]

This is a specimen of arbitrary philologizing: of what Hall termed 'instinctive legislation' – and which of us can claim total immunity to it? But in the work of the Fowlers there is a recurrent conflict between judgements arising out of personal instinct and those based on the authority of usage. Things are wrong because they are just wrong, because they sound wrong, because no decently educated person could suppose them to be right, because that would be immoral. (Otto Jespersen called H. W. Fowler 'an instinctive grammatical moraliser', and Fowler was pleased to accept the title.) Such messages can be read between the lines, and often in the lines, of more than one passage in *The King's English*.

The Fowlers do not devote any chapter of their work specifically to the topic of jargon. In the sections devoted to grammar and construction they refer to journalese (the word was fairly new in the 1890s), and in their chapters on vocabulary they have a great deal to say about *slang*, under which head they treat instances of what we would now call jargon. We gather that the good-citizen-in-the-middle is passively receptive to 'slang' of different kinds, coming at him from different quarters:

> To the ordinary man, of average intelligence and middle-class position, slang comes from every direction, from above, from below, and from all sides, as well as from the centre. What comes from some directions he will know for slang, what comes from others he will not.[40]

What comes from 'below', it seems, is the uncouth usage of the lower classes – the examples cited are *bike, nice* (as in 'a nice day'), *awful* (as in 'an awful storm'), and *chronic*, of which the authors say that 'it has been adopted by the masses, as far apart at least as in Yorkshire and in London, for a mere intensive, in the sense of *remarkable*'.

Other words come from 'regions that to most of us are overhead' – that is, from the studies of philosophers, historians and critics. Among the examples cited are *phenomenal, immanence, epochmaking, inwardness, cryptic, philistine,* words which the Fowlers obviously perceived as items of show talk, specimens from some general Jargon of Pretension. Then there is the 'slang' that 'comes from different sides or from the centre', meaning 'the many words taken originally from particular professions, pursuits, or games, but extended beyond them'. There could be no clearer description of shop talk, or Jargons of Profession. The Fowlers provide 'a short list of slang phrases or words that can most of them be referred to more or less of certainty to particular occupations':

> To *hedge, the double event* (turf); *frontal attack* (war); *play the game, stumped* (cricket); *to run* – the show, &c. – (engine driving); *knock out, take it lying down* (prize-ring); *log-rolling, slating, birrelling* (literature); *to tackle* – a problem, &c. – (football); *to take a back seat* (coaching?); *bedrock, to exploit, how it pans out* (mining); *whole-hogging, world policy* (politics); *floored* (1. prize ring; 2. school); *the under dog* (dog fighting); *up to date* (advertising); *record* – time, &c. – (athletics); *euchred, going one better, going Nap* (cards); *to corner* – a thing – (commerce) – a person – (ratting); *chic* (society journalism); *on your own, of sorts, climb down, globetrotter, to laze* (perhaps not assignable).[41]

This list is a random compilation, and the last five items ('perhaps not assignable') are certainly not products of any occupational shop; however, the Fowlers' point is made, and interestingly made for those of us who have not heard of *birrelling,*[42] or who had not realized that in the colloquial English of the 1890s *up to date* was particularly associated with the language of advertising. ('Up to date' was presumably how one described the 'state of the art' before 'state of the art' replaced 'up to date'.)

The Fowlers are ready to concede that 'slang' has some place in the development of language, but gravely warn their readers against its corrupting effect in literary usage. They also present a code of five principles designed to protect the user against other potentially corrupt practices. The principles are:

1 Prefer the familar word to the far-fetched.
2 Prefer the concrete word (or rather expression) to the abstract.
3 Prefer the single word to the circumlocution.
4 Prefer the short word to the long.
5 Prefer the Saxon word to the Romance.

Readers are then advised that 'different kinds of composition require different treatment', and that consequently 'in this fact may be found good reasons for sometimes disregarding any or all of the preceding rules'.

These recommendations have greatly influenced twentieth-century prescriptive or corrective writings on usage and composition. Twenty years after *The King's English*, Sir Arthur Quiller-Couch published his lectures *On the Art of Writing*, in which he not only refers to and endorses the Fowlers' five principles, but in his chapter 'On Jargon' adds some recommendations of his own:

> The first is: Whenever in your reading you come across one of these words, *case, instance, character, nature, condition, persuasion, degree* – whenever in writing your pen betrays you to one or another of them – pull yourself up and take thought.
>
> . . . . . .
>
> Next, having trained yourself to keep a look-out for these worst offenders (and you will be surprised to find how quickly you get into the way of it), proceed to push your suspicions out among the whole cloudy host of abstract terms.
>
> . . . . . .
>
> Let us turn to another trick of Jargon: the trick of Elegant Variation, so rampant in the Sporting Press . . .
>
> . . . . . .
>
> For another rule – just as rough and ready, but just as useful: Train your suspicions to bristle up whenever you come upon 'as regards,' 'with regard to,' 'in respect of,' 'in connection with,' 'according as to whether,' and the like. They are all dodges of Jargon, circumlocutions for evading this or that simple statement: and I say that it is not enough to avoid them nine times out of ten, or nine-and-ninety times out of a hundred. You should *never* use them.[43]

The essential Fowlerian doctrines are developed here, in warnings about mode words, about sloppy connectives, and above all about the dangers of the abstract noun. Having laid down his prescriptions, Quiller-Couch goes on to present a cautionary text, a translation into jargon of Hamlet's soliloquy *To be or not to be*:

> To be, or the contrary? Whether the former or the latter be preferable would seem to admit of some difference of opinion; the answer in the present case being of an affirmative or of a negative character according as to whether one elects on the one hand to mentally suffer the disfavour of fortune, albeit in an extreme degree, or on the other to boldly envisage adverse conditions in the prospect of bringing them to a conclusion. The condition of sleep is similar to, if not indistinguishable from, that of death; and with the addition of finality the former might be considered identical with the latter; so that in this connection it might be argued with regard to sleep that, could the addition be effected, a termination would be put to the endurance of a multiplicity of inconveniences, not to mention a number of downright evils incidental to our fallen humanity, and thus a consummation achieved of a most gratifying nature.[44]

This brilliant assault on the twin bugbears of abstraction and wordiness implies the conviction which Quiller-Couch shared with Jonathan Swift, that jargon is a weevil working its way into the mind and insidiously corrupting reason and perception. His lecture 'On Jargon' concludes with a declaration of stylistic faith:

> So long as you prefer abstract words, which express other men's summarized concepts of things, to concrete ones which lie as near as can be reached to things themselves and are the first-hand material for your thoughts, you will remain, at best, writers at secondhand. If your language be Jargon, your intellect, if not your whole character, will almost certainly correspond. Where your mind should go straight, it will dodge: the difficulties it should approach with a fair front and grip with a firm hand it will be seeking to circumvent. For the Style is the Man, and where a man's treasure is there his heart, and his brain, and his writing will be also.[45]

That goes a stage or two beyond those earlier evaluations of usage as an index to the best minds and/or the best society; here it becomes a definition of superior morals.

Quiller-Couch's morality of usage was certainly shared by George Orwell, who in more than one place echoes, paraphrases or reproduces the principles and prescriptions of Quiller-Couch and the brothers Fowler. In his best-known piece on usage, 'Politics and the English Language', Orwell writes:

> When you think of something abstract you are more inclined to use abstract words from the start, and unless you make a conscious effort to prevent it, the existing dialect will come rushing in and do the job for you, at the expense of blurring or even changing your meaning.[46]

Orwell's particular quarry was the English of public transactions: as he puts it, 'official English, or Stripetrouser', 'the political dialects to be found in pamphlets, leading articles, manifestos, White Papers and the speeches of Under-Secretaries'. The purpose of Stripetrouser, he considered, was to confuse, to mislead, to lull with clichés, abstractions, cynical euphemisms. (As when 'pacify' is used in the sense 'to overpower and subjugate by force of arms', or more briefly, 'to bomb'.) Orwell perceives these things as the symptoms of a sick society. His programme for stylistic defence, or what the modern jargonist might call 'consciousness raising', owes everything to the Fowlers:

i   Never use a metaphor, simile or other figure of speech which you are used to seeing in print.
ii   Never use a long word where a short one will do.
iii   If it is possible to cut a word out, always cut it out.
iv   Never use the passive where you can use the active.

v   Never use a foreign phrase, a scientific word, or a jargon word if you can think of an everyday English equivalent.
vi Break any of these rules sooner than say anything outright barbarous.

These rules appear again in the writings of Sir Ernest Gowers, a distinguished civil servant, whose teachings in *Plain Words* – followed by *More Plain Words* – followed by *The Complete Plain Words* – have in our time claimed an authority comparable to that assumed by *The King's English* in the 1890s and the early decades of the twentieth century.[47] The titles of the books tell their own tale. Gowers is not concerned with English fit for kings, or even queens; Civil Service English is his business, and his object is the rehabilitation of Stripetrouser. See how the time-honoured prescriptions are recalled:

> Use no more words than are necessary to express your meaning, for if you use more you are likely to obscure it and to tire your reader. In particular do not use superfluous adjectives and adverbs and do not use roundabout phrases where single words would serve.
> Use familiar words rather than the far-fetched, if they express your meaning equally well; for the familiar are more likely to be readily understood.
> Use words with a precise meaning rather than those that are vague, for they will obviously serve better to make your meaning clear; and in particular prefer concrete words to abstract, for they are more likely to have a precise meaning.[48]

You could hardly be blamed for thinking that recommendations have hardened into rules, and that rules have expanded into a creed, regularly and devoutly chanted, by schoolteachers, by editors of journals, by Disgusted of Tunbridge Wells, by sinners of every capacity. The Fowlers, Quiller-Couch, Orwell and Gowers represent the modern, century-long orthodoxy in questions of usage, and have given us a very effective method of inquisition; for if I cannot convict you of stylistic heresy under one head (say, your fondness for abstract nouns), I can surely damn you under another (perhaps, your inclination to use long words when short ones would do). One comfort for the student troubled by an obscure feeling that this severe theology of usage in some way fails the user, is that those arch-inquisitors would not emerge with total credit from an examination of their own writings, or of the reasoning underlying the principles they profess.

Certainly they have good reasons on their side, and their principles are generally useful to the journeyman in language, but still, the modern orthodoxy – which has grown out of the ancient prejudice – is not wholly a matter of reason. The road out of Jonathan Swift has been a journey among feelings, to which reasons have been attributed from time to time. There is the feeling that language can be – must be – evaluated as 'good' or 'bad'; and that 'good English' is 'plain', or better still, 'pure'; and that the best English, this plain, pure English, will always pass the test of purity because it will be understood by 'ordinary people' (a category like 'the taxpayer', embracing citizens of no established identity); that some words or expressions are inherently bad, convicting the user of mental sloth and the surrender of the individual will to the mindless whims of the masses; that clear thought will beget clear language, and that clear language will beget right action, which in its turn will foster true relationships in the good society. Unfortunately, such feelings have rarely been nurtured in a charitable and hopeful spirit – rather, in exasperation, scorn, despair, even rage; and though the rules constructed from them may well have served as useful guides to practice in speech or writing, they have also promoted division and dissent.

(XXXI)
... AND SO BACK TO THE HERE AND NOW AND WHY

All attacks on jargon express or imply the fear that it is a symptom of a declining culture. We are never what we used to be: never as concrete as Shakespeare, as majestic as the King James Bible, as clear as Swift, as trenchant as Burke, and if there were any health in us we would get rid of jargon altogether – set up committees to report on it – publish a White Paper promulgating measures to combat the proliferation of undesirable practices – and return to the simplicities of those olden, golden ages of English style. So we would.

But jargon is not to be got rid of, not by the best teachers, the best writers, the sternest and most fastidious guardians of our culture; because while it may be a literary disease it continues to be a social necessity. Give us this day our daily phrase, and forgive us our jargoning, for it makes things so much easier. It helps to sustain the fabric of society – so effectively that it seems at times to *be* the fabric, and everything else mere pattern and colouring. In its simplest function it marks the dealings of professionals who share a calling, as they explain positions, expound arguments, signify agreement, banter with each other. We have workmates; jargon is a token of mateship.

It is also a token of social pretensions, a claim to be seen, heard and identified as an acceptable sort of animal. A politician, reputed to be a man of some refinement, who abruptly quits the even tenor of his ordinary discourse in order to declare himself 'gobsmacked', or to denounce the 'porkies' of his antagonists, or to predict a 'double whammy' threatening the British public should the opposition prevail, is in effect shouting 'Look at me, lads!' while he proclaims his emphatic solidarity with citizens in the economic classes C1 and C2.[49] Never mind the philosophy, his instinct tells him, go out and get yourself gobsmacked. His instinct is right; we identify ourselves – or identify our *preferred roles* – by our slang and our jargon. If I allude to 'the community charge', I allow my hearers to make certain assumptions about my politics; or to put it another way, talk of the 'poll tax' might not be well received at the Conservative Club. In the same way, *enterprise culture* would raise hackles at a Labour Party Rally; *caring society* goes better with a red rosette.

More often than we are aware, jargon is the sly servant of ideology. In political cant especially, but also in various kinds of publicity and copywriting, whole philosophies, essential beliefs and compelling doctrines are compressed into words and short phrases, slogans which proclaim a stance. In this way, because it confines argument to mere labelling, ideological jargon is *reductive*. At the same time, because its slogans forestall questioning, resist critical analysis, and generally inhibit discussion in any further terms other than those they generate or imply, they are *directive*. They tell you where to put your cross. Phrases like 'freedom of choice' and 'the enterprise culture' are ideological slogans which presume the acceptance of some preliminary trains of argument (for instance, that 'freedom' is morally superior to and socially more desirable than 'equality'), and anticipate or rule out the possibility of subsequent argumentation (by implying, for instance, that 'enterprise' needs no definition and is self-evidently better than some of the other things that might characterize a culture, e.g. 'planning', 'collective action').

It is not hard to identify the social functions of jargon; and very easy to devise a jargon for labelling them. There is an interpersonal function, in the communications of shop talk; a 'membershipping' function, a way of claiming inclusion in some social class or category, in various styles of show talk; and an ideological function, in political and commercial sales talk. But knowing *how* jargon works in our day-to-day experience does not wholly explain *why* we resort to it so frequently. Talking about a 'function' leads to the assumption that the jargonist *chooses* the material of his or her jargoning, and designs an effect. It averts attention from the possibility that jargoning is a *habit*, or a response conditioned by certain stimuli; that its use may be found pleasurable, or funny, or reassuring; and that users may frequently have no very clear consciousness that their usage verges upon jargon. One writer's jargon is another's method, serving no intention other than that of denoting a meaning as briefly as possible. Will we, for example, invariably denounce as jargon the word (or phrasal compound) *decision-making*, because it frequently turns up in such jaded and journalistic rigmaroles as 'involving the people in the decision-making process'? Will we not agree that *decision-making* might sometimes offer a useful alternative to *[the] making [of] decisions* in 'the making of decisions is a great burden', or 'she worried about making decisions', which may be reconstructed as 'decision-making is a great burden', 'decision-making worried her'? The impulse to form compounds like 'decision-making' need not lead to something identifiable in itself as jargon. It is only one symptom among many of *jargoning*, and jargoning is not so much a state as a style – a stylistic response to complex psychological promptings.

Some of those promptings are respectable, others less so. As a rule, shop talk is honestly prompted. It arises from the most congenial of motives, to make sense of the world in terms that make sense of one's everyday activities and dominant concerns. The jargoning of horsey folk who talk about 'hard going', 'taking your fences', 'an outsider', 'ready for the off', 'under starter's orders', 'bar none', 'past the post', 'coming up the home straight', etc., may be construed as the style of people comfortably translating the vagaries of life at large into the relative simplicities of the race track. Let society be Epsom or Aintree, then its leaders are the favourites, its members in general are the runners, its failures are the also-rans, its problems are fences, its general condition is the 'going', and so on. Such simple transferences endow the common tongue with expressions that eventually settle into cliché, but often retain some of the colour of figurative language and some of the comedy of slang.

A less worthy motive is the desire to separate the knowing sheep from the ignorant goats, thus establishing one's claims as a fleecy insider, one of the prize flock. Jargoning works to exclude and include. If, as so often happens, I cannot understand the art criticism in some periodicals, I feel excluded, resent the pretentious manner of these pieces, and grumble about jargon. But the critic almost certainly does not think of himself as a jargonist; his talk of 'exquisitely plain encaustic two-tone harmonies', of a 'process of modification and defacement elevated to a leveller ethic', of 'expansive, ultimatum qualities, achieving on average a kind of vasty blare' (all examples from one of the weekend supplement mandarins) may sound to me like Osric on the South Bank, but to him are legitimate tokens of knowing what he is talking about. Your language tells the world that you know your stuff, and that your stuff is the right stuff to know.

The impulse to proclaim one's insidership has a corresponding desire, to be shielded from the suspicion of being an outsider, an unsophisticated ignoramus. Everybody is vulnerable, nobody likes to confess 'I don't know', still less 'I don't understand'; and so the emperor's clothes are sedulously woven. Those who attend committee meetings and have suffered the tedium of many boards and assemblies will know the difference between people who speak to the point and others who speak in a kind of desperate litany, jargoning busily. Do these committee-jargonists feel threatened by the solemn professional circumstance, or is their motive rather to be described as a sense of decorum? The urge to adopt the appropriate style of speaking, and the feeling of exposure and embarrassment if one fails to do so, is almost as powerful as the instinct to wear the right sort of suit. A sense of occasion is undoubtedly one of the motives of jargoning.

But here is a link with another motive, the sense of verbal adequacy. Jargon provides in ready-made gobbets the verbal material that will pass for thoughtful discourse. Jargoning is language at work, but periodically nodding on the job; it dozes through the struggle for telling expression, the individual account of thought and experience, the unremitting stress of seeking precision and of having to compromise with imperfect solutions, and wakes to find the text accomplished. (As Orwell puts it, 'unless you make a conscious effort to prevent it, the existing dialect will come rushing in and do the job for you'.) Jargon offers an automatic facility of which most of us are content to avail ourselves now and then; it even allows a small margin of creativeness, enough to persuade us that we are expressing ourselves cogently, perhaps vividly, demonstrating an assured command of language. What it seems to offer above all is a recipe for that treasured modern condition, 'togetherness'. Around the workplace, in the office, over at the club, in the minutes of the meeting, in the draft paper, the report, the review, everyone can slip into the appropriate jargon if the effort to speak as individuals becomes so awkward as to hinder easy communication, or perhaps to hinder the process by which things are not only communicated but are seen to be communicated. I formulate and submit: you evaluate and respond. (Translate: I speak, you reply.)

(XXXII)
AT THE END OF THE DAY, AT THIS MOMENT IN TIME

So at the end of the day, at this moment in time, togetherness is what jargon is about. Membership rules, OK? – and showing, through your language, that you have paid your dues, of sense, of sympathy, of sycophancy, is an obligation laid upon you whenever you discuss the daily news, or the financial situation, or hemlines, or hooch, or anything in the teeming corporate life of This Great Country Of Ours. Much jargon is a token of recognition, like a regimental tie or a Masonic handshake; and tokens are elaborated by further tokens. Consider, for instance, the interesting phenomenon of *political correctness* (or *PC*), a club-making power of such formidable clout, particularly in academic circles, that the liberal, the eccentric and the solitary are obliged to keep what is fashionably known as a low profile. *PC* engenders a great deal of jargon. It not only decrees that spokes may go with persons or even with crats (like aristos) but never with men; that the average person-in-a-wheelchair may be said to be disadvantaged but never crippled, not disabled but differently abled; that the wicked are socially under-motivated; that the blind are unsighted and the deaf acoustically deprived; that the ugly are aesthetically challenged; that sex shall be known as gender, and the old-time battle of the sexes as new-style gender politics; that henceforth the expressions 'black comedy', 'black moment' and that fine old weather-wisdom 'it's getting a bit black over Bill's mother's' shall be deemed not to exist, except in the forms 'macabre entertainment', 'extremely unpleasant episode', and 'there is a heavy concentration of cloud over the East Midlands area';[50] that lust shall be called 'sexuality', or better, 'sexual orientation', to account for diverse tastes; not only these, but more, much more, for it begets in addition the manifold *-isms* that define the politically incorrect. There is, of course, racism, and sexism too; but also ableism and ageism and heightism and fattism. These words and expressions are created in response to the rules of right-thinking association, which decree that you shall be relied upon always to conduct your discourse with irreproachable humanity and tact, and thus avoid the suspicion of harbouring Fascist ideas and of having the general disposition of a misogynistic storm trooper.

Jargon begets jargon, as word-forms suggest other word-forms. Jargon also attracts jargon, as a stylistic principle; when a piece of jargon settles on a line of text, in come its cawing, ragged, black-winged (or for PC's sake *Afropenniform*) relatives, all perching in a row, 'politics of choice' next to 'classless society' next to 'people's charter' next to 'value for money', or 'environment' with 'ecological' with 'biodiversity'. Being of a feather, the birds flock noisily together; and much as one bird cries the same message as its neighbour, so, in jargon, one word caws in stylistic variation with its partner – *benefit culture*, for example, doubling with *dependency culture*, or *command economy* with *planned economy*. Words are about other words. Names replace, or elaborate, or play variations on names, and in this respect jargon differs from the technical language and shop talk that are so often absorbed into jargoning; for a technical term is bound to the contract supposedly existing between a signifier and a signified, or a word and some kind of 'thing', whereas true jargon, vintage, jargonist's jargon, requires only that a word should be a word, with other words in view.

There is something of metaphor in this; but the primary purpose of metaphor is to illuminate and explain, which jargon rarely does. There is also something of the fashionable variation of slang, but jargon can seldom make slang's claim to picturesque, uncompromising vigour; *senior citizen* is a euphemistic, jargoning variation on *old age pensioner* (or *OAP*, to spare the subject the embarrassment of having it spelled out), but slang goes its vivid, heartless way and calls the poor creature a *wrinkly* or a *crumbly*. At least *crumbly* recalls some sort of something – a picturesque ruin, maybe, or a loaf of dry bread – and there is consolation in the illusion of substance; but *senior citizen* is sealed in the senseless sense of 'meaning in other words'. Yet we use such expressions happily enough, and deliberately choose to make use of them. If I accompany my friends to a circus or an exhibition of paintings, I do not ask to buy tickets for a couple of wrinklies and the odd crumbly. I say 'three senior citizens', and feel pleased enough to consider myself a beneficiary of the caring society. The jargon does very nicely, like the American Express card, for it helps us through a world of transactions and pantomimes, where the mobled queen runs barefoot up and down and we need to find a good word or two for whatever is going on. Jargoning is wording, and words are increasingly what we have to live by at this shadowy moment in senior citizen time, before the end of the crumbly day; for as Dr Johnson once said, words are the daughters of earth, but things are the sons of heaven, and he surely knew what he was talking about.[51]

Notes

1 Popular etymology identifies *way* (meaning 'motion') with *weigh* (as in 'weigh anchor'). Thus 'under way' = 'under weigh', and the seaman's phrase 'under way, making way' = 'under weigh, making way', i.e. with the anchor lifted and the ship in motion. But neither the comparable Dutch expression, *underweg*, nor associated words and phrases such as 'headway', 'sternway', 'losing way', 'getting some way on her', lend much colour to the suggestion that in one particular instance *way* = *weigh*. 'Under way, making way' may be paraphrased 'in motion, gaining momentum'.

2 W. Strunk and E. B. White, *The Elements of Style*, 3rd edn, New York: Macmillan Publishing Co., 1979.

3 For an explanation of 'economical with the truth', see the glossary in Part II. Mandy Rice-Davies spoke her celebrated piece – 'Well he would, wouldn't he?' – in the course of the Stephen Ward trial, which took place in London in 1962. Ward, an osteopath with a number of fashionable or aristocratic friends and clients, was charged with living on the immoral earnings of prostitutes; but the trial had a political significance, since it involved the reputation of a leading member of the Conservative government, and Ward (who committed suicide before the end of the trial) was something of a scapegoat. Much of this is now forgotten, or half-forgotten, but 'Well he would, wouldn't he?' remains as a cynical way of saying 'That is only to be expected, and why are you surprised?'

4 *Mens sana in corpore sano*, from Juvenal's 10th Satire, and *Quis custodiet ipsos custodes*, from the 6th, are not so much misquoted as misapplied, through ignorance or faulty recollection of the contexts in which they occur. The poet does not imply a causal relationship between states of mind and body (if your body is healthy your mind will be sound), as teachers of physical education commonly suppose; he bids us, as we grow older, to 'pray for a sound mind in a healthy body'. As for the guardians, Juvenal suggests that a man with a lascivious wife might ensure her chastity by paying people to watch over her – 'but who will watch the watchers?'

5 A contributor to the *Spectator* (Ian Buruma, 2 February 1991) notes the

common tendency of sporting talk and fighting talk to chop and change with each other: '. . . the jargon tends to get confused; hot-dog fighter pilots talk about how it's "still early in the game", while television sportscasters speak of "massacres", as in, for example, the massacre of the Raiders by the Bills.'

6   The 'broken cricket bat' came in a speech made to the House of Commons by Sir Geoffrey Howe, justifying his resignation of the post of Foreign Secretary. He complained that the Prime Minister (Mrs Margaret Thatcher) had by intervention and subversion so impaired his freedom of action at the conference table as to make him feel like a batsman whose captain had deliberately sent him in with a broken bat. In the subsequent debate Mrs Thatcher scornfully observed that all he had to do in that case was get a new bat; she apparently did not take into account the alternative possibility, of getting a new captain.

7   See Jonathon Green, *Dictionary of Jargon*, London: Routledge & Kegan Paul, 1987. This comprehensive work replaces the same author's *Newspeak, a Dictionary of Jargon*, London: Routledge & Kegan Paul, 1984.

8   Nicholas Abercrombie, Stephen Hill and Bryan S. Turner, *The Penguin Dictionary of Sociology*, London: Penguin Books, 1984.

9   From C. Juncker, 'Writing (with) Cixou', in *College English*, 50, pp. 426–7. I am grateful to Susan Peck MacDonald for drawing my attention to this passage. See note 16 below.

10 The reference to G. M. Young occurs in the 2nd (1973) edn of Sir Ernest Gowers' *The Complete Plain Words*, Harmondsworth: Penguin Books, p. 133.

11 Talcott Parsons, *Societies: Evolutionary and Comparative Perspectives*, p. 9. Englewood Cliffs, NJ: Prentice-Hall, Inc., 1966 (Foundations of Modern Sociology Series).

12 Reg Melton, 'An Alternative Approach to Assessment', in *Teaching at a Distance*, 23, p. 49. Milton Keynes: The Open University, summer 1983.

13 Diane Bailey, 'Samuel Smiles Revisited: Helping Yourself in the Open University', in *Teaching at a Distance*, 23 (see note 12 above), p. 10.

14 *Spectator*, 7 December 1991.

15 Donald Pease, 'J. Hillis Miller: The Other Victorian at Yale', in Jonathan Arac, Wlad Godzich and Wallace Martin (eds), *The Yale Critics: Deconstruction in America*, p. 75. Minneapolis: University of Minnesota Press, 1983 (*Theory and History of Literature*, vol. 6).

16 F. Jameson, *The Political Unconscious: Narrative as a Socially Symbolic Act*, p. 218. Ithaca, NY: Cornell University Press, 1981. I first came across this passage, as well as the extract from C. Juncker's 'Writing (with) Cixou', quoted on p. 55, in Susan Peck MacDonald's paper, 'The Literary Argument and its Discursive Conventions'; see Walter Nash (ed.), *The Writing Scholar: Studies in Academic Discourse*, pp. 31–62. Newbury Park: Sage Publications, 1990. Dr MacDonald's comments are more ample than mine and not so ill-humoured.

17 Daniel O'Hara, 'The Genius of Irony', in Jonathan Arac *et al.* (eds), *The Yale Critics: Deconstruction in America*, p. 119.

18 Rodolphe Gasche, 'Joining the Text: From Heidegger to Derrida', in Jonathan Arac *et al.* (eds), *The Yale Critics*, p. 168.

19 In his Forword to G. C. Spivak, *In Other Worlds: Essays in Cultural Politics*, New York: Methuen, 1987.

20 For an excellent study of Puritan Jargon, see M. van Beek, *An Enquiry into Puritan Vocabulary*, Groningen: Wolters-Noordhoff, 1969.

21 For illustration of the polite jargon of duelling, see the report in *The Times*, 8 April 1803, on a duel between Colonel Robert Montgomery and Captain James Macnamara, RN. See further the reports on the inquest on Montgomery (*Times*, 9 April), and on Macnamara's trial (*Times*, 23 April).

22 Eric Partridge, *The Penguin Dictionary of Historical Slang*, Harmondsworth: Penguin Books, 1972.

23 Byron's fluency in low-life jargon may have had sources other than 'professors' of the noble art of boxing. In his day, Francis Grose's *A Classical Dictionary of the Vulgar Tongue* (1785) had been republished under the title *Lexicon Balatronicum* (1811); and in 1811–13, the sporting writer Pierce Egan had published his *Boxiana; or Sketches of Antient and Modern Pugilism* (enlarged, 1815–29).

24 'Tap your claret' = 'to draw blood'. 'Claret' for 'blood' goes back to the early seventeenth century, but Partridge notes 'from ca 1770, mostly in boxing circles'. He also notes the use of 'claret' as a verb, quoting Egan's *Boxiana*: 'Purcell's mug was clareted'.

25 On the derivatives of 'laser', see Kerstin Klasson, *Developments in the Terminology of Physics and Technology*, Stockholm Studies in English, XLII. Stockholm: Almqvist & Wiksell, 1977, p. 167. I am indebted to Dr Klasson's monograph for a number of examples of technological word formation.

26 Edward Tenner, *TechSpeak, or How to Talk High Tech*, London: Kogan Page, 1989, p. 13.

27 It is typical of Swift that one of his poetic squibs – 'On the Day of Judgement' – clinches its final line with a cant word. When humanity presents itself for judgement, the Almighty is angrily amused, in true Swiftian style. Says God, 'I damn such Fools! – Go, go, you're bit' (meaning 'you've been conned').

28 'Walls have ears' was a saying in common circulation during the Second World War, when it figured often in posters and bills warning the public against careless talk that might be overheard by a spy. ('Careless talk costs lives', the companion legend ran.) But no one ever added 'Hedges have eyes'.

29 Lord Chesterfield, *Letters*, ed. Bonamy Dobree, London: Eyre and Spottiswoode, 1932. Letter 123.

30 James Boswell, *Life of Johnson*, ed. R. W. Chapman, Oxford University Press, World's Classics paperback reprint, 1983, p. 825 (entry dated Sunday 14 September 1777).

31 Boswell, *Life of Johnson*, p. 873 (Tuesday 23 September 1777).

32 Boswell, *Life of Johnson*, p. 1235 (Thursday 15 May 1783).

33 Crispinus' (or Marston's) 'windy words' include 'inflate' 'reciprocal', 'retrograde', 'conscious', 'spurious', 'strenuous' and 'defunct', along with 'lubrical', 'turgidous', 'ventosity', and 'obstupefact'. See Arthur H. King, *The Language of Satirized Characters in Poestaster*, Lund Studies in English, X. Lund: C. W. K. Gleerup, and Copenhagen: Ejnar Munksgaard, 1941.

34 Archibald Campbell, *Lexiphanes*, 2nd edn, London, 1767, p. 126.

35 Boswell, *Life of Johnson*, p. 1099 (year entry, 1781).

36 Boswell, *Life of Johnson*, p. 1251 (October 1783).

37 Richard Owen Cambridge, article in *The World*, 12 December 1754.

38 FitzEdward Hall, 'English Rational and Irrational', in *The Nineteenth Century*,

vol. 43, 1880. Reprinted in W. F. Bolton and David Crystal (eds), *The English Language*, vol. 2: *Essays by Linguists and Men of Letters, 1858–1964.* Cambridge: Cambridge University Press, 1969. For the quoted extract, see p. 38.

39 H. W. and F. G. Fowler, *The King's English*, Oxford: Oxford University Press, 3rd edn, 1931; repr. paperback 1979, p. 52.

40 *The King's English*, p. 58.

41 *The King's English*, p. 60.

42 'Birrelling' is the Fowlers' spelling of 'birling'; and 'birling' is synonymous with 'log-rolling'; and 'log-rolling', in the jargon of the 1890s, was a metaphor for what we would now call 'puffing' or 'hyping'.

43 Sir Arthur Quiller-Couch, *On the Art of Writing*, Cambridge University Press, 1916, pp. 87, 90, 93, 94.

44 Quiller-Couch, *On the Art of Writing*, p. 96.

45 Quiller-Couch, *On the Art of Writing*, p. 103.

46 George Orwell, 'Politics and the English Language' (1946); in *The Collected Essays, Journalism and Letters of George Orwell*, vol. 4, New York: Harcourt, Brace, Jovanovich Inc., 1968.

47 The most recent issue of *The Complete Plain Words* is the 3rd, extensively revised edn by Sidney Greenbaum and Janet Whitcut (London: HMSO, 1986).

48 Sir Ernest Gowers, *The Complete Plain Words*, 3rd edn, p. 48.

49 The allusion is to Mr Christopher Patten, who, as Chairman of the Conservative Party, used these expressions during the British election campaign of 1992. Mr Patten shortly afterwards became Governor of the Crown Colony of Hong Kong.

50 In the dialect of South-East Derbyshire, the saying 'it's gerrin a bit black ower Bill's muthas' portends the advent of a thunderstorm.

51 A similar remark is attributed to one Samuel Madden (1686–1765): 'Words are men's daughters, but God's sons are things'.

Part II

Such as in Cases of the Ensuing Nature
A Glossary of Additional Instances and Further Comments

Note

What follows is not a lexicon; it is only a device for saying 'furthermore', and 'by the way', and 'what do we say about this?'. Readers of our so-called 'quality' newspapers, viewers of prime-time television and reflective persons in general will have no difficulty in adding further furthermores. (For more than furthermore, and numerous ways by the way, there are some excellent dictionaries of jargon and new words; see the Biblio-graphical Note on pp. 208–9).

Since it cannot be comprehensive, my glossary is bound to seem arbitrary in its selections. Why should I include in it some words and phrases to the exclusion of others which a reader may consider more obvious examples of jargon? This, indeed, brings everything back to the difficulty of defining jargon in the first place. It eludes simple definitions; its *parameters* are uncontrollably plural; it soapily evades the grasp; every day we meet it, revile it, rejoice in it, ignore it, know all about it, and yet there is no definition of jargon so firm as wholly to satisfy an enquirer. Must a word be put down as jargon because it is new? Not so, a wise friend reminds me. Some of the ripest jargon is made out of old words. And yet the status of new words, if not as jargon then as *adjuncts to jargoning*, is something that must always puzzle the collector. There are current words and phrases that seem to me to be jargon-like, or on their way to becoming jargon – words that have 'jargon potential', to put it jargon-wise. Then again, there are words that enter into the *aggregate* of jargoning, stylistic fellow-travellers, associate members of the gabbling academy, and they ought not to be left entirely out of account. Much that strikes me as jargon does so by peripheral qualification – it smells and smacks of the thing – or by the relative power of being jargon in one place but not necessarily in another.

Here are puzzlements enough for any critic. As for the criteria that have guided me, not always with logical certainty, I would list the following:

1   Word forms. Certain types of word formation are very productive in jargoning, e.g. prefix-formations ('Euro-', 'macro-'), suffixing ('-ize', '-ify'), phrasal nouns ('care package'), acronyms (in techspeak), grammatical shifts (e.g. noun–verb shifts as in 'target', 'access'). On this, see pp. 10, 19–21.

2   Shop talk, of two kinds, i.e. (i) 'pure' shop, the distinctive terminology of a profession, craft, or practice, old or new, and (ii) 'borrowed' shop, as when one jargon supplies another. (Thus, 'a difficult one to call' is sporting shop – the umpire makes the call – borrowed into the language of political or administrative decision-making.) On shop talk, see pp. 7–9, 13–14.

3   Social group language; the exclusive/inclusive usage of a subculture, e.g. rockspeak, youthspeak, drugtalk. See pp. 77–9.

4   'Cant' – the phraseology of politicians, PROs and pundits, civil and moral. 'In the public interest' and 'family values' are specimens of cant. Those in high office speak it all the time, or – if they are not sufficiently talented to produce it for themselves – have officials and speech-writers to create it for them.

5   Journalese, including the language of broadcasters, news-readers and 'sportscasters', the latter being assiduous purveyors to the general public of what the *Readers Digest* used to call 'picturesque speech and patter'.

6   Mode words and phrases. On this important matter, see p. 16–18, *et passim*.

7   Some slang. This is a very fuzzy, subjective category; slang overlaps with jargon (the Fowlers considered the two things as much the same, see p. 93), but not all slangy sayings are stuff for the jargonist. This makes for capricious decisions. Why do I keep **plonker** and drop **stonker**? Why bring in **wimp** and **naff**? (Do I contradict myself? Very well then I contradict myself.) In general, I think that slang has a jargoning impulse (a) when it is the language of a subculture, (b) in providing a source for the jargonist – as when, for instance, **double whammy** enters the language of electioneering polemic, and (c) in furnishing a type of affective terminology for casual use in social or political discourse. Discussions of political leadership often include **wimp**; architecture, interior decoration, fashions, may be decidedly **naff**.

8   Allusive, figurative and 'metaphrastic' expressions; e.g. 'winter of discontent', 'well he would, wouldn't he?', and, for an example of a metaphrase on top of a metaphor, 'haemorrhage' = 'leak' = 'illicit disclosure'. See pp. 21–2, 24–6 on allusion and metaphor; p. 11 on metaphrase.

It will not take a philosopher to see how some of these categories are a little less than categorical, or how, in many of the words listed below, one 'category' may be seen to overlap with another. But jargon is not a philosopher's business (though philosophers are capable of producing it as abundantly as the next chatterbox); it is the common talk of fallible folk, set down here to set folk talking.

Most of the words and phrases cited in Part I are not re-listed here, though for inconsistency's sake I have included one or two. Within each entry, **bold type** is used **either** to direct the reader to another entry, or occasionally to amplify the scope of the headword. (Thus **approach**, for example, includes the item **skills approach**, and **bottom out** is 'amplified' by **bumping along the bottom**.) In repeating the headword, or in citing examples for which no separate entry is provided, *italics* are used. Of the quotations occasionally used in illustration, many are taken from newspapers and journals, duly acknowledged; others are undocumented, being of conversational origin or of my own (plausible, I hope) invention.

A

AB This coded reference denotes, in economic/demographic shop, the upper and professional middle classes: 'While the AB groups (the professional classes) have become markedly more pessimistic about the future, the rest of the population (including the electorally crucial C1s and C2s) have continued to cheer up' – *Observer*. See also **C1, C2**; and **DE**. Such stratifications have been anticipated in imaginative literature. The infants in Aldous Huxley's *Brave New World* are taught to cry 'I'm glad I'm an alpha!' – or a beta, or a gamma, etc., according to their allotted station in life.

ableism Discrimination in favour of the able-bodied. If your employer has reservations about your glass eye, he (or, to avoid the charge of sexism, she) is an ableist, or rather, a *disableist*. Note the word form; -isms are the current masters of the abstract noun. See also **PC**.

about, that's what X is; alt. **X is what that's about** This formula, a candidate for the George Orwell Prolespeak Award, if there were any such thing, defines the purpose and function of all variants of X. Thus, Goals are what football is about (alt., Football is about goals); Athletics are about effort (alt., Effort is what athletics are about); People are what life is about; Neighbours are all about helpfulness; Christmas is about children; Handkerchiefs are what blowing your nose is about; and Babbling inanely while they measure you for your straitjacket is what **banging on** like this is about. This phrase obeys the jargoning principle of talking big and meaning little; mainly a sportscaster's formula, it also enjoys favour among bar-room moralists.

abuse Maltreatment of children and tennis rackets; misuse of Evo-Stik, lighter fluid, and other volatile and narcoleptic substances. See, accordingly,

child abuse, racket abuse, and **solvent abuse.** A mode word, verging on cant, or at least on social euphemism, since *child abuse* too easily and queasily accounts for so many unspeakably abominable acts.

acceptable/unacceptable Adjectives denoting what politicians and financiers think they can or cannot get away with; or what we, the public, are prepared or not prepared to put up with – always supposing that we know what is going on. Thus, 'acceptable levels of pollution'; 'the unacceptable face of capitalism'; 'the risks of transporting such wastes long distances by sea and road are unacceptable'. *The unacceptable face of capitalism* (sharp practice in the market, **insider dealing**) has become a package phrase with possible extensions: 'They have formed their own political party . . . which has been described as the acceptable face of anarcho-Thatcherism . . .' – *Observer.* This modish piece of jargon often keeps stylistic company with **sensitive.** See also **issue.**

access This is a verb. Its meaning is not 'to give physical access to', but 'to make available'. The back door may give access to the garden, but prayer accesses the Almighty, with, in some cases, restricted facilities.

accessible Another mode word, meaning fairly easy for your ordinary sort of chap to understand; not uncomfortably abstruse; requiring some effort, but well worth it, really. 'X's ideas are fairly accessible' means 'I am not lost in bewilderment after the first three sentences', and 'Y is an accessible author' means that Y is a cut above Jackie Collins, but not as hard as James Joyce. Accessibility, however, is not in all cases **acceptable:** 'All great music can be accessible, but it's totally selling an audience short if you pretend you can sell the Brahms violin concerto like a pop video' – *Independent.*

accountability The principle historically established in the Parable of the Talents, that servants are answerable to their masters and must accordingly be prepared to give an account of themselves; from which it is thought to follow that governors are answerable to the governed, whose interests they serve. This is a **sensitive issue.** See also **open government** and **economical with the truth.**

acid house It is necessary even for **crumblies** to understand this phrase, which unites rockspeak and drugtalk. *House* is a style of rock music, originating in Chicago, depending more on the accompanying production of dazzling or deafening electronic effects than on the talent of the performing musicians. *Acid house* is a youthful festivity involving the assembly of large numbers of participants who dance to the strains of *house* and 'trip out' on hallucinogenic drugs (LSD, or lysergic acid, and of recent times **Ecstasy**). See further **festival.**

across the board Affecting or including all categories in a particular scheme or proposal: 'There will be salary increases across the board, from junior grades to top management'; 'The agreement proposes a 20% reduction across the board of tactical and strategic nuclear weapons'. This piece of jargon is now so comfortably lodged in the common usage of negotiators that its figurative origins ('board' = 'table') are all but forgotten.

act, getting it together   Getting your act together is the current version of the process once solemnly known as 'bringing some order into your affairs'. Alternative phrases are *getting your ducks in a row* and *sorting yourself out* (alt., *getting yourself sorted*). The shorter form, 'getting *it* together', has the same meaning, but may also signify success in dealing with a **problem** – 'he had a drink problem, but now he's got it together'; 'her folks are a bit of a problem, she can't seem to get it together with them'. Success in overcoming mental illness or drug addiction may be called *getting your head together*.

activist   One who takes an active part in promoting political and social causes; as in 'Labour activist', '**green** activist'. Forms in **-ist** are less common than the **-isms**; *-ist* is nevertheless a productive suffix for the jargon-maker.

actressocracy   Portmanteau words are often the comedians of jargon (but not in techspeak, where they are deadly serious). Here is a portmanteau of 'actress' and 'aristocracy', meaning actresses who have married into the aristocracy. For a comparable blend (portmanteau) form, see **artocrat, spokescrat**. Earlier examples of this kind of playful formation are *plutocrat, squirearchy*.

adultify   To treat children as adults, the converse being **infantilize**: 'If there is one feature of our society more troubling than the adultifying of children, it is perhaps the infantilising of adults' – *Guardian*.

aerobics   In nineteenth-century techspeak, an 'aerobe' meant a microbe living on oxygen supplied by the ambient air. The term was coined by Louis Pasteur, in the form *aerobie*. Thence came the adjective 'aerobic' ('having to do with aerobes'), and then, of recent years, the noun **aerobics**, in plural form, like *mathematics* or *gymnastics*. Aerobics is a **high-impact** form of gymnastic exercise, not connected with microbes, but designed to stimulate the intake of oxygen, fortify the fit, and induce the collapse of stout parties. Those who prefer drowning may take a course of *aquarobics*, the waterborne version of this exercise.

Afrocentrism   One of the latest **-isms**. In reaction against European assumptions of cultural dominance (sometimes denoted as **Eurocentrism** or **Eurocentricism**) it promotes the claims of Africa as a founding centre of civilization.

ageism   A politically incorrect disposition to question the capacities, talents, motives and entitlements of the elderly, i.e. anyone more than five years older than oneself. The term *senior citizen* is an attempt to correct the ageist sentiments lurking in colloquialisms such as *gaffer, codger, old bat, old biddy, old fart,* and, of recent times, **wrinkly** and **crumbly**. See **P(olitical) C(orrectness)**.

agenda, hidden In the political mode, *the hidden agenda* means the complex of **sensitive issues** that make up the potentially **unacceptable** items of someone's **ideology** – meaning what they don't tell you about what they intend to do if they get half a chance. Old phrases like 'ulterior motive' or 'concealed purpose' might do at a pinch, but somehow lack the **clout**. This is a very modish expression. Do not say 'Some parish councillors are trying to get rid of the old fish-and-chip shop *on the sly*'; say 'The progressive streamlining of local catering facilities is evidently an item of high priority on the council's hidden agenda'. See also **curriculum, hidden**.

agitpop In rockspeak, a portmanteau of *agitator* and *pop* (i.e. *pop*ular music). Meaning music turned to the service of political propaganda, this word is based on an earlier blend, *agitprop*, from the name of a bureau of the Communist Party Central Committee in the Soviet Union, the *Agitpropbyuro* (*agit*atsiya + *prop*aganda). Most agitpop is neither very beguiling as *pop* nor very effective as *agit*.

agony uncle This playful piece of journalese updates the long-established **agony aunt**, a woman employed by a newspaper to give worried readers helpful advice on sundry painful topics – e.g. broken marriages, faithless lovers, refractory children, glue-sniffing (a.k.a. **solvent abuse**), menstruation, adiposity and acne. The advent of the agony uncle, a representative of the **new man**, reflects the progress of **consciousness raising** and **gender politics**.

agribusiness A glum portmanteau of 'agriculture' and 'business'; a specimen from the shop talk of those who never held a spade but can turn over a profit.

airhead In the language of the young and easily scornful, this means one of little brain: *a blockhead, deadhead, dickhead, dunderhead, fathead, linthead, rubblehead, thickhead*. In militarese [noted during the Gulf War of 1991], it signifies a place for landing troops from the air; modelled on earlier *beachhead*.

Albanianize To create a politically repressive, economically backward, isolated, God-forsaken nation-state; this used to be called *Balkanization*. 'Nowadays, its Balkan neighbours mischievously speak of Romania's "Albanianization"' – *Economist*. Further, see **Kuwaitization, Benidormification**.

alphabetism A parodic -**ism**, invented by a contributor to *New Scientist* (Ian Stewart, 22 Oct. 1987). It means discrimination on the grounds of alphabetical order. If your name begins with *A*, your application is first in the pile, if it begins with Z you are **disadvantaged**. See also **extremilexic**, **fundilexic**.

alternative Occurring in phrasal compounds, e.g. **alternative lifestyle**, **alternative medicine**, **alternative comedy**, **alternative culture**, this does not imply a choice between equal options. It denotes a rejection of the current orthodoxy. Alternative lifestyles reject the notion of living in style; alternative medicine renounces pharmacology; alternative comedy eschews old-fashioned funny men; alternative culture turns a righteous back on society. See further under **lifestyle**, **New Age**.

alternativist One who chooses or supports an alternative lifestyle. 'Things began to go sour in the Eighties when the old hippies and alternativists found themselves ill at ease in a world which had spawned "crusties" and various post-punk types' – *Independent*.

among the medals 'He looks like being among the medals' = 'He will probably be placed 1st, 2nd or 3rd in this foot-race/long jump/hammer-throw/[other] international athletic event.' 'Britain is out of the medals' = 'We are not going to win anything this year, either.' This grandiosely inane phrase is a specimen of (British) sportscasters' telebabble at its most pretentious. See also **in contention**, **on the pace**, **up to speed**, and **left for dead**. Generally, runners are in contention as long as they stay on the pace, but if they cannot keep up to speed they will literally be left for dead and forfeit their chances of finishing among the medals. Some commentators grow hoarse with bellowing nonsense of this kind; but always recover to shout another day.

animalist Another *-ist* word: an advocate of **animal rights**, i.e. an opponent of hunting, and of laboratory experiments on animals in the name of science and medicine. In the latter meaning, it is replacing the much older 'anti-vivisectionist'. An *animal rights group* is a covey, gaggle, skein, pride or herd of animalists.

anonymize To render anonymous. A useless word that ought to be dememorialized as soon as possible. Tests taken anonymously, questionnaires anonymously completed, are said to be *anonymized*: 'The anonymised screening, he said, went ahead only after careful consideration by the hospital's ethical committee' – *Independent*.

approach One of the educationist's indispensable mode words (see Part I, p. 58), an 'approach' means a way of teaching, or a way of teaching about teaching, or possibly a way of thinking about teaching about teaching. Teaching approaches may be *teacher-centred* (chalk and talk and avoid the individual eye), or *subject-centred* (supply cumulative book-lists, and give reading assignments on which tests will be held), or *pupil-centred* (allow questions). There are **skills approaches**, **audio-visual approaches**, and **continuous assessment approaches**. The phrase **alternative approach**

may be taken to imply that all other approaches are useless. In more general usage, 'approach' is a useful idiomatic adjunct to 'question', or **problem**; in medicine, 'an approach to the management of terminal cases' would signify 'dealing with the dying', and in law, 'approaches to a rational sentencing policy' might mean 'making the punishment fit the crime'.

area   Every day, in every modish way, enough is said or written about *areas* **in terms of** *dimensions, departments, aspects* and *general connections*, to make further comment unnecessary. It is worth noting, though, how deftly a skilled political performer can manage the word, finding a place for it in the most effective position, at the end of a sentence: 'Mr Hurd insisted that Britain would support a deepening of cooperation between states in the judicial area' – *Independent*. This must mean that Britain would be **proactive** in broadening the scope of international collaboration in the legal sphere.

artocrat   A person highly placed in the administration of the arts. (For the portmanteau form, compare **Eurocrat, spokescrat**.)

asking the questions   Not, as one might suppose, a phrase culled from the usage of the sardonic film detective ('*I'll* ask the questions, if you don't mind'), but an indispensable phrase out of the sportscaster's book, meaning 'attacking', 'challenging the opposition with skilful play', as in 'Arsenal are asking all the questions now'. The origin of this curious sample of picturesque speech and patter is unknown. Usually the players do the figurative talking, but recently an American golf course was reported (on TV) as asking some awkward questions of the competitors in a championship tournament. As yet, no one has been subjected to the ruthless interrogation of a snooker table, but the day may come, and the odd croquet hoop may yet pose a devilish query.

as such   In Standard English, this handy adjunct (see p. 23) is equivalent to the Latin *per se*, and means 'in itself', or 'as commonly defined': thus, 'I do not object to smoking as such, it's your blowing it in my face that I find objectionable'. The jargonist uses it somewhat differently, in senses paraphrasable as 'in my opinion' or 'what you might call', and also with the nuance 'in particular': 'He's not a good footballer as such' = 'I wouldn't call him a good footballer'; 'It's been a bad week for business as such' = 'It's been a particularly bad week for business.' Other meanings are 'therefore', 'thus', 'consequently', 'because of that': 'The approach is most likely to appeal to course teams which see concepts and skills within their subject areas as building very much on one another, and as such the approach is likely to be of greater interest to course teams in the science, mathematics and technology faculties.' (See Part I, p. 58.)

at the end of the day   We used to say 'When all's said and done', or 'in the end', or 'after all'. *At the end of the day* has little to do with time, and a lot to do with emphasis; it sounds wearily wise and sagaciously long-sighted, but at the end of the day it doesn't mean a great deal. Politicians are fond of it. See p. 22, on *package phrases*.

at this moment in time Another package phrase: in plain English, *now*; or, with emphasis, *here and now*; or, in plain American, *right now*. *At present* would also do nicely. But the implications of 'at this moment in time' are often neither momentary nor temporal. 'At this moment in time we do not anticipate any shortages as such' = 'To tell you the honest truth, we do not know if there will be shortages, and if there are, we will probably not call them shortages.' 'At this moment in time' may be a way of taking your oath, and **as such** is a fitting companion for **in any way, shape or form**, and also **basically**.

attitude problem See generally under **problem**. To have an attitude problem is to resist, or be critical of, conventional codes of behaviour, postures of civility and deference, etc.; to be wanting in **commitment** to your trade or your professional duties; to be reprehensibly frivolous about serious matters; in extreme instances, to be sullen, foul-mouthed and aggressive. Attitude problems come out of a sense of being hard done by, or of being forced into an inferior position. They may also arise out of other problems – *cash-flow problems, drink problems, marital problems*. But essentially it is the cat who spits at a king that has an attitude problem.

audiophile The smart word for someone who collects gramophone records. A mark of the genuine state-of-the-article. As philatelists are to stamp-collectors, so is the audiophile to the mere record player. See further under **digitization**.

auteurist An adjective (usually; but also occurring as noun) denoting the fashionable theory that it is the director, rather than the scriptwriter, who is the true creative power, or 'auteur', in film-making. Derived from the French, an excellent language **as such**, but in transposition a fertile source of what used to be known as kiddology. *Plus ça change, plus c'est la même chose.*

authentic It is not easy to determine the sense of this word, which is often used as a synonym for 'authoritative': 'an authentic performance', 'an authentic statement', 'an authentic personality'. It also doubles with **genuine**: 'it's absolutely genuine and authentic'. In the language of music criticism, 'authentic performance' often refers to a performance of early music (usually seventeenth–eighteenth centuries) strictly confined to the use of 'period' instruments and techniques that the composer would have recognized. 'Traditional' is a related sense, shading into **classic** (which means heaven knows what, see Part I, p. 51). The sentence 'We were treated to a display of authentic flamenco dancing' might therefore imply that the dancing was authoritative, genuine, stylistically pure, traditional and classic.

authored   In the lamentably humourless jargon of the academic CV – *curriculum vitae*, a respected form of **docufiction** – *authored* means 'originally written', as opposed to merely 'edited' or 'compiled'. There is also a verb **co-author**, which, like **author**, is usually found in the past tense or in the past participial form. (Or even in a modalized past: a recent communication asks me to 'state the titles of any books you may have co-authored' – but does not go so far as to ask for the names of any children I might have co-parented.)

aware   A modish adjective, usually linked with a designating adverb, as in 'environmentally aware', meaning actively conscious of the need to take care of our physical environment. Also **awareness**, e.g. 'She displays a high degree of awareness in ecological matters'. People are also 'politically aware', whereas at one time – notably in the 1930s – they were 'politically conscious' (an epithet usually applied, however, to members of the Communist Party).

awfulize   To make something inherently awful seem more awful yet, as in 'awfulizing the future'. This awful word, more awful even than **anonymize** and **adultify**, seems to be of American origin, a circumstance which must surely proactivize and mimeticize patriotic British jargonists: 'we have a tendency towards awfulizing and catastrophizing' – *Newsweek*.

B

-babble   A derogatory suffix, denoting empty or inflated talk, gob-bledygook: *Eurobabble, telebabble, psychobabble*. The first element in these compounds is customarily (a) Graeco-Roman, and (b) disyllabic. This rhythmic principle may reduce the likelihood of 'sportsbabble' and 'governmentbabble', but you never can tell. For an alternative word formation, see **-speak**.

baby-boomer   Someone born during years of high birth-rate, or 'baby-boom'; specifically in the period 1945–52. 'Once zestful baby-boomers are now in their forties' – *Independent*. 'What Teeter was discovering was that as baby boomers were having families, they were concerned with "family values"' – *Guardian*. (See **value**.) The jargoning converse of *boom* is *bust*; hence, a **baby-buster** is someone born during a period of declining birth-rate.

back to back   Used adjectivally, this phrase means 'occurring in immediate succession', e.g. *back to back centuries* (in cricket), *back to back engagements/appointments*, etc. It is the kind of 'racy' jargon that might fall under the heading of pseudo-metaphor. It serves no indispensable purpose, since in most instances the word 'successive' would do as well, or the phrase 'one after the other'.

badmouth Perhaps to be reckoned slang rather than jargon, this is worth noting at least as a sample of word formation. It is a verb (transitive), meaning to miscall, malign, disparage, speak ill of. There is no such word- form as 'goodmouthing', but then there is no procalling, boligning or conparaging. Badmouthing is a constituent of what is known in youthspeak and black English as *dissing* – to 'diss' meaning to treat dismissively or insultingly.

balance Also known as *even-handedness*; the impartial representation, in the *media*, of opposing views and conflicting circumstances. Raucously demanded by parties who take offence when they get it; a specimen of political cant. 'Possessing highly professional talent, and the illusion of impartiality (a venerable illusion, with its lexicon of "balance", etc.) as well as occasionally dissenting programmes, 'public service broadcasting' developed into a finely crafted instrument of state propaganda' – John Pilger, in the *Guardian* (7 Sept. 1992).

ball A sporting metonymy; some account of its significance in sport-scasterese and general shop is called for. Most of the British usages come from soccer: the *long ball*, as in 'playing the long ball', 'the long ball game' (when the ball is persistently kicked upfield); the *through ball*, meaning the pass through the defence, to a waiting player; and the *fifty-fifty ball*, meaning the ball for which opposing players compete, with equal chance of sustaining a moderately crippling injury. In rugby, *quality ball* means possession which can be developed into attacking play; quality ball is supplied by the forwards to the backs. In cricket *the throat ball* is a delivery (from the bowler) calculated to pop up and strike the batsman somewhere between the chin and the adam's apple; compare *bean ball* in (perhaps outdated?) baseball talk. Here is a rich vein of sometimes alarming shop talk, as a sentence like 'All afternoon he's been laying on his lovely little balls' (noted during a television soccer sportscast) must surely demonstrate. Some 'ball' phrases are well established, e.g. *play ball with me, throwing a curve ball, the ball is in your court.*

ballpark figure Book-keepers' and statisticians' shop: a general, round-figure estimate of a large number. Originally used to denote the probable size of the crowd at a baseball game, this American expression was subsequently extended to any estimate of population, expenditure, budgetary outlay, etc. 'How much is this project going to cost? – I don't want it down to the last penny, just give me a ballpark figure.' Britons tend to confuse 'ballpark' and 'ballgame' – but that is a whole new ballpark.

bang on A quasi-figurative word form, *bang on* replaces, with heightened emphasis, earlier phrases such as 'drone on', 'witter on'. (On this process of 'heightening' in slang and jargon, see Part I, p. 18.) It means to talk insistently and at boring length: 'This **wally** went banging on about his Rover.'

barnstorming > brainstorming In the 1920s *barnstorming* was the province of travelling showmen, and specifically of itinerant post-war pilots putting on displays of aerobatics for the benefit of impressionable rural communities. It has developed the political meaning of 'vigorous campaigning' (in rural and provincial areas); and recent usage suggests some confusion, whether playful or unintentional, between a barnstorm and a brainstorm: 'Among the subjects covered at the brainstorming session on 22 June, according to inside sources, was the necessity to take journalists out to lunch and write their stories for them ...' – *Independent*. The current slightly mistaken use of *barnstorming* may have taken colour from *storming*, meaning 'irresistible' (as in *stormin' Norman*, a nickname conferred on General Norman Schwarzkopf, the officer commanding Allied forces in the 1991 Gulf War).

basically Increasingly, this word is used as an adverbial disjunct, introducing a sentence or declarative clause with the sense of 'in fact', 'actually', 'to be honest'. 'Basically, I realised that a new approach was required' – *Independent*. ' "Basically, I'm going to tell them to shove it", he said' – *Guardian*. Like **at this moment in time** its main purpose is often to affirm the statement that follows.

basket of currencies In financial shop talk, a 'basket of currencies' means a selection against which the value of anyone's money might be measured: 'The pound has fallen against a basket of currencies including the D-mark and the yen.' The homely, housewifely feeling that this is all a matter of bread and cheese and a rasher or two of streaky bacon is quite illusory; there is no source-jargon here, only a little word-play. Note that in his *Dictionary of Jargon* Jonathon Green defines *basket* as a political term denoting 'a group of interrelated issues or topics, especially those that are scheduled for discussion at a national or international conference'.

benefit culture See under **culture**.

Benidormification The process of turning a small, charming coastal settlement into a vulgar sprawl of multi-storey hotels, casinos, Olde Englysshe Taverns, vomiting hooligans clad in Union Jack boxer shorts, souvenir shops, and Clubs with Karaoke Nites for the stupendously and shamelessly untalented. From Benidorm, one of the lost villages of old Spain. Also called **Benidorming**: 'Its presenter ... was concerned with the means by which tourism is 'spoiling the world', and specifically with the Benidorming of Turkey' – *Independent*.

benny See **wally**, and, indeed, the whole thesaurus of youthful miscalling and multiform **badmouthing**, e.g. **dink, dork, dweeb, nerd, plonker, wimp**, and all the sub-species of dunce and **airhead**.

big bang Financial/political shop, from a scientific source-jargon (on source-jargons see pp. 30–8): a popular name for the **deregulation** of the (London) stock market in 1988. Alluding to the cosmological theory which postulates that the universe began with an enormous explosion, 'big bang' implies an act of total creation or re-creation. In that sense it can be used with reference to any process of vigorous and fundamental change.

bimbo A young woman (occasionally a young man, or 'pretty boy') of great sexual endowment and little else. In reference to men, it has some of the sense of earlier 'gigolo', in that a male bimbo is often a kept man – see further, **toy boy**; in reference to women, it suggests the character of what used to be called the 'enthusiastic amateur' (at the time of the Restoration, the word would have been 'punk' – see Part I, p. 78). The form **bimbette** is sometimes used to distinguish the female of the species, with **bimboy** or **himbo** for the male. American politicians with old love-affairs or incautious 'flings' to conceal have learned to appreciate, at election time, the danger of the **smoking bimbo,** or mistress in the closet – a pleasant journalistic play on 'smoking bomb'. British politicians are perhaps more keenly aware of the lurking danger of imprudent *obiter dicta* and ill-considered jibes – the threat of the smoking *bon mot,* so to speak.

bio- This word-forming prefix is growing in public esteem as a voucher of 'scientific' status, an example being *biodegradable*: 'biodegradable waste' consists of organic material which will conveniently rot away into the good green earth, or lend itself to **recycling** in the form of (say) wrapping-paper or cat-litter. 'Biological' is a favoured adjective among copywriters selling cosmetics or washing powder. In marketing jargon, the prefix **bio-** has suffix-allies in **-free** and **-friendly**. If it's biological it's pollution-free and environment-friendly. See **environment, pollution.**

biodiversity Holier than shop, this is a word out of the **green** litany. High on the list of **ecological** and **environmental** priorities, *biodiversity* denotes the multitudinous species of plants and animals which we must observe, record, respect and rescue. Biodiversity is to be seen everywhere, though more in the rain-forests of Brazil than in, for example, Ealing.

blow the whistle on In the source-jargon (football of any code) 'blowing the whistle' refers to the referee's action in stopping the game because the rules have been infringed. As transferred into general usage, the phrase refers to the action of an employee, subordinate, member of staff, etc., in company or government service, who reluctantly draws public attention to institutional misconduct. A whistle-blower is an informer, but one who may claim some moral credit for his/her action.

blue-chip More source-jargoning. In the casino, the blue chips carry the highest monetary denomination. In the world of finance, 'blue-chip stocks' represent the most reliable investment. Thus the epithet *blue-chip* comes to mean 'most expensive', 'costly', 'of a quality only affordable by the rich': '... long-established blue-chip galleries have closed at a frenetic pace' – *Observer*.

bolt-on In carmanspeak (see p. 39) 'bolt-on goodies' are additional fitments literally bolted on to the car by its proud owner: wing mirrors, bumpers, tow-bars, lights, chrome-plated ornaments. There are current signs that *bolt-on* may become established in other fields; e.g. a law, an act of Parliament, a manifesto, etc., may have 'bolt-on' provisions, a schedule of prices may have 'bolt-on' supplements, etc.: 'Getting a nasty shock when the invoice arrives because of bolt-on charges to the basic price is another source of misery' – *Sunday Times*.

bonk journalism The reporting, mainly in the **tabloid** press, of the sexual activities of **celebs** and even **royals**. *Bonk*, meaning 'to copulate', has overtaken the earlier *bang* (verb) and *bunk-up* (noun). Inasmuch as *bonk journalism* relies on contributions from paid informants, it is a sub-species of *cheque book journalism*, the competitive acquisition of tall tales in return for large sums of money.

boot[strap] Before a computer can be *up and running* (see Part I, pp. 4–5) it must be 'booted (up)', i.e. supplied with its basic programs. The verb is derived from the noun 'bootstrap', and what is playfully implied is that the computer, in running through its preliminary self-instructional routines, is 'pulling itself up by its own bootstraps' – a feat impossible to human beings, but within the compass of the indispensable machine. The usage may spread; in commerce, for example, a *bootstrap operation* is one requiring no money or assistance from external sources, a 'self-financing' project.

bottle This best-of-British word means 'steady resolve', 'fortitude', 'nerve', 'guts', as in *he's got a lot of bottle. You're losing your bottle* = 'You're getting cold feet'; *She bottled out* = 'She lost her nerve'. The etymology is a little mysterious. I am inclined to think that it can be traced back to eighteenth- and early nineteenth-century low-life jargon (see p. 73), in which *bottom* had much the same meaning, although no one in those days 'bottomed out' or 'lost their bottom'. Eric Partridge lists the sense 'stamina, GRIT', dating this meaning from 1747, and quoting one Captain Godfrey, who states, in his *The Science of Defence*, 'Bottom, that is wind and spirit, or heart, or wherever you can fix the residence of courage'. My *Shorter Oxford Dictionary* quotes Byron: 'He died all game and bottom.' But a bottom was also a backside. Dr Johnson once referred to a certain lady as having 'a bottom of good sense', and when his companions were convulsed with laughter angrily insisted, 'The *woman* was *fundamentally* sensible'.

bottom line The bottom line of a bill, account, column of figures, etc., denotes the total amount; hence, figuratively, the price that has to be paid for anything. 'Go into Europe by all means, but the bottom line has to be some surrender of sovereignty'. **Bottom-line** also occurs as a transitive verb: 'You cannot bottom-line a job until it has been time-costed' – *Daily Telegraph*.

bottom out Phrasal verb, meaning to sink to the bottom, to reach the lowest point on a downward curve: 'The recession is bottoming out.' A piece of political pop-talk. The figurative reference may be to the shape of the sea-bed; this appears to be the metaphor implicit in **bumping along the bottom**, e.g. 'the economy is bumping along the bottom' – meaning that the economy has 'bottomed out' but has not begun to come up again. See **turn the economy round, upturn**.

brilliant Here is God's plenty: militarese, wine-writer's shop, youthspeak. In weaponry, a missile so finely programmed as to be capable of very precise self-guidance, is 'brilliant'. Brilliant weapons replace earlier marvels, which were merely **smart**. In wine-talk (see Part I, pp. 48–50) 'brilliant' conventionally describes a superior vintage. In youthspeak, 'brilliant', contracted to *brill*, means much the same as *fab*, *bad* and *wicked* – in other words, great and super and generally pretty OK, OK?

broadsheet A newspaper of large format, not easily handled on the Piccadilly Line; has close print, complex sentences, long paragraphs, intellectual pretensions; the opposite of a **tabloid**. *Broadsheets* are sometimes called 'quality' papers, or, less formally, 'posh' papers, and now and then, because of their content, *the heavies* – epithets never applied to tabloids. It is presumably the necessity of having a discursive antonym to *tabloid* (for one would not wish to speak of 'the tabloids and the poshes', or even 'the tabloids and the qualities') that has fetched *broadsheet* out of its occupational hutch and into the general run of usage. A very dignified word. Broadsheets are read by the **pontificating classes**.

broker (vb) In the sub-diplomatic jargon of *peace-keeping missions*, negotiations between warring parties, agreements to suspend hostilities, etc., are *brokered* by neutral agents. The source-jargon is finance (as in 'stockbroker', 'insurance broker'), but the immediate impulse is from *honest broker*, in the sense of an impartial and trusted intermediary. 'Meanwhile, the latest ceasefire between federal and Croatian military leaders, brokered in Sarajevo by the UN special envoy, Cyrus Vance, appeared to be taking hold' – *Independent*.

brutalize Originally an intransitive verb, meaning 'to behave brutishly', and then a verb usually constructed in the passive, e.g. *to be brutalized* = 'to be made brutish', this is now frequently a transitive verb with the sense 'to treat brutally', e.g. 'The court was told how some officers brutalized the prisoners'. The usage lends itself to metaphrase (on which see p. 11); 'some officers brutalized the prisoners' means 'some officers maltreated the prisoners', or simply 'some officers beat the prisoners'. A noun,

brutalizing, has developed: 'There was one question left by this ... film. Why did the MoD want it made about the brutalising and humiliation of two fliers now back on duty?' – *Guardian*.

bubble Financial shop, becoming familiar in these monetary times. A sudden downward fluctuation in the market, trade-figures, share index, etc. An antonym of 'boom': 'But the real trouble set in when the monetary policy smoothed the path from boom to bubble' – *New Statesman and Society*.

bufferism The new word for good old *Blimpishness*. Not, as the form might suggest, the **politically incorrect** act of persecuting old buffers, but rather the behaviour (petulant, splenetic, reactionary) of angry old fogeys. On fogeyism, see **young fogey**.

bum bag Not exactly a phrase from the lexicon of *haute couture*, (see pp. 52–3 on fashion talk) but nevertheless a fashionable word for a large pouch fixed to a belt and generally (despite the name) worn at the front – in effect, as a 'tum bag' – where the wearer (usually female) can check its security. The American word is *fanny pack*. Bum bags are *de rigueur* on the Costa del Sol, not unknown in Stratford-on-Avon, but seldom remarked in Rotherham.

bump Airline shop, a verb meaning to cancel a passenger's flight, even though he/she has booked a ticket: 'Last Tuesday, passengers who had bought their tickets months ago were "bumped" after they had queued for three hours to check in' – *Observer*. The quotation marks in that example suggest that the writer is a little nervous about admitting the word to common usage, though the practice is common enough.

bunce, buncing Though this street-traders' jargon is listed among the new words in at least one recent collection, it is far from new around the barrows and market-stalls; variations, as *buns, bunse, bunt*, occur from the eighteenth century onwards. (For nineteenth-century stable-lads, a *bunt* meant the pooling of their tips, and hence applied to the box in which the tips were kept.) **Bunce** as verb means 'to overcharge'; **bunce** as noun means a margin of profit to allow for pilfering; **buncing** means the practice of adding the marginal overcharge, for whatever reason. The etymology is unclear, but it may be derived from 'bonus'.

buoyant, buoyancy Financial jargon, denoting a prosperous economy – the opposite of one that is **bumping along the bottom**. 'Commenting on a record 181 billion ryals budget ... they added that only an oil price upheaval could disrupt the new buoyancy in the economy' – *Independent*.

buppie A black **yuppie**.

C

C1, C2   More economic-demographic shop: group labels for the white collar (C1) and skilled working (C2) classes. See also **AB, DE**.

cabin   Carmanspeak, in figurative vein, meaning the interior of a car; the passenger space: 'better equipped, with a well-furnished cabin' – *Independent*. In some cars the cabin is accessible through a *hatch*. See pp. 39–40, 47–8 on *carmanspeak*.

cannibalize   Not, as might easily be supposed, 'to behave like a cannibal'. This is scrap-dealers' and auto-wreckers' jargon, meaning to break up old machines, usually cars, in order to retrieve any usable or saleable working parts, or even to incorporate the retrieved parts in the construction of a new vehicle. A cannibalized engine is one constructed from such a miscellany of parts.

cap (vb), cap, capping (n.)   Current political jargon: to stop the flow of public money, set a limit on levies raised from local taxation, as in 'some Labour councils have been capped'; 'rate capping', 'charge capping'. A metaphor, from 'capping' an oil well. This figure may have more than parochial scope: 'Mr Yeltsin has asked not only for $10 bn to $12 bn to buy imports, but also for a $45 bn stabilisation fund to defend the rouble and put a cap on inflation' – *Independent*. The use of **cap** as a count-noun is also established: 'David Blunkett, Labour's spokesman, condemned the caps as a further centralisation of power' – *Independent*.

capability   In military jargon, the possession of large supplies of arms and equipment: '. . . cautious observers credit Iraq with a formidable capability' – *Observer*. In 1985/6 the Conservative government in Britain was deeply divided on the question of Britain's *helicopter capability*.

capacity   A socio-political mode word, roughly synonymous with 'room', 'space', 'site', 'premises': 'He said that there had been a threefold increase in planning applications for toxic incineration capacity' – *Independent*. Note how *capacity* takes the stink out of *toxic incineration*. 'Space for toxic incineration', or 'buildings to burn poisons in', would have seemed smellier by far.

cardboard city   Figurative expression for a foul circumstance: a collection of flimsy shelters crudely constructed from carboard packaging by communities of homeless people who spend the night in some convenient archway or underpass. See **underclass**; also drop in on **property-owning democracy**.

care package   Arrangements for taking care of a sick, handicapped/ elderly/mentally ill person: 'They have slipped through the care package. There should be a proper care package for every mentally ill patient discharged from a psychiatric hospital, and no hospital should close until that can be arranged' – *Independent*. See further **package**.

carer   General mode word for nurse, **minder**, attendant upon the child, the invalid or the aged; a member of 'the caring professions'. A modern Cain would enquire, 'Am I my brother's carer?'

casual sex   Promiscuity; copulation with a passing acquaintance; disregard of contraceptive precautions; an expression in the very latest mode, the phrasal antonym of **safe sex**. For the young a habit, for the old a hypothesis; as the French say, *si la jeunesse savait, si la viellesse pouvait*.

catastrophize   Make a catastrophe out of a mishap; foredoom catastrophe where the worst **scenario** is no worse than casual and customary **cock-up**. Nearly as awful as **awfulize**.

celeb, celebrity   A popular entertainer; one who has achieved public fame, whether by telling jokes, singing, acting, **hosting** a quiz-show, or some comparable means. (See also **royals**.) The epithet **pro–celeb**, a contraction of 'professional–celebrity', is applied to games of golf in which, to raise money for charity, professional golfers (who do not qualify as celebrities) agree to enter into partnership with celebrities (who barely qualify as golfers).

challenged   In the language of **political correctness**, the second element of compounds denoting varieties of physical or mental affliction, e.g. *intellectually challenged* (backward), *aesthetically challenged* (ugly), *orthodontically challenged* (buck-toothed). Perhaps seriously intended to overbid *disadvantaged* or *deprived* or *handicapped* in the lexicon of underprovision; but difficult to take in sober earnest.

chaos theory   In physics, an argument challenging the traditional Newtonian assumption of a systematically ordered universe, governed in accordance with a retrievable set of mathematical rules. **Chaologists** deny that things are so simple, or that all systems work as one system. The phrase *chaos theory* is sneaking into common usage as an expression with a smart, 'scientific' cachet, approved among the **numerati**, and signifying, for the less numerate, not much more than the pardonable futility of attempting to explain the ins and outs of a funny old world. It used to be the custom to refer to unpredictable events as *acts of God*; now, in less pious times, we may appeal to *chaos theory*.

charter   A prime-cut piece of political cant and electoral flim-flam. In the nineteenth century, 'charter' and 'chartist' referred to a programme of radical reform (the Chartist Movement of 1838) and to those campaigning for it. Recent usages rely on the **resonance** of the word: *Charter 88*, a campaign for a British Bill of Rights; *The Citizens' Charter* (giving guarantees of satisfactory service from public institutions), *The Passenger's* [*sic*] *Charter* (for the benefit of the railway traveller), and *The Patients' Charter* (for hospital patients, or **customers**). The last three are governmental inventions, and are declarations of benign intent rather than 'charters' in the nineteenth-century radical/political sense. But the show goes on apace; the tally of governmental 'charters' has now (June 1992) exceeded twenty.

chattering classes A rare thing, this; a phrase which is bandied about as jargon (among the classes to whom it refers), and yet can be traced to its creative source. It makes derogatory reference to those who read, muse, and impotently talk while others act; *the chattering classes* enjoy more privilege than the 'working classes' and much less power than the 'ruling classes'. They include professors, teachers, social workers and the like, and they subscribe to **broadsheet** newspapers, but do not always have beards or wear sandals. This phrase was invented by a journalist, Frank Johnson, and made popular by Alan Watkins (of the *Independent*).

child abuse The maltreatment, possibly including sexual molestation, of little girls and boys. A euphemism for incarceration, neglect, beating and buggery, practised by some parents, or worse, by some **carers**, in 'homes' designated for child care. In general, a crying shame to This Great Country Of Ours; but officially described as though it were some form of reprehensible over-indulgence. After such knowledge, what forgiveness?

chocoholic See under -oholic.

choice A huckster's word, borrowed into the cant of the hustings. In political jargon, something freely available to the rich – choice of schooling, choice of hospital, choice of transport, choice of lawyer – and a promise for the not-so-rich when the **classless society** is achieved. *Choice* is to the right wing of British politics what **caring** is to the left. Those who believe in choice naturally advocate the choice of care; and care, like anything else, has to give **value for money.**

clarification Ministryspeak, meaning anything but clarification. Its general sense is 'excuse', 'lame attempt at plausible explanation': 'Last night, the Home Office conceded that "clarification" was needed over the admissibility of computer records, the issue at the heart of the confusion' – *Independent.*

classic On this indispensable mode word, see p. 51. The following quotation shows its use in conjunction with **design**: 'Vron Ware is a freelance journalist and design consultant . . . co-author of *At Women's Convenience*, a classic design manual on public toilets' – *Observer*. It is not altogether clear from this whether the design, the manual or the toilets are classic, but such considerations rarely matter when *classic* gets into a sentence. Its shimmer invests the whole, like tinsel on a tree.

classless society A political notion, cultivated, paradoxically, by Conservatives, whose very existence requires a sense of social classification, and held suspect by Labour politicians, whose traditionally declared ideal is to abolish class distinction. In a classless society, Labour politics would presumably be **dead in the water.** See **one nation conservatism.**

clout A foolish, modish noun meaning 'power', 'influence'; from the blow that hits the right nail on the head, or boxes the appropriate ear with gratifyingly prompt and profitable results. Clout is usually political or economic, and is idiomatically 'carried'. Ministers of State, company directors, senior Civil Servants and merchant bankers all carry clout; teachers, nurses, foundrymen, steeplejacks, bus conductors, etc., are obliged to get along without it (having no **choice**), but are sometimes awarded the British Empire Medal by way of compensation.

cocktail From 'a mixture of alcoholic ingredients', the sense 'mixture of chemicals' has developed: e.g. 'a cocktail of drugs', 'a deadly cocktail of radioactive substances'. But the usage comprehends other disagreeable mixtures: '. . . beneath that seemingly trivial dispute [over the name of Macedonia] lies a cocktail of ethnic and territorial rivalries that threatens not only to touch off a war but to cause another calamitous Balkan refugee crisis and to sow the seeds of decades of instability and paranoia' – *Independent*. Here a cocktail, lying beneath a dispute, threatens to touch off a war and sow seeds of paranoia. Metaphor is a wonderful thing. Another example, from the *Guardian*: 'But eventually it [borrowing to support the currency] will prolong industry's exposure to the lethal cocktail of high interest rates and an overvalued pound.' In the same *Guardian* article the writer, varying his figure, refers to 'this anorexic diet of high interest rates and an overvalued currency'. Exposure to lethal cocktails will certainly bring on the ultimate anorexia.

cock-up theory The theory that social and political emergencies are the result of 'cock-ups', i.e. of human incompetence having arbitrary consequences; as opposed to the **conspiracy theory** which argues that such emergencies are foreseen and deliberately planned. *Cock-up theory* is the sociological equivalent of the cosmologist's **chaos theory**.

cohabit In government or in international politics, to coexist and even collaborate with nominal opponents. The European Community may be said to be an exercise in cohabitation. The word may also be used of rival currencies' equable coexistence: 'the D-mark became Europe's leading currency, while the yen and the dollar cohabited' – *Business*. The origin of this usage is in the French *cohabitation*, which can mean 'coexisting' in senses broader than the 'living together' of two unmarried individuals. Strictly speaking, then, this is French political jargon transposed into English, as if we did not have enough of our own.

cold calling Salesman's jargon: the practice of calling on a prospective client or entering a potential market without a preliminary introduction or recommendation. 'Before arriving' (at the Cannes Film Festival) 'she researches the trade papers, discovers who will be here and what projects they are keen on. Then she braces herself for some "cold calling" at the luxury Majestic and Carlton hotels' – *Independent*.

collateral damage Militarese or General Staffspeak for 'civilian casualties'; as when a missile hits the wrong bunker, or a computer unwittingly demolishes a hospital. This may happen in the course of **interdiction bombing.**

collectable Used as noun or adjective; in the world of antiques, bygones, and curios, 'collectable' means whatever people are collecting and will pay money for. Wig-stands, wind-up toys, snuff boxes, china dolls, Nazi daggers, silver decanter-labels are collectables. For a comparable word form, see **renewable.**

collectivism In political jargon, a philosophy based on the principle of collective ownership of the means of production and distribution; in a wider, looser sense, the practice of government as a relationship with collective institutions (e.g. trade unions) rather than with individuals.

colour-coordinated From the original meaning, 'designed in matching colours' (e.g. of a woman's dress and accessories, or the decorations and furnishings of a room), a new sense has developed: 'advised as to the appropriate way to dress for public appearances'. Thus Simon Hoggart in the *Observer*: 'I run into my old friend Austin Mitchell, MP, who tells me that he has been "colour-coordinated" by a fashion expert for £150. This, I am told, is all the rage in the Labour Party.' See also **style counsellor.**

command economy Political shop; also **planned economy.** An economic system regulated and directed by central government, in accordance with a political doctrine, rather than by free response to the demands of the market. The military **resonances** of 'command' are strong enough to suggest that this is a pejorative term, implying rigid, dictatorial imposition, as opposed to the more **flexible** disciplines of the *market economy*, or *monetarist economy*. It is generally assumed that *command economies* are socialist or communist (socialists prefer the term 'planned economy'), whereas 'market economies' are an expression of true-blue democratic capitalism.

commitment 'Commitment' is faith amply demonstrated by works. Football teams show their commitment, or *dedication*, when they are **motivated** and consequently 'believe in themselves'; they then go out to **do the business, give one hundred and ten per cent,** and **get a result.** Industrialists and businessmen also have commitment: 'With commitment and care, renewables will grow to maturity within the next 20 years' – *Independent*. (See **renewable.**) People who express too many doubts and queries do not have *commitment*; they have **attitude problems.**

commodification In accordance with the principles of the **market,** the reduction of an apparent imponderable (art, health, the enjoyment of leisure) to a commodity that can be bought, sold, and indexed. Even money can now be commodified, so arcane are the rituals of brokerage.

We await with interest the commodification of the Holy Ghost, a project surely not beyond the range of British marketing expertise; it is all a matter of **presentation**.

community charge Also called the **poll tax**, the former expression being preferred by the (British) Conservative government, the latter by the Labour Party in opposition. A form of taxation *per capita* (whence 'poll' = 'head') to raise money for services chargeable to the local (town or district) budget. This levy was introduced by the government to replace the earlier *rating system*, a charge on property and the householder, generally felt to be unfair in its workings; the poll tax/community charge, however, proved equally unpopular, and was phased out in 1992, to be replaced in its turn by a **council tax**, based on the assessment of property values. From the beginning, the expressions *community charge* and *poll tax* connoted opposing socio-political positions: 'Employers, many of them feeling guilty about their windfall gains from the community charge, will settle too generously with employees who are demanding compensation for their poll tax losses' – *Independent*.

compassion fatigue Although not invented by him, this ironic phrase is associated in British minds with the singer Bob Geldof, who has devoted a great deal of energy to relieving the plight of the sick and starving, especially in the Horn of Africa. Mr Geldof noted the necessity of raising money quickly from a willing public, before 'compassion fatigue' sets in – that is, before the givers become wearily used to watching, on their TV screens, scenes of suffering and deprivation.

conceptual art A phrase with a shimmer of show talk. A form of art theory, or elaborated hokum, according to the disposition of the reader, which examines the role of ideas in art, including the ideas of the theorist. See Part I, p. 60. See also **conceptualize**. The concepts of 'conceptual art' are sometimes reflected in the contrivances of **installation art**.

conceptualize To organize in a system of concepts, i.e. to develop theories, of art, of film, of literature; to state and elaborate the concepts thought to underlie the production and form of some phenomenon, e.g. art, films; to posit, as it were, the phantom skeleton under the solid flesh; or, like a critic, to assume that the cart has natural precedence over the horse. There is no end to this. 'Unlike Pauline Kael who had no interest in conceptualising the medium [the cinema] Daney was concerned with the medium as a whole...' – *Independent*.

confidence In the shop talk of the financial **market**, this ordinary word has the particular nuance of knowing that one's money is safe and sound, and that the pound sterling is not about to become the pound stalling. 'The Bank of England is concerned that if the phenomenon spreads, consumer confidence would suffer, affecting the speed of the economic recovery, or, in the worst scenario, leading to runs of deposits on banks and building societies' – *Independent*. The quotation illustrates the propensity of jargon to grow on jargon: *consumer confidence* shares a sentence with 'economic **recovery**' and 'worst **scenario**'.

confrontational, also **confrontive** Disposed to meet opposition directly, aggressively, even violently, as with truncheons or handbags: 'With hindsight the police could have adopted less confrontational tactics' – *Independent*. 'With hindsight' is a style-companion to 'less confrontational'; a useful way of saying 'if they had bothered to think about it', just as *less confrontational* signifies 'less heavy-handed'. See further **judgemental**.

confrontationism The philosophy of confrontation, or aggressively direct response to opposition; a **knee-jerk** disposition towards what is known in the United States as 'kicking ass' (which, however, implies unilateral confrontation).

consciousness raising Making people actively aware of their mental habits, their social behaviour and assumptions, their rights and obligations as citizens; in particular, directing attention towards the **issues** of alternative **lifestyles** and **gender politics**. 'Myself and a few others went off in the direction of educational camps, consciousness-raising camps. If you like, New Age camps' – *Independent*. See further **New Age**.

conspiracy theory See **cock-up theory**.

constraint A mode word, perhaps drawn from academic shop, in which – for example – a 'constraint' upon a proposition would define the conditions under which that proposition did not apply. More widely, we now have *political constraints, social constraints, constraints upon fiscal policy*, etc., meaning whatever it is that stops you from doing whatever it is. *Constraint* keeps house with words like *thrust*; an argument either has a *thrust* or there are *constraints* upon it.

consumer durables Things that can be bought, but not eaten, worn out, or used up – in short, what used to be called *hardware*, a word now reserved for a different use. Consumer durables include *white goods* – e.g. refrigerators, dish-washers – and *brown goods* – e.g. TV sets (because of their cabinets of brown plastic or veneered wood). The concept of **shelf life** cannot apply to consumer durables, which never reach their **sell-by date** but simply vanish from the show-room. Old Hoovers never die, they only fade away.

contented majority, the The majority of people who are happy with economic things as they are. Modelled on *silent majority* and *moral majority* (which, however, have somewhat different meanings) this phrase appears to have been the invention of a senior politician in the British Labour Party, John Smith, MP: 'Labour must develop policies that appeal to "the contented majority" but also produce economic and social progress, John Smith said yesterday in the latest stage of his campaign for the leadership' – *Independent*. See, however, under **culture**, the phrase **culture of contentment**.

context   The master mode word, perhaps rivalled only by **problem**. In literary shop it means 'surrounding text' (e.g. 'What does the word X mean in this context?'); social anthropology gives us 'context of situation' ('The significance of an action is determined by the context of situation'). In the weaker, jargoning form of the latter meaning, the sense is 'background', or 'connection': 'the place is well known in a cricketing context'; 'Mr Major was asked to put his own policies into the context of Thatcherism' – *Independent*; 'this ship was conceived in the context of a great tradition' – cruise line brochure, see Part I, p. 41.

corner, to fight one's   The expression is political, the source-jargon is sport – specifically, boxing. 'To fight your corner' means to defend your own interests, or to follow a plan of action laid down for you (as boxers fight under instructions from their 'cornermen', their trainers and seconds): '. . . government representatives are obviously expected to fight their corner' – TV political commentator. See further **where he's coming from**.

corporate patronage   In the arts, patronage by a corporate body rather than by an individual; e.g. by a bank, an insurance company, a manufacturing industry. It has links with **commodification**.

couch potato   One who rejects heroic action and favours the vegetable existence of sitting on the couch and watching TV. From the USA, where 'boob tube' (= 'television') produced 'boob tuber', one who watches the boob tube; and thence, punningly, since a potato is a kind of tuber, 'couch potato'. Other playful forms, yet to come into common circulation in Britain, are *vidspud* and *telespud*. Flaunting one's tuberous **lifestyle** is called *spudismo*, on the analogy of *machismo*. But is *couch potato* jargon, or simple slang? The case invites argument, as do others in this Glossary.

counter-inflationary   A fairly recent addition to words with the 'counter-' prefix. It means 'designed to reduce the level of inflation': 'That is why he and his team have attached such importance to developing a set of counter-inflationary proposals' – *Independent*.

counter-productive   Of a course of action in politics or personal relationships = 'producing the opposite of the effect intended'. 'If you wanted him to be kind to birds, buying him an airgun was counter-productive.' But seriously: 'The proximity of the election means both devaluation and an interest rate rise would be counter-productive' – *Independent*.

cowboy   The various jargon-senses of this word include (a) an incompetent and dishonest workman, as in 'cowboy plumber', 'cowboy double-glazing firm' (the common current sense in Britain), (b) in Northern Ireland, a member or associate of a sectarian gang, and (c), in the USA, a factory worker who ignores (and exceeds) the piece-work norms set by his colleagues.

creamaholic See **-oholic**.

credentialism The principle that a PhD goes farther than an MSc, or that status and promotional prospects depend mainly if not exclusively on qualifications. It may be noted that very few people in senior positions are credentialists, and very few people in junior positions can afford to be anything else.

credibility A mode word in current politics, denoting the capacity of a party to attract belief in its competence and possible fitness to govern: 'Given the collapse of its policies at the end of the Seventies it has taken [the Labour Party] a long time to regain credibility' – *Independent*. The word has risen in the world, from its earlier, disguised role in **street cred.**

credibility problem If, as a politician, you have a credibility problem, you are unelectable because no one believes you can do the job – not necessarily because you are suspected of lying, though you may well be as dishonest as the day is long. (In politics, credibility and veracity need not go together.) But see **problem**.

credible Having **credibility**; presenting a convincing front: 'He has always been aware of the need for Labour to be credible on inflation' – *Independent*.

cross-party fertilization A miscegenation of political ideas; the pollination of Conservative flowers by Labour bees; or the impregnation of Democratic sensibility by Republican sentiments. It can happen, with occasionally **green** results.

crumbly An aged person, in general decomposition one stage beyond a **wrinkly**. (These expressions are glossarized out of consideration for the author of this book.) See further under **-ie/-y**.

crusty A vagabond, called 'crusty' somewhat unflatteringly, not solely on account of **attitude problems**, but also because his/her skin and clothing have parched and coarsened through weathering and infrequent washing. 'Things began to go sour in the Eighties when the old hippies and alternativists found themselves ill at ease in a world which had spawned "crusties" and various post-punk types' – *Independent*. See also **New Age**.

culture The top of the show-talking shop, almost impossible to define other than by a specifying epithet. The **benefit culture**, also called the **dependency culture**, goes with the **planned economy**, and (its opponents claim) weakens the morale of its beneficiaries by allowing them to depend on support from the state; as opposed to the **enterprise culture**, which encourages them to go forth into the market-place, take up their risks, and prosper enormously until the receivers are called in and the bailiffs arrive. Ill-natured people sometimes call the enterprise culture the **greed culture** (derisively echoing the sentiment 'greed is good', propounded by the character of the ruthless entrepreneur Gordon Gecko, in the film *Wall Street*). Other sub-species of culture are **youth culture**, **drug culture**, and **rock culture**. The **counter-culture** is the rejection of whatever social and institutional practices John Citizen may deem 'respectable', 'conventional', or 'established'. See **alternative**. The economist J. K. Galbraith has coined (as the title of a book) the phrase **culture of contentment**, meaning a system of economic and political management that placates the comfortably-off and encourages them to ignore the plight of the so-called **underclass**.

curriculum, hidden   Formed after **hidden agenda**, the 'hidden curriculum' implies an unacknowledged and potentially subversive content in school and university courses. This content is supposedly 'progressive' – i.e. devoted to the demolition of the three Rs, traditional **values**, and the social structure which has served so well This Great Country Of Ours.

customer   Currently dominant notions of the **market** and **value for money** have modified the use of this word, taking it out of the **context** of simple shopkeeping. It can now mean a 'client' (in law practice); a 'passenger' (in air transport, etc.); a 'student' (in universities and colleges); or a 'patient' (in hospitals). It is a synonym of 'consumer' and **punter**, and is associated with the socio-political cant of **charters**.

customize   To adapt a general product to the needs or requirements of a particular customer; e.g. to furnish a car with eye-catching coachwork designs, a Texas longhorn bumper, drinks cabinet and a horn that plays The Stars And Stripes Forever. (Other schemes may be available on enquiry.)

cut   A general-purpose prop-word or phrase-filler, meaning a reduction of public expenditure, or, in some **contexts**, the reduction of a charge or levy. Usually in the plural, e.g.: *economic cuts*, *defence cuts*, *education cuts*, *health cuts*, *tax cuts*. A *cut* is more drastic than a 'squeeze' (but see **differential squeeze**) and no less painful than a **cap**.

cutting edge, at the   *At the cutting edge* is where what it's all about is happening; the forefront of the action, the state of the art. Also *at the leading edge*. The figurative origins of the term are not altogether clear; 'leading edge', however, is probably from aerodynamics (it is the leading edge of the aerofoil that 'cuts' the airflow, creating a 'lift'). But there is no feeling of flight in the following: '. . . the teachers are at the cutting edge of a culture which has no aesthetic sense, no common values' – *Guardian*. That suggests the coalface rather than the wing.

D

DE Social/economic indicator of those with limited purchasing power, and hence little significance in the real world, e.g. the unskilled classes, pensioners, **crusties**. See also **AB, C1, C2**.

de- Formative prefix, as in *desensitize, defuse, devalue*, **de-accession, de-communize, deregulation, de-skilling**.

de-accession Also **de-acquisition**. A cowardly, snivelling, guilt-ridden euphemism for the selling off of books by a library, or paintings by a gallery, or objects by a museum. It would be no less than justice were the inventor of this ghastly unword to spend eternity in penitential harness with Esau, who de-accessed his birthright for a serving of classic peasant cuisine.

dead in the water A ship is dead in the water when her engines are disabled. This phrase, however, is socio-political rather than maritime; policies, proposals, schemes, electoral ambitions are dead in the water when support for them runs out and **funding** fails.

deal This salesman's noun, originally signifying an exchange, a division of goods and money, has developed the meanings 'bargain' (*do a deal* = 'strike a bargain', in American *cut a deal*) and 'arrangement', 'provision', 'agreement', as in *hostage deal*, an agreement to exchange hostages, *package deal*, an agreement to include several elements in one transaction, *pension deal*, the terms under which an employee is pensioned at the end of a period of service or whenever he/she is too worn out to be of further use, whichever is the sooner.

deccie An enthusiastic (amateur) interior decorator. For a comparable formation, see **foodie**. See further -**ie**.

de-communize To purge [a society, nation, organization] of all symptoms of communism. This follows the European events of the 1980s, rather as *de-Nazification* followed the events of 1939–45. The Western world now waits to be *de-tribalized*.

deconstruction A currently fashionable branch of philosophy, devoted to the study of meaning in literary texts, and principally associated with the names of the Belgian-American Paul de Man and the French *philosophe* Jacques Derrida. Since its advocates repeatedly assert that it is not so much a method, more a state of mind, its tenets are difficult to present concisely. Its central position, however, is the assertion of the linguistic primacy and autonomy of written texts; for the deconstructionist, writing is the true representative of *langue*, a mental system, of which speech, with its pragmatic acts of social behaviour, is a secondary product. Texts thus have precedence over ('real-life') conversations; and texts do not 'mean' in the way that conversations 'mean', with the assumption that words (signifiers) regularly relate to non-words, objects, ideas, conventions, *realities* (things signified). According to the deconstructionists 'meaning' is not to be finally captured in this way; access to meaning is repeatedly put off, or 'deferred'. A text has no closure in reality. It is language in continual and supplementary reference to language, words unpacking words, incomplete meanings endlessly generating possibilities of meaning. What the deconstructionist critic does is to attempt to follow and define in the most exacting detail the process here called, metaphorically, 'unpacking'. (An expression which may in its turn need to be unpacked, or *supplemented*.) Such a view confers a new status upon the critic, whose work is no longer seen as an auxiliary service to literature, still less as a way of encoding the principles of composition, but as a form of literature in its own right, subject to the same ambivalences and figurative shifts that inform the texts with which it engages. Much of this is very interesting, but there is unfortunately a good deal to be said, mostly in four-letter words, about critical notions of literary style. (See, however, Part I, pp. 61–4.) There is, furthermore, the paradox that while deconstructionists deny the classical principles of signification in literary texts – arguing, in effect, that a text can 'mean' whatever you see in it – they are almost arrogantly insistent on the rigorous rightness of their own meanings, and of the sanctified status of the jargon in which they express them. See **post-structuralism**.

deficit, democratic deficit A currently modish political phrase. From 'budget deficit', a shortfall in the nation's finances, new meanings develop: 'Many of the EC's staunchest supporters are worried about its democratic deficit, the fact that EC regulations and directives emerge without direct, popular input' – *Independent*. See **input**.

definitive A term of approval, close in meaning to **authentic**. Youthful jargon contracts this to *def*, which consorts with *fab*, *brill*, etc.

democratization The creation of democratic institutions in society and politics. 'I think you've got a democratization of the whole European process' – comment made during a TV interview. ('You've got' = 'there is'; an existential construction.)

de-recognize To withdraw official recognition from a person or an organization. A trade union or a credit card may be de-recognized. There is a Carrollian whimsy about this; it would have brought out the best in the Mad Hatter and the March Hare. See further **deselection**.

deregulation The removal of rules and **constraints**, originally those thought to impede trading in stocks and shares (see **big bang**). Since applied to the process of removing any enterprise (e.g. transport) from the control of a public authority. In this sense deregulation is synonymous with **privatization** and an antonym of **interventionism**. See also **self-regulation**.

deselection   In [British] politics, the withdrawal of support, by a constituency party, from a currently sitting Member of Parliament; the Member is 'deselected', because his (or her) constituents will not choose him/her to stand as their representative at the next election. This frequently happens because the electorate persists in confusing the notions of 'representative' and 'delegate'; people are deselected for not fulfilling the delegated wishes of the folks back home, whose interests they have been doing their best to represent.

desertification   The reduction of fertile land to barren waste, e.g. through the destruction of forests, with consequent drought and soil erosion. A product of human folly, worse even than **Benidormification**.

designer   Occurs freely in journalism and social commentary as a phrasal prefix, e.g. in 'designer water' (mineral water of a fashionable brand), 'designer stubble' (once disapprovingly known as 'five o'clock shadow', now a stylish ornament of the carefully unshaven male). The use of 'designer' as epithet or prefix began reasonably enough with things designed, e.g. designer clothes, designer accessories, designer tableware, designer wallpaper. Usage has since expanded, and the word can now suggest meanings paraphrasable as 'chic', 'costly', 'exclusive', 'available to those who move in the most affluent circles': e.g. 'designer lawyer'.

de-skilling   In industry, through technological advances, rendering the *skilled worker* unnecessary. 'It is now in the US and UK, where the implementation of the style [= the technology] is proving difficult, that it is doing most to increase inequality; destroying whole industries, de-skilling occupations, weakening unions . . .' – *Guardian*.

des. res.   Estate agent's shop, meaning desirable residence w. dble. glzing throughout, full gs-frd cntrl hting, lrge 25ft lnge, dng rm, stdy, 4 bdrms incl mstr bdrm w. bthrm en suite, games rm, lndry, dble grge, lrge gdns frnt and rear. But *des. res.* is fast becoming yupspeak (see **yuppie**) for 'a house, a home'. Every *des. res.* has a *Bimmer* or a *yupmobile* of comparable status in the dble grge. Persons who can refer to a home as a *des. res.* are not above asking for things to be done *a.s.a.p.*, which their fathers called *p.d.q.*

destabilize, -ization   In political jargon, this somewhat sinister term implies the deliberate attempt to subvert a foreign government by covertly attacking, through intelligence operations, the institutions on which it relies, its economy, and the constitutional procedures – e.g. elections – on which it is founded. A way of keeping socialism out of the neighbourhood, or hemisphere; at one time thought to be a proprietary skill of the CIA, now something that the natives can do for themselves.

differential squeeze   This is a Stripetrouserism (see p. 95), meaning a corrective balancing of sums of public money granted in aid to different regions of the United Kingdom. 'Stand by for a different type of public expenditure: the differential squeeze' – *Guardian*. *Squeeze* is a family relation of **cap** and **cut**.

digital, digitizing, digitization   These flowers of techspeak grow out of the application of computer technology to the making of sound recordings. In computertalk, 'digital' refers to the breakdown of data (an **input**, a message) into a code consisting of digits. *Digital recordings* are those resulting from such encoding, or *digitization*. Older recordings, of *analogue origination* (on vinyl disc), may be *digitized* for *CD* ('compact disc') playing. A letter to the *Guardian* explains: 'Once subject to digitization, a recording is best played digitally at home on a CD player and not transcribed further into the vinyl format. Vinyl will inevitably become marginalized in historic and specialist audiophile applications whatever the debate concerning relative sound quality.' Read that, and make what you can of your old Beatles and Joan Sutherland albums.

dimension   This is the word to use when *connections* fail, *fields* are full, and **area** came two sentences back. *Dimension*, however, often has the sense of something added – a *historical dimension* or a *dimension of hope* – for the benefit of those addressing themselves properly to any **problem** or **issue**.

dink   A fool, a *dickhead*; also, in the plenitude of youthspeak, a **dork** and a **dweeb**, not to mention a **nerd**. See further under **wimp** and **wally**.

dirty tricks   This is political shop talk; it means *mud-slinging* and *smearing* and *rumour-mongering*; it means any unscrupulous expedient to which some politicians and their *sleazebag* (or *scumbag*, or *scuzzbag*) hirelings will resort in order to discredit and humiliate those who oppose them. Dirty trickery is becoming an almost respectable feature of electoral politics.

dis-   An important contemporary prefix, notably in **disbenefit, disincentive, disinformation**. In such formations, 'dis-' represents a peculiar kind of antonymy, an opposition within the same field of reference, not across contrasting fields. 'Drawback' and 'discouragement' are (rough and ready) antonyms, i.e. *contrasting* partners, of 'benefit' and 'incentive', but 'disbenefit' and 'disincentive' are *companion* partners of those words. That I must wait six months before I am allowed to withdraw savings from a high-interest account is not a *discouragement* from saving; it is a *disincentive* to save in that particular account. That I am obliged to pay tax on my pension is not so much a *drawback* as a *disbenefit*. 'Disinformation', consequently, is not an antonym (or contrasting partner) of 'knowledge'. It is information of a sort, generally synonymous with 'misinformation', except that whereas one might unintentionally misinform somebody, disinformation is deliberate and is designed to have harmful effect. In wartime, another name for disinformation was *black propaganda*, a phrase now seldom encountered because almost any use of the word *black* may be condemned as *racist* (from earlier *racialist*) and not **politically correct.**

disadvantaged In this age of **political correctness** it is not allowed to speak of the down-and-out, the deaf, or the crippled; they are respectively the 'unwaged', the 'hearing-impaired' (or perhaps 'acoustically challenged') and the 'disadvantaged' or 'differently abled'. Further disadvantages are insanity, cancer, multiple sclerosis, and haemophilia, all of them **health problems**: ' "They [haemophiliacs] were doubly disadvantaged as a result of their hereditary condition, compounded with the problems they now face with the onset of HIV", she told the Commons' – *Independent*. A notable aspect of current social jargoning is the proliferation of euphemisms which put other people's agonies at a comfortable distance.

docudrama (also dramadoc), and docufiction A portmanteau of 'documentary' and 'drama' (or 'documentary' and 'fiction'), indicating that a dramatic (fictional) work contains some documentary (factual) elements.

dork See **dink**; refer also to **airhead, nerd,** and **wally**; also to **plonker,** meaning 'prick' – which, anatomically speaking, is what *dork* means. Youthspeak from the American West.

do the business This counts as sporting jargon. It is football managers' cant, and it means 'do the job', 'do what is necessary' (i.e. to win the game). See under **commitment, get a result,** and **give one hundred and ten per cent.** The phrase has powerful overtones of physical conflict – of 'doing' the opposition before they incontinently 'do' you. See **putting oneself about.**

double dip recession The economist's version of a really bad **scenario**: a recession (i.e. a failure to grow and prosper economically) which has to go on **bottoming out** after it has **bumped along the bottom** or even shown an **upturn**; a process of sinking by starts, or plunging on the instalment plan, as portrayed in graphs and charts. 'The prospect of the economy moving into a "double-dip" recession sharpened yesterday with news that house-building activity and consumer confidence continue to slide' – *Guardian*.

double whammy Septuagenarian devotees of the Li'l Abner comic strip or the Phil Silvers show will recall that 'putting a whammy on someone' meant casting a spell, and that a 'double whammy' was a curse of peculiar power. In the cruder sense of 'a double blow' (like *the old one-two*), the phrase has made a recent debut in British political jargon, beginning with the election campaign of 1992, when a huge billboard displaying two large red boxing gloves warned Conservative voters to beware of Labour's 'double whammy', higher taxes and rising inflation. See p. 97, and note 49.

dough-nutting The tactic of surrounding a party leader or minister of state with a close company or *posse comitatus* of loyal henchpersons, readily apparent to the eye of the TV camera, even when the back benches are deserted; a useful and necessary stratagem during election speeches, question-time in the House, etc., giving comfortable substance to otherwise empty phrases like 'my right honourable friend'.

down-market (adj. and adv.) Adverbially, 'down-market' is where the less-than-rich folk of economic class C and the sturdily impoverished of D and E are thought to dwell. Car manufacturers 'go down-market' when they produce rattling mobile kennels for indigent piano tuners and retired teachers of English. 'Down-market' is also the adjectival form: 'a down-market concept'; 'a down-market trend'. An alternative (nominal) phrase is **the lower end/bottom end of the market**. See (consequently) **up-market**.

down side The 'down side' complements the **up side**. The down side is the bad news, the **disbenefit**, the catch. The up side dispenses free beer on Wednesday, the down side being that today is Thursday. Sometimes spelt as one word: 'The downside is that the motorist remains a tempting source of very big and easily collectable tax revenues' – *Independent*.

dream ticket Political slang, imported into British English from the USA, where the phrase originally denoted a supposedly ideal partnership of running mates in a Presidential election. It has kept its political significance (with appropriate shifts of reference) in British English, but it has also developed a more general sense of 'best imaginable pairing': 'A double-CD set with the same pieces [by Mozart] on a modern piano would have been the dream ticket' – *Independent*.

drink problem A euphemistic synonym for 'habitual drunkenness'. 'He has a drink problem' = 'He is a drunkard'; the latter word, however, has almost gone out of use, being no longer **politically correct**. A deaf old man who cannot hold his liquor is a hearing-impaired senior citizen with a drink problem. See further **attitude problem** (a deaf old man who cannot hold his liquor and gets into fights with the police has one), and **problem** generally.

-driven Modish suffix, conveying the sense 'impelled, guided, directed by', 'taking motive and shape from'. Whence, 'theory-driven', 'deficit-driven', 'market-driven'. Some academic courses are theory-driven; others are humanely taught. See further **-led**. This formal and semantic model, expressing the notion 'directed', 'impelled', is now extending to include other hyphened elements, e.g. *-inspired, -induced, -oriented*: 'The campaign temperature is becoming noticeably warmer, so an attack of poll-inspired collywobbles would be far from surprising' – *Independent*; 'The moment the Chancellor decided last March to add to the industry's recession-induced woes by burdening it with yet more taxes' – *Independent*; 'It is this kind of disparity that first attracted the attention of the harmony-oriented EC' – *Independent*.

dweeb Alas, a *dork*, and by all accounts a pretty wimpish one.

E

ecology, ecological, eco- Ecology is the study of the relationship between organisms in a symbiotic system. In popular usage it denotes concern for the common **environment** and the attempt to reduce the effects of **pollution**. The inevitable abbreviation, *eco-*, makes a handy prefix for the word-coiner: 'The eco-doomsters prefer to frighten the public with threats that the planet will be uninhabitable' – *Independent*. Also *eco-awareness*, *eco-crisis*, *eco-tastrophe* (abbreviated from 'eco-catastrophe'), *eco-freak*, *eco-politics* and many another in these ecomanic times.

economical with the truth Mendacious by default. The phrase was invented, and its applications demonstrated, by Sir Robert Armstrong (now Lord Armstrong), Secretary to the [British] Cabinet and Head of the Secret Service, who when called as a witness in an Australian court, in the course of the so-called 'Spycatcher' trial, would not admit to lying, but cheerfully confessed to having been *economical with the truth*. The phrase has entered the language, and joins Winston Churchill's invention, *terminological inexactitude*. Perhaps in time the **fun** lexicon of friendly fibs will be augmented by Lady Archer's phrase *inaccurate précis*, describing her husband's gift for telling a flowery autobiographical tale. See **porky**.

economism The systematic reduction of any **issue** or **problem** to economic terms; insistence on economic priorities. Mr Micawber's analysis of happiness in *David Copperfield* is a classic example of economism. ('Annual income twenty pounds, annual expenditure nineteen nineteen six, result happiness. Annual income twenty pounds, annual expenditure twenty pounds ought and six, result misery.')

Ecstasy A **designer** drug, a.k.a. **E**, alias **XTC**, otherwise **methylenedioxy-metamphetamine**, which is **MDMA**, or **Adam**; reportedly inducing euphoric hallucinations in those who take it. The current choice for the **festival** or a night at the old **acid house**.

eighty-six This verb has recently been borrowed into British English from American popular usage, where it appears to have meant 'to refuse to serve a customer' – the form being rhyming slang with 'nix' ('nothing', 'emphatically no'). Its current meaning seems to be 'to refuse firmly': 'Attempts to breach the sanction of his [Vladimir Nabokov's] private life were firmly eighty-sixed' – *Independent*.

electoralism In politics, the tailoring of policies to please the electorate. Readily observable before an election, subsequently less obvious. Loosely related to **populism**.

elitist As noun or adjective, a pejorative term, denoting a disposition to believe that all undertakings properly give rise to an elite, a class of persons qualified through merit, through industry, through inherited capacity, to be leaders in their chosen field. This is a not altogether popular point of view. The meaning of *elitist*, however, tends in some usages to lapse into the broader, merely sullen senses of 'stuck up', 'too big for his boots', 'excessively literate', 'able to read French', 'awfully good at sums'. Thus, 'What a pity J. Danforth Quayle cannot spell "potato"' could be taken for an *elitist* remark.

energy pricing Deciding how much the public can be persuaded to pay for supplies of gas and electricity; subsequently persuading them that **in real terms** they are paying less than formerly, and are in fact getting **value for money**. Value for money in real terms constitutes what the economically primitive citizen calls a *rip-off*.

enterprise culture See **culture**.

entrepreneur, entrepreneurial The ascendancy of this word is symptomatic of an exciting development in British culture, for the entrepreneur – called by our Elizabethan forebears the *undertaker* – is a folk hero whose achievements ensure that **customers** of all kinds shall have **value for money** through a wider range of **choice**. It is not only merchant bankers, stock-jobbers and company directors who claim the entrepreneurial palm; professors, head teachers, general practitioners, museum directors, theatre managers and others have learned to revel in the *disciplines of the market* and cast off the shackles of the **benefit culture**. We are, as Adam Smith almost said, and Napoleon may have done, a nation of entrepreneurs.

entropy In strict scientific terms, this should denote a measure of the breakdown and dispersal of energy put into any closed system (e.g. a combustion engine). In a degraded meaning, however, it merely signifies 'a state of confusion', 'a mess': see John Updike, in *The Witches of Eastwick* (Penguin, 1985, p. 216): 'The women returned hellos, and in the Armenians' hardware store tried, like everybody else, to describe with finger sketches in the air, the particular thingummy needed to repair a decaying home, to combat entropy.'

entryism The political **strategy** of entering an organization in order to assume ultimate command of it, by covert acquisitions of power and influence; a traditional tactic of the old communist parties in their relationship to popular movements such as trade unions.

environment, environmental, environmentalist The modishness of 'environment' and its derivatives is guaranteed (in Britain) by the appointment of a Minister for the Environment. The environment is mainly vegetable (greenery) with some mineral accessories (rocks, watercourses) and animal intrusions (see **wildlife**). The environment is threatened by **pollution**. It is the main object of **green politics**. Environmentalists are the natural allies of **Greens** and **animalists**. Environmentalism thrives on *projects*: 'Granted permission to film Prince Charles in Wales as he presented awards for environmental projects in the principality, we were issued with three passes' – *Independent*. Wise manufacturers woo the public with products – toilet-paper, washing-up liquid, etc. – deemed **environmentally friendly**. Wise purchasers view these claims with some scepticism. See also **ecology**.

equal opportunities employer An employer committed to the principle of recruiting staff equally from applicants in all social or racial categories – male and female, white and black, one religion or another. 'Although keen to insist that the Royal Household was an equal opportunities employer, Mr Anson had eventually to concede that it had only nine ethnic minority people working for it out of a total of 891 – 1 per cent' – *Independent*. See **ethnic**; see also **positive discrimination**.

Essex man, Essex girl That there has always been something odd about the county of Essex is suggested by some historical usages recorded by Eric Partridge, who informs us that in the 1570s a native of Essex was an 'Essex calf' (much as, to this day, natives of Guernsey are 'Guernsey donkeys'); further, that by 1620 an 'Essex lion' meant a calf – Essex being noted for its calves; and that an 'Essex stile' was, in fact, a ditch. (See Partridge, *The Penguin Dictionary of Historical Slang*.) *Essex man* is the modern caricature of a confident, philistine, chauvinist, blatantly self-interested, **upwardly mobile** man of business. The *Essex girl* is his partner, the local version of the old 'dumb blonde' stereotype, naive, venal, not greatly gifted, the butt of *sexist* jokes. All that Essex has done to deserve its raucous repute is – probably – to be close to London and the money market.

ethnic This most curious of mode words has the sense 'pertaining to those of non-European racial origin' – ignoring the fact that, etymologically speaking, we are all 'ethnic' wherever we come from. *Ethnic art*, for example, may refer to Navajo bead-work, West African wood-carving, Australian aboriginal painting, but not to the exhibits at the Royal Academy Summer Show. *Ethnic rock* and *ethnic pop* refer to styles of Western rock music incorporating Afro-Asian elements. 'Ethnic monitoring scheme planned for armed forces' (headline in the *Independent*) refers to a proposal to scrutinize the recruitment figures for blacks and Asians. What is curious is that this expression, cultivated in the cause of **racial equality**, is in effect racist in its patronizing implications of separate categories and special cases. Usages such as *the ethnic vote* smack of the ghetto. Civil war in the Balkans – specifically, between Serbs and Bosnian Muslims – has produced the ghastly phrase *ethnic cleansing*, meaning the killing or expulsion of those considered to be of alien race. It was in this spirit that the Nazis industriously strove to render their communities *Judenrein*. Also, **ethnicization**: 'The ethnicisation of participatory television – long overdue – was bound to creep in once the issue of tokenism had been fought out' – *New Statesman and Society*.

Euro- As prefix, yields Eurobore, Eurocrat, Eurofanatic, Europhobia, Eurosceptic and many others. We are all Eurobabblers now. Note *Europol*: 'European police coordinating agency' (modelled on earlier *Interpol*).

Europeanism Assiduous cultivation of the state of being **Euro**; the -ism for Euroenthusiasts.

exercise Now a little overworked and due for superannuation, *exercise* is a smart synonym for 'process', 'undertaking', 'course of action', or simply 'event'. 'What's the point of this exercise?' = 'Why are we getting married/ buying three pounds of stewing steak/spying on the next door neighbour/ flying to Majorca/having a quarrel?' In the vocabulary of politics it harmonizes with other mode words: 'The whole exercise had been an attempt further to marginalise the Jackson liberals within the party' – *Spectator*. It rarely has anything to do with exercise as in jogging, learning a language, or playing the piano.

extremilexic A humorous coinage (see **alphabetism**) denoting the placing of a surname at the beginning or end of the alphabet; Mr Atkins and dear Mrs Baker are extremilexics, but so are Miss Young and crumbly old Mr Zimmer. See further **fundilexic, medilexic, summilexic.**

F

faction A portmanteau of 'fact' and 'fiction', meaning a fictional narrative with a strong basis in recorded fact, e.g. Thomas Keneally's novel *Schindler's Ark*, or J. G. Ballard's *Empire of the Sun*. See also **docudrama, dramadoc, docufiction.**

factor A powerful socio-political mode word; most useful as a discourse-filler for TV commentators and broadsheet columnists having trouble with their sentences. It is roughly synonymous with 'thing': 'TV may be the most influential factor influencing people's perceptions' (Geoffrey Joynson-Smith, *Newsnight*, 3 January 1992); 'I'm convinced that she [Mrs Thatcher] may be a factor in us winning the next election' (Jeffrey Archer, *Newsnight*, 3 January 1992); 'Perhaps some exogenous factor – such as the fear of a Labour Government – is worrying the professional classes' (*Independent*). For 'some exogenous factor' read 'something else'. In some usages *factor* is modified by a word indicating the sort of thing that constitutes the thing; e.g. *causation factor, Falklands factor, feel-good factor*: 'Speeding and tailgating are the two main causation factors of accidents on the motorway' – policeman, speaking on BBC TV broadcast. That Mrs Thatcher and her government presided over a military victory in the Falkland Islands was thought to be a 'factor' ensuring her increased popularity and subsequent re-election. More recently, the *feel-good factor* (sometimes spelt *feelgood*), meaning an assurance that all is for the best in the best of all socio-political worlds, has been invoked in support of the Conservative Party's (1992) election campaign. Thus Mr John Major, as reported in the *Independent*: '. . . if we put things in place, but every aspect of the feel-good factor isn't there, so be it'; and from the same newspaper, 'Measured in this way the "feel-good factor" will be entirely missing from the coming election campaign'. From all of which it must appear that if the appropriate factors are endogenously in place they will be influential in influencing every aspect of something or other. This is called *the language of politics*, and we are meant to feel good about it, heaven help us.

fast food   Food quickly prepared, to be quickly consumed by people in a hurry: e.g. hamburgers, cheeseburgers, wackyburgers, Big Macs, hot dogs, French fries, choc-bars, toothsome chicken nuggets, sesame buns. Dispensed in *fast food joints* which are usually links in a *fast food chain*, e.g. McDonalds. Sometimes called **junk food**, implying the gastronomic equivalent of **junk mail**, or just plain **junk**. Swallow in haste, repent at leisure.

fast lane   Where life is metaphorically lived by folk who know **where it's at**, and who take it fast and easy (with designer clothes, designer cars, designer careers, designer drugs, drink, dalliance, and – in due course – designer death). The source-jargon is motorway terminology, the *fast lane* (a term traffic policemen dislike and avoid) being the 'third', or 'outer', or 'overtaking' lane (which is another term traffic policemen dislike).

fattism   Politically incorrect prejudice against people who are *aesthetically challenged* or **disadvantaged** by excess of weight. Words such as 'slob', 'tubby', 'jumbo', 'fatso', 'meatball', 'greaseball' and 'Billy Bunter' are presumably fattist. Is 'belly-laugh' fattist?; we should perhaps speak of abdominally sited mirth. It may be noted that aircraft once known as *jumbo jets* are now usually referred to as *wide-bodied*; a modest victory, perhaps, for FAF (Flyers Against Fattism). Of all the fatuous -isms, this one is least likely to survive the impact of laughter; but then the word may well have been coined with humorous intent.

federalism, -ist   Current political jargon: the movement to create a political federation of European states. Anathema to some, who refer to this as *the F-word*.

feedback   A complex technical term with simple social meanings. In electronics, **feedback** is that part of the **output** of a system which returns as **input**; *positive feedback* increases the strength of the input signal. Socially, *feedback* means information denoting the effect or success of some undertaking, and *positive feedback* has the sense of 'good report': as in 'we've had some pretty positive feedback from your seminar students'. (See **positive**.)

festival   This recent usage implies – as **sub-text** – the convergence of **acid house** and **New Age** (but see also **rave, raver**); a *festival* being a celebration, usually lasting for several days, of the combined potency of rock music, young bodies, hallucinogenic drugs, and the unlicensed freedom of an **alternative lifestyle**; resulting in the invasion of common land, the infraction of the Queen's Peace, the apoplexy of farmers, and the aural endangerment of anyone living within a radius of two miles. Not to be confused with relatively decorous events such as the *Edinburgh Festival* and the annual *Garden Festival*. *Festivals* are also called *raves, rave-ups*.

first past the post   The package phrase (see p. 22) is political, the source-jargon sporting. On the racetrack the winner is the first horse past the post; in electoral politics the 'first past the post', and hence the outright winner of the election, is the party securing an overall majority of seats in the legislative assembly. A *first past the post system* operates in Great Britain, where it is considered easy for a robustly simple electorate to understand; other countries, where the voters are justly credited with some creative powers of mind – e.g. the Republic of Ireland – favour a form of *proportional representation*, an equitable system justly decreeing that, in the immortal words of the Dodo, '*Everybody* has won, *all* must have prizes'.

flavour of the month   Figuratively, the 'flavour of the month' means whoever or whatever is currently high in popular esteem – a personality, a politician, a policy, a purchase. The source is the storekeeper language used to tempt the consumer to buy ice-cream, pastries, packaged desserts, etc. See further **sliced bread, the best thing since**.

flexible, flexibility   In the jargons of administration and business organ-ization, *flexibility* is a virtue, testifying to the possession of an open mind and **management skills**. Anything that can be changed, adapted, or adjusted (including, of course, an **approach** or a **strategy**, or even a **structure**) is *flexible*: 'With better training, growing professionalism and more emphasis on personal initiative, flexible management structures become possible' – *Independent. Flexibility*, furthermore, is such a word as educationists love to mouth: 'Our modular system and the implementation of credit accumu-lation and transfer are further developments in the cause of increased flexibility and therefore increased access to higher education for people with home or work responsibilities' – letter in the *Guardian*. Here the writer scores heavily, placing *flexibility* firmly in the **context** of *modular, implementation, credit accumulation and transfer,* and *access*. Even *development* shows a fair little colouring of jargon.

foodie   The word was once *gourmet*, which had to be distinguished from *gourmand*; but our democratic, non-elitist foodie is both *gourmet* and *gourmand*, a connoisseur, cook, and enthusiastic consumer of food. The word is sometimes used in half-disparaging reference to journalists who write about meals and entertainer-chefs who prepare them before a TV audience.

foot, to shoot oneself in the   The source is military, referring to the self-inflicted wound of the soldier desperately hoping to be taken out of the front line and sent to hospital. The expression is an old one (in its literal application at least as old as the First World War) but it has taken a new lease of life in current political jargon, with the sense of [to score] **an own goal**, that is, to make a costly mistake. This transferred sense is out of strict keeping with the original signification. The soldier who shot himself in the foot did so deliberately, in the hope of gaining something from his act; the politician who 'shoots himself in the foot', with an imprudent remark, an ill-considered proposal, a rash liaison, an act of risible stupidity (such as publicly insisting, on a visit to a school, that the word *potato* is spelt with a final *e*), does so quite unintentionally, though in some cases you would never know. There are public figures who have the terrifying ability to shoot themselves in the foot *while* they are scoring an own goal.

forex   A word form newly come out of the money **market**; **for**eign **ex**change – whence *forex dealers*, *forex speculators*. 'Forex frenzy nets £900m' – headline in the *Guardian*.

fractionalization   The reduction to fractions, fragments, shards, shoots, slivers, bits, bobs, of – it seems – a political programme, party, or conference: 'The convention seemed to spin out of his control before it began, though the fractionalization reflected Bush's fragmented character' – *Guardian*.

fragrant   This is scarcely a mode word, though it might be called a mode unword, since its use in current British English has been seriously compromised by a court case (the Jeffrey Archer libel case, 1987) in which the presiding judge, addressing the jury, admiringly commended Mr Archer's wife with the words 'You saw her. Wasn't she fragrant?' – this by contrast with the crumpled, tear-stained creature who was the principal witness for the defence. In the current jargon of picaresque London, the phrase *an Archer* reportedly signifies 2,000, this being the sum allegedly donated with charitable intent by Mr Archer (now Lord Archer) to a sad young woman, in a railway station, to encourage her to go away and live a more fragrant life. *Fragrant*, like **gay**, has become a word to be used with circumspection.

framework   Very modish, especially in educationese, where it consorts affably with **approach**, **context**, **model**, and **strategy**. One might, for example, devise a strategy for teaching table manners within the framework and general **parameters** of a behaviourist **approach**. *Framework* also has its uses in political jargon, in references to the 'constitutional framework', 'legal framework', etc.: 'Much more needs to be done to improve the legislative framework' – *Independent*.

-free   Like **-driven**, **-friendly**, and **-led**, this is a modish suffix. It is especially popular among copywriters and public relations people: 'lead-free', 'cholesterol-free', 'pollution-free', 'alcohol-free', 'sugar-free'. A now out-worn usage is 'nuclear-free', as in 'nuclear-free zone', meaning an area, tract of land, etc., without nuclear weapons (e.g. S. E. Derbyshire).

freebie Fairly recent in British English, much older in American usage (whence we have it), this means the free gift that comes with your purchase at the store, supermarket, or demonstration. A freebie may be called a *stocking filler* or a *bagstuffer*, the latter being a free brochure, booklet, etc., presenting a product or range of products, dispensed at the sales counter and popped into the purchasers' bags or stuffed into their hands while they struggle to get their bags under control. The ultimate freebie would be a carrier for carrying your freebies, or the bag they stuff into the bag containing your bagstuffer.

free marketeer Not quite a privateer or musketeer, still less a buccaneer, a free marketeer nevertheless has strong **entrepreneurial** instincts which require the **deregulation** of markets at home and abroad. The phrase **free market philosophy** is sometimes used, to give an intellectual cachet to nakedly acquisitive enterprises. There is not much philosophy about a commodity broker in full cry.

-friendly Second element in numerous adjectival compounds. Probably the earliest example was *user-friendly*, in reference to computers or other machines designed for the comfort of the non-technical user. This has proved to be a productive pattern, some examples being *computer-friendly*, *earth-friendly*, *eco-friendly*, *environmentally friendly*. The popularity of *-friendly* seems to depend on the noble if wishful thought that we are each and every one the best of buddies, full of good will towards all creatures and keyboards and substances and the many machines that need us and love us in return. This notion can only have originated in the United States of America, that phenomenon-friendly land.

friendly fire In war, bombardment, shelling, strafing, fusillading, etc., from your own side; a tragically common occurrence, with a long history in war. (Stonewall Jackson was a victim of friendly fire.) This euphemism, originally an American usage, broke into British English with a much-discussed incident of the Gulf War against Iraq (1990–1), when 17 British soldiers were killed as a result of a mistaken attack on their troop-carriers by planes of the US Air Force.

front runner In sporting jargon, one of the athletes who lead the race; sometimes, a runner who takes the lead in order to set the pace for others. In a transferred sense, a leader in any competition, especially in political elections, or in the competition for commercial contracts, or among the nominees for an artistic or literary award.

fudge and mudge In the vocabulary of politics, this phrase, used as a noun, means a compromise that evades responsibility for clear decisions;

as a verb, it means to be evasive and imprecise in declarations of intent and implementations of policy. The etymology is uncertain. Eric Partridge (*The Penguin Dictionary of Historical Slang*) has a long entry for *fudge*, which includes the senses 'to interpolate', 'do impressively very little', 'contrive with imperfect materials', 'botch, bungle', 'tell fibs'. *Mudge*, presumably, goes along for the sake of rhyme and rhythm.

fun As adjective, means 'amusing', 'pleasurable', as in 'a fun idea', 'a fun thing to do', *a fun run* – the latter being a long distance race in which the participants are amateur athletes raising money for charity.

fundamentalist Primarily, one who upholds the fundamental doctrines of a religion, appealing directly to scriptural authority. The common current usage, however, refers to Muslim theologians, to sects within Islam, and to the political and military representatives of such sects. In a wider sense, a *fundamentalist* is one who believes in starting at the bottom and sticking to the basics.

fund-holder, fund-holding A fund-holder is a general medical practitioner, or a group of partners, whose practice is financed by a direct budgetary allocation enabling doctors to 'shop', on behalf of their patients, for clinical and consultant services. 'Nearly half of family doctors in England will become eligible to become fund-holders and buy hospital care for their patients'; 'Robin Cook . . . while condemning the extension of fund-holding, welcomed the pilot studies' – *Independent*.

fundilexic Humorous coinage; indicates **extremilexic** names at the end of the alphabet, e.g. Williams, Yorath, Zander. See **alphabetism, medilexic, summilexic**.

funding [n.; also vb, to fund] The supply of money for specific purposes, usually in education, the arts, medicine and science. 'The imminent departure of the team of Alzheimer's disease researchers from St Mary's Hospital Medical School . . . raises some fundamental questions about science funding in this country today' – *Independent*. Note the phrase-form, *science funding*; comparable phrases in current use are *arts funding, education funding*.

G

-gate The *-gate* suffix is enjoying a long life. The first *-gate* was *Watergate*, a building in Washington DC, which in 1972 gave its name to the malpractices and the political scandal leading to the downfall of President Richard Nixon. Since then there have been frequent *-gates*: in the USA, for example, *Billygate* (1980), named for Billy Carter (President Carter's brother) and his dubious connections with the Libyan regime; and *Irangate*, after a disreputable scheme involving arms sales and the support of South American 'contra' rebels. In Britain there have been *Westlandgate* (1985–6, a dispute in the British Cabinet over the purchase of helicopters), *Stalkergate* (1986, the controversy surrounding the withdrawal of Deputy Chief Constable John Stalker from the chairmanship of an enquiry into the conduct of police in Northern Ireland) and *Lawsongate* (1988, involving allegations that the Chancellor of the Exchequer, Nigel Lawson, had deceived the public about the state of the economy).

gay   Hardly to be considered as jargon, so firmly is the word now established in general usage, *gay* nevertheless deserves comment, particularly for the benefit of those who lament the fate of 'such a nice word'. The specific sense of 'homosexual' is very recent. In vulgar usage of the late eighteenth and early nineteenth centuries it meant 'libidinous', 'sexually active'. A *gay girl* was a prostitute, a *gay house* a brothel, and the penis was the *gaying instrument*. A lady of easy virtue (as they used to be called – now, perhaps, a worker in a specialist branch of the entertainment industry) was said to be *gay in the arse*, or *groin*, or *legs*. (The French had a similar expression, *avoir la cuisse gaie*.) It may be worth noting, if it can be done without offence to the Court of St James, that among my grandparents' generation in the working-class North of England, a popular and affectionate nickname for King Edward VII, who had many a gay time in his youth, was *Merrylegs*. (Eric Partridge defines *merry-legs* as 'a harlot: low coll: C19–20'.)

gender   Once a grammatical term (as in 'nouns of the feminine gender') this word now fatuously denotes a biological category, as in 'persons of the male gender'. In this function it seems to have all but displaced **sex**, which word now refers (a) to *coitus*, which is something 'had' – one 'has sex', usually (though not mandatorily) with a person of the opposite 'gender', or (b) to the *pudendum muliebre*. Persons of the female gender are no longer to be accounted members of *the fair sex* or *the gentle sex*, and to describe a woman as *a credit to her sex* might be considered an ambiguous compliment. Late twentieth-century usage apparently reverses the colloquial practice of the nineteenth century, when *gender* could connote *pudendum*, as in the naughty schoolboy rhyme: '*Amo, amas*, I loved a lass, / And she was tall and slender; / *Amas, amat*, I laid her flat / And tickled her feminine gender.' (Captain Marryat quotes this in his novel *Jacob Faithful*, 1834.) *Gender studies* are now an academic discipline, though not, of course, in the Marryat sense. See further **gender politics**.

gender balance   The principle of balancing or fairly proportioning the numbers of men and women employed in any institution or enterprise, including the House of Commons: 'Mr Cormack had spoken out against a Private Members' Bill introduced by Teresa Gorman . . . which would have brought gender balance to the House of Commons' – *Independent*. (Mr Cormack said 'I have never in 22 years in this House heard a more silly proposition'.) See also **gender politics**.

gender politics   For feminists, this signifies an **ongoing** form of negotiation between female and male, designed to establish the rights of the one and the obligations of the other, possibly without offering too much satisfaction to either. A typical **issue** in British gender politics is the number of women on the Conservative benches of the House of Commons. In January 1992, the tally was 17. Labour politicians, many of them virtuous products of **consciousness raising**, could boast of higher aspirations to **political correctness**; in their ranks were 44 persons of the female gender. From America, via the *Independent*, comes the following comment on the campaigning fortunes (in June 1992) of presidential candidate H. Ross Perot: 'If any group is wary of Mr Perot's can-do authoritarianism it is women: last week's *Time/CNN* poll showed his support at 45 per cent among women – a gender-politics gap if ever there was one.' See above under **gender balance**.

gentrification   Most commonly, the transformation of a working-class neighbourhood into a fashionable area of middle-class housing. The verb is **gentrify**; anything that can be moved **up market** can be gentrified, but it is usually houses that are the objects of this process. This is a very British, indeed superlatively English word. Only the English have *gentry*; other nations have rich guys, fat cats and high society.

genuine   A difficult word to classify. As an item in the jargon of popular moralizing, it signifies 'having integrity, probity, utter willingness, dedication'. To their admiring parishioners, parish priests are genuine, even *very* genuine, or in particularly favoured instances, *absolutely* genuine. Horses and football players are 'genuine' when they give of their best. In another sense, *genuine* is a partner to **authentic**.

geographical deprivation   Among pedagogues and those who teach at a distance, this refers to the peculiar disadvantage of living off the beaten track and far from centres for the propagation of learning, e.g. in Auchentinny or Zennor. It is a **down side** not without its **up side**: 'In the Open University self-help is often the offspring of geographical deprivation' – *Teaching at a Distance*, 23 (OU Publications).

geometry   In carmanspeak, the design of mechanical structures functioning in parallel or counterpoise: 'steering geometry' (the turning angles of the front wheels), 'suspension geometry' (the balanced operation of springs at front and rear). There is a current tendency to use the word *geometry* in the general sense of 'design', 'formation'; discussions of the formation of the European Community, for example, have included the term *variable geometry*, indicating the relationship of the various member-states to the central constitution. Founder-members are 'concentric'; later entrants may be somewhat eccentrically placed. And here is *geometry* as applied to the choice of a 'ticket' – i.e. of partners running for office – in a presidential election: 'Bill Clinton, the Democratic candidate, has defied the traditional geometry of presidential ticket-building in yet another way' – *Independent*. (The 'traditional geometry' takes partners from opposite wings of the party; Mr Clinton chose Al Gore, a fellow *centrist*.)

get a result In soccer jargon, to be the winner or at least to tie the game. A defeat is not considered a result. See **do the business**.

getting in touch with one's feelings This is much the same as **having access to one's feelings**. It means finding out about all the feelings one has been suppressing, or losing in the accelerated scamper of life in **the fast lane**. ' "Gonna go out there", said one, "run around in the woods, get in touch with our feelings" ' – TV review in the *Independent*. This kind of activity is characteristic of **New Age** people. Old age people (if a personal observation is in order) would on the whole rather stay out of touch with their feelings; detachment makes for lovingkindness and safer driving.

give one hundred and ten per cent Athletes, particularly those in team games, demonstrate their **commitment, motivation,** and determination to **do the business** and **get a result** by *playing their hearts out, playing out of their skins,* and *giving one hundred and ten per cent*; more than which no manager or coach can ask, though many reportedly do.

glitterati Shiny and enviably successful people, who glitter because of their fame or because of their jewels, gold chains, Rolex watches, and other tokens of conspicuous wealth and **up-market lifestyle**. The form is based on *literati*; see **jazzerati, numerati**.

golden parachute This is the severance payment – the *golden handshake* – contractually offered to those who may be made redundant and have to descend from high executive places. Lesser folk are given **tin parachutes**. Others come under the umbrella of the State.

grassroots Now a fairly old specimen of political cant, this still turns up regularly, especially as an adjective: 'To the dismay of many grassroots idealists, seasoned professionals in Dallas are taking control of the campaign' – *Independent*. The *grassroots* are **where it's at, in terms of** ideals and **commitment**. Party workers and **activists** are located at the *grassroots* (often in places where grass seldom grows).

green As adjective (in *green politics, green issues, green candidates, green revolution*), or as a noun (*the Greens*), means 'concerned politically with **ecological** and **environmental** matters'; whence **Greenpeace**, an international movement with a programme of pacifism based on the protection of the environment and of the earth's resources. Can be used as a verb, *to green*, meaning to create awareness (cp. **consciousness raising**) of **green issues**. The word is rapidly spawning derivatives, some of them humorous and even disparaging: *greenery* (the doctrines of the Greens), *greenie, greenster* (adherent of the movement), *dark green* (deeply committed to greenism, extreme in professing the creed). Dark greens, or green **fundamentalists,** are sometimes called *fundies.*

gridlocked Jammed in the works; brought to a complete standstill by some organizational malfunction. The source-jargon is the language of traffic control in the USA, where most towns are build on the classical 'grid' pattern. If cars block the streets and intersections (e.g. during peak hours), traffic becomes gridlocked.

growth A mode word from the jargon of economics, now generally signifying an expansion in profitability, trading value, etc.: 'Zinc galvanises itself for gradual increase in growth' – playful headline in the *Independent.* Thence *a growth industry, growth area.* A **recovery** may be *growth-led* (amounting to much the same thing as *consumer-led*).

guppie A guppie is a **yuppie** who is (a) **gay,** or (b) **green,** or possibly both, Lord bless him.

guru This word, borrowed from Hindi, formerly signified 'teacher', but now generally (and often with pejorative connotations), denotes 'expert'. An Indian pupil once explained to me that a *guru* could be any person, animal, or even *thing,* from which a moral or spiritual lesson was learned. Thus, the spider was Robert the Bruce's guru. Currently, however, a guru is usually a Civil Service guru or an economic guru; rarely if ever an arachnid guru.

H

haemorrhage Uncontrolled flow, initially of information; replacing or 'metaphrasing' (see p. 11) the earlier metaphor, *leak;* when information is leaked (surreptitiously disclosed) too generously, it becomes a *haemorrhage.* Subsequently, in a wider sense, any metaphorical outflow or loss: '... it looks as if the Tories will avoid the kind of haemorrhage of support they have suffered in previous by-elections' – *Independent.*

handbagging Of old, press-gangs and robbers 'sandbagged' their victims, i.e. struck them over the head with a sock full of heavy sand; but *hand-bagging* is a form of ferocious verbal assault, in the gangways and corridors of politics. The metaphor of a woman irascibly swinging her handbag at any who dare to oppose her is particularly associated with Mrs (now Lady) Thatcher, and was very popular with reporters and cartoonists during the 1980s. Hers is a personal weapon of fearsome journalistic repute: 'John Major believes in aid to the Third World. Unlike his predecessor, who railed against "handouts" and took a steel-tipped handbag to the aid budget, he realises that it is essential for the health of the world's economy...' – *Observer.*

handle In colloquial usage this verb replaces 'cope with'. Bad news, unwelcome ideas, 'pressure', are *handled*: 'I don't want them to tell her she has cancer – she couldn't handle it'; 'On top of that, Stich had to handle the pressure of being the new, and unexpected Wimbledon champion' – *Observer*.

hands-on Adjective, meaning 'practical', 'direct', as in *hands-on experience*. The original hands-on experience was the trainee's first touching of the computer keyboard; now the expression can apply more diversely – for example to a medical student's first attempts at the clinical examination of a patient, or a learner-driver's practical training in handling the controls of a car. The epithet *hands-on* may also be used in application to persons; 'The question hardly anyone dare ask in Washington . . . was whether the crisis could have been averted in the first place by a more hands-on president' – *Observer*. From *hands-on* follows **hands-off**: 'Mr Lilley . . . has traditionally taken a hands-off approach to industry' – *Guardian*.

happening In youthpatter, this is an adjective, like **fun**. Birmingham is a happening place (maybe), but Brighton is a fun place (possibly). Happening places are places **where it's at**, and where you do happening things with happening people and fun people and pill-popping, roaring, barely intelligible, demi-semi-literate people.

hard Not jargon **as such**, but a jargon-maker. Commonly used, with its antonym, **soft**, as an index of extremes, e.g. *hard core* (pornography), *hard left*, *hard liner* (politics), *hard sell* (commerce), even *hard gambling*. 'And what about casinos? There are barriers to entry to non-nationals in several countries, but if these are removed, surely a new method of policing hard gambling will need to be introduced' – *Independent*.

hardware In computer technology, *hardware* denotes the machinery of the computer, the working centre that processes the **input** from **software**, i.e. disks containing programmes (or rather, *programs*) of instruction. It used to mean 'ironmongery' before it started to mean 'guns and tanks' (military hardware); now it means chips and disk-drives and such, a comforting development.

harmony Eurotalk: the moderation and coordination of regulations applicable throughout the European Community. Whence **harmonize**, **harmonization**. 'Ireland is the only country to ban casinos completely, but it does have a thriving local bingo industry . . . It is this kind of disparity that first attracted the attention of the harmony-oriented EC' – *Independent*.

headhunter This ferocious noun has nothing to do with the habits of warring tribesmen in Papua or Borneo, but indicates a hunter of a more sophisticated sort: one who 'scouts' for talent, usually in the fields of business, the Civil Service, and the learned professions, trying to persuade highly qualified personnel to move out of their existing posts and into the department/section/institution/managerial team whose interests the head-hunter represents. 'Headhunters are trawling the field for candidates from within and outside television' – *Independent*. 'Trawling the field' is a wonderfully mixed metaphor; but see under **trawl**. There is a verb *to headhunt*, which allows the passive transformation *to be headhunted*. In older sporting jargon, the process was known as 'scouting' or 'talent-spotting'; as a reprehensible practice once indulged in by wealthy families looking for good servants, it was called *poaching*.

heightism An absurd addition to the **-isms** that represent obstacles to **political correctness**, heightism signifies prejudice against those who are felt to be too short, or too tall, or perhaps 'stature-challenged'. See **ableism, ageism, alphabetism, fattism,** and then imagine how our heartless society treats tubby little old one-legged ladies called Wotherspoon. We are all guilty.

he would, wouldn't he? See Part I, p. 103, on Mandy Rice-Davies and the Stephen Ward trial. In rough translation, the phrase means 'that is only to be expected': 'Mr Ashdown dismisses this theory as nonsense, although he would, wouldn't he?' – *Independent*.

high concept An idea that can be presented in a brief, compact form. '[This] lame addition to Channel 4's portfolio of late-night chat-shows reeks of "high concept" (a supposedly sure-fire idea that can be encapsulated in one sentence) and cultivated controversy' – *Independent*. It is not easy, however, to see how that definition might serve to clarify the following adjectival usage, from a newspaper review of a production of *Twelfth Night*: 'This production may be low-budget-looking and it is not high concept, but it shows all the virtues of having been closely pondered' – *Independent*. Perhaps the general sense of *high concept*, as applied to productions and programmes, is (noun) 'a powerfully generative idea', and (adjective) '**driven** by an idea or theory'.

high-impact Denotes any vigorous exercise involving much jumping, pumping, or thumping. **Aerobics** is *high-impact*. 'We have one high-intensity, high-impact class a week and that's it. It's all gone. Aerobics is over' – *Independent*.

hi-tech, high-tech Not only characterized by advanced technology, but by a technology so advanced that it all but eliminates the need for human fingers and thumbs. 'High-tech wars are still fought by people' – *Observer*. Originally *high-tech* expressed an attribute (as in the quoted example), but it is now also used as a noun, meaning a general type of product, or hardware. A computer is a piece of hi-tech. See p. 81 on techspeak.

hole in the wall, hole-in-the-wall machine Popular mode of reference to an Automated Teller Machine, also called a *cash point* or a *cash dispenser*; the purpose of which is to dispense money to a customer holding an account at a designated bank, upon insertion of a valid bank card. This perhaps comes under the heading of 'new word' rather than 'jargon'; but it is worth noting that *hole in the wall* has a longer history, as a phrase meaning a location with no obvious distinguishing features. *Collins English Dictionary* defines *hole in the wall* as 'a small dingy place, esp. one difficult to find'. The phrase has been used to identify bus stops on rural routes, and public houses in urban back streets.

homophobic Hostile to homosexuals. A convenient and unfortunately necessary formation, although as a combination of *homo* ['same'] and *phobic* ['fearing', 'disliking'], it does not add up to the desired sense. Strictly speaking, *homophobic* should mean 'disliking or fearing those of the same kind'. It is not a straightforward Greek derivative, however, but a portmanteau of *homosexual* and *phobic*. The stages of formation appear to have been: *homosexual* abbreviated to *homo* (a form now listed in dictionaries), to which *phobia* is added. This gives the noun *homophobia*, and the adjective *homophobic* follows. As yet it seems that there is no antonymic form, *homophilic*, although *homophile* is listed in some dictionaries as 'a rare word for homosexual'. Perceptions of the meaning of *homosexual*, etc., have been blurred by the confusion of Greek *homos*, 'same', and Latin *homo*, 'man'.

host Occurs as epithet in, for example, 'host nation' (the nation that plays the part of host to visiting football teams, convention delegates, etc.) and as verb in 'to host a conference'. This represents a transfer or extension of meaning of the original *host*, which refers to an individual; hosting a conference or a tennis tournament is a matter of collective organization. Some operations, however, are hosted by individuals: television *chat shows*, for example, are *hosted* by **celebs**.

hyperactive See p. 48 on 'hyperactive hatches'. The source-jargon is psychiatric medicine, but the word is getting into common use with the meaning 'nervously busy', 'unrelaxing', applied to almost any pursuit: 'But Schiff himself is to blame for pecking at the finale of the famous little C major Sonata like a flock of farmyard hens, and his sonata first movements tend to be hyperactive' – *Independent*. It also characterizes energetic people: 'At 67 the hyperactive Mr Bush may turn health consciousness into a parody...' – *Independent*. The abbreviation *hyper* has been noted: '*Who will love Billy* concerned a slightly hyper 13-year-old orphan...' – *Sunday Times*.

I

ideology, ideological This mode word, a favourite with sociologues and smart-art critics, refers not so much to a set of explicitly formulated ideas as to the pattern of beliefs implied in someone's writing, painting, film-making, behaviour, style of government, etc. In the sense of 'a covert programme', it goes along with **hidden agenda**. Some literary critics see it as their business to **deconstruct** the ideologies of the authors they study, the authors themselves being allegedly blind to their own tendencies. In political usage, *ideology* customarily connotes 'left wing', 'crooked' and 'obscure', the ideologies of the right being presented as plain straightforward common sense, and you'd better believe it.

-ie/-y Popular formative suffix, as in **buppie, crumbly, deccie, foodie, freebie,** *oldie,* **wrinkly,** *yeepie, yottie.* The way is open to many more: 'Surely Yuppies, Foodies and . . . Deccies are under a bigger umbrella which shelters ambition, food and decorating – they are Housies' – *Observer.*

impact on As phrasal verb, suggests 'make an impact', 'affect', 'modify'. It is presumably derived from *make an impact on.* 'I'm not sure how it [the Gulf War] will impact on a range of things' – Prime Minister John Major, in a television interview. Mr Major's style adroitly combines the firm (*impact on*) and the floppy (*a range of things*) – like a boxer battering a bolster. But the phrase is not exclusive to Mr Major: 'Dr Brian Bailey, Infolink's chairman, described the month as disappointing, and warned that "threats of a rise in interest rates seem likely to impact on consumer confidence in August"' – *Guardian.*

imperative A modish noun, signifying something that must/ought to be/by and large had better be/could be perceived by interested parties as needing to be/done. 'Military imperatives . . . have served to expose the ambivalence of intentions underlying this crisis' – *Observer.* That sentence metaphrases (see Part I, p. 11) the text 'What the soldiers want makes lying nonsense of what the politicians claim'.

implement As verb, means 'put into effect', 'put into practice', with reference to policies, legislation, regulations. It upgrades other usages, e.g. *apply, bring in, introduce,* and smartly alternates with 'put **in place**'. It has the particular connotation of getting on with the job and putting your muscle where your mouth is; no politician can afford to be without this powerful verb, available now in almost any newspaper. (But see p. 91; FitzEdward Hall, writing more than a century ago, mentions *implement* as a 'Scotch' usage.)

impose yourself on the game This burly specimen of sportscasterese means 'take control of the game', whether by skill or by physical intimidation (the latter is also known as **putting yourself about**). The point of imposing yourself on the game is to **do the business** and **get a result**.

in any way shape or form Is equivalent to *by any manner of means,* but being a word or two longer carries more emphatic conviction. People who say *at this moment in time* are also likely to say *in any way shape or form.*

Note that this expression always occurs with negative assertions. You may say that you have never been the worse for drink in any way shape or form, but oddly enough we do not say that the licensing laws are strict in every way shape and form. Furthermore, it is unidiomatic to say *in any form shape or way*, or *in any shape way or form*. This fixed phrase, a **sound bite** stalwart for union bosses and football managers, is not to be tampered with in any way shape etc.

in contention   Having a chance of winning an athletic contest, usually a foot-race, but also a field event or a boxing match. In foot-races, those who are in contention are **on the pace** and out with the **front runners**; consequently they may find themselves **among the medals**, if there are medals to be among **at the end of the day**. In ripe old sportscasterese, it may be said that those who are not *in contention* have been **left for dead**.

in-depth   The hyphenated form is always used adjectivally – 'an in-depth study', 'in-depth survey', etc.; in adverbial use – 'interview in depth' – the hyphen is omitted. The adjective commonly keeps company with a sub-modifying phrase, e.g. 'Specially commissioned in-depth study', 'Exciting new in-depth survey'. If it means anything, it means 'extensive and detailed', but its true purport may be something like 'taking up a whole page of the **broadsheet**'.

indicator   Socio-economic shop: a measurement of things as they stand, from where the commentator stands. 'However, the index should be seen primarily as a political indicator – a measure of the 'feelgood factor' – and not as an economic forecast' – *Independent*. See also **factor**.

industry   Used to honour and beautify things hardly industrious and not at all industrial, e.g. *the amusement industry, the gambling industry, the leisure industry*, even *the bingo industry*. 'Ireland is the only country to ban casinos completely, but it does have a thriving local bingo industry' – *Independent*.

infantilize   To treat adults as children. See **adultify**; see in general -ise/ -ize.

in-form   Occurs as adjective in sporting reportage, e.g. 'an in-form batsman'. In-form athletes are **on song**.

information society   One in which information is said to be freely accessible and communicable, thanks to modern technology. 'We are told constantly we are living in an 'information society' when, in truth, we are living in a media society in which unrestricted information is unwelcome, even a threat . . .' – *Guardian* (see under **balance**).

infrastructure   In the Marxist analysis of society, the infrastructure is the basic organization of the workers and doers; consequently it refers to *things*, or concrete assets – roads, railways, schools, hospitals, etc. As a mode word it suggests, vaguely and portentously, any kind of institutional apparatus: thus, 'art infrastructure' implies the administrators, committees, premises, societies, professional bodies, etc., concerned in the public presentation of art. For the writer of solemn reports, it provides an escape from such undignified expressions as 'the general set-up'.

initiative Now a fairly well-worn political mode word – hardly *à la mode* but not wholly *demodé* – this means 'a suggestion', 'a proposal for discussion or action', 'a possible solution', put forward or *initiated* by someone who then assumes credit for having done something while everyone else is morosely bent on doing nothing. It is not unknown for the initiator of the solution to be the originator of the problem; as, in the past, with 'trade union initiatives' to 'overcome deadlocks' in 'labour relationships'. Initiatives lend themselves admirably to mixed metaphor: 'How long the seven will continue to send their senior ministers is imponderable, but once they start substituting juniors it might be said that last year's initiative is running out of steam' – *The Times*. When initiatives run out of steam they are **dead in the water**.

innovative This mode word is the pretty sister of *new-fangled*; it means 'tending to introduce new ideas, concepts, proposals, **lifestyles**, gadgets, fashions'. An item in a newspaper supplement announces: 'Habitat is not as innovative as it used to be'. The form *innovatory* also occurs: 'It conveys a portrait of a composer, charming, cultivated, convinced of his innovatory mission, yet helplessly amused at his own neuroses' – *Independent*.

in place 'Ready', 'available for use', 'about to take effect'. 'But what we are sure about are [*sic*] that the basics are still in place to ensure that we have the most precious of gifts when it [the British General Election, 1992] occurs: non-inflationary growth . . .' – Prime Minister John Major, reported in the *Independent*. Little did he know that the time was out of joint, even though the basics were in place.

input A word of diverse meanings. In electronics and computer technology, it means the signal fed into a circuit, or the data put into a system. Current usage goes beyond technology; an *input* may be, for example, a contribution to a debate, or work done in support of a collective, **ongoing** effort, or research programme. The effectiveness of such social input may be reflected by **feedback**. See also **throughput**.

insider dealing, insider trading Stock market shop: trading in stocks and shares, using privileged information not available to clients in the open market. The phrase is a kind of euphemism, and indeed the practitioners of this form of dishonesty do not seem to regard their activities as criminal, or even as misdemeanours: 'Mine was a very private mistake. Insider trading is a victimless offence' – Dennis Levine, an American financier, reported in *Observer Magazine*. Tell that to your small shareholder.

insightful A pretendedly unpretentious adjective, for which *perceptive* will serve perfectly well. It occasionally happens that an Anglo-Saxon word form is considered more stylish and **up-market** than the Latin; here perhaps the **sub-text** is that the eyes of insight see deeper than those of mere perception. Professional critics may be *insightful* about Film or Dance; others make perceptive comments on their way home from the Odeon or Sadler's Wells.

installation art Art which uses the gallery as its 'canvas', laying out objects (bricks, stones, common furniture) in considered relationship to the space of the building; a revelation or a load of quasi-intellectual rubbish, according to the eye of the **insightful** beholder.

-intensive Common as a second element in hyphenated compounds usually in socio-economic jargon, e.g. 'labour-intensive', 'capital-intensive', where it means 'using up a lot of'. For this tendency in compound formation, see also **-driven, -friendly, -led**.

interactive technology; interactivity In techspeak, the linking of different systems of information storage and communication – e.g., at a crude level, the interaction of the human brain and the camera. Computers are interactive with display systems. 'Interactivity is the techie word for this happy marriage of computing power and TV' – *Guardian* (describing a 'simulator' used in training engine drivers). *Interactive technology* produces **virtual reality**.

interdiction A military euphemism, familiar from the reporting of the 1991 Gulf War, meaning 'blockade'. The sponsor who brought you *human remains pouches* brings you this word. **Interdiction bombing** means the bombing of transport, roads, bridges, the means of access and egress.

interface In computer technology, an *interface* is a device serving to link systems in the machine. In psychotherapy, 'interfacing' is the forming of relationships, e.g. between the therapist and the patient, or between one patient and another. In educationese, an 'interface' is a frontier between compatible disciplines: one 'explores the interface between linguistics and sociology', etc. 'The aim of the INTERFACE series is to examine topics at the "interface" of language studies and literary criticism . . .' – Publisher's notice (Routledge).

in terms of This loosely connects an A with a B, denoting 'in the form of', or 'such as', or 'in connection with', or simply '='. Thus, 'The economy is recovering in terms of the Gross National Product' means 'Increase in the Gross National Product = Recovery of the economy'. In the following example, 'in terms of' means 'in the form of': 'The aim is to enhance the brand identity of ITV but it will also prevent independent producers building up capital in terms of programme rights' – *Independent*. See further p. 23 on *handy adjuncts*.

internationalize To bring [a nation] out of the closed circle of its own customs and traditions and into the wider sphere of international practices. 'Even the agonised debate on 'internationalising' Japan is reflected into the same world' – *Independent*. (The conductors of the 'agonised debate' are the Japanese; the 'same world' is Japan itself.)

interventionism The philosophy of intervening to put things right – or turn them to your liking – in the market, in society, in the currency exchanges, in the world at large. The antonym of interventionism might conceivably be *abstentionism* – a word waiting to be called into use. Governments with the most loftily abstentionist claims (e.g. that of the Baroness Thatcher of Kesteven) are noticeably the most determinedly interventionist in practice.

in the case of This is an old bugbear to purists and prescriptivists, listed among the phrases forbidden by the Fowlers, Quiller-Couch, and Orwell (see Part I, p. 94). It is now somewhat overshadowed, as a jargonist's connective, by **in terms of** and **as such**. 'In the case of drinking water, these two issues come together' – *Independent*. (The **issues** are **subsidiarity** and the **democratic deficit**. One might re-phrase, parodically: 'These two issues come together in terms of drinking water', or perhaps 'Basically, in terms of drinking water as such, these two issues come together'.)

into, to be A package phrase (see p. 22), a quick fix for smart talkers, used by people who have no time for 'have an interest in', or 'be an enthusiast for', or 'take up as a hobby': 'She's into alternative medicine'; 'He's really into antiques'. Those who are into the English Language in a big way may consider that basically we must be free as such or **literally** die, in terms of speaking the tongue that Shakespeare spake and holding the faith and morals that Milton held at a particular moment in time.

-ise/-ize Powerful verb-forming suffix; the spellings -ise and -ize vary from nation to nation and newspaper to newspaper, from author to author, and even from writer to the same writer, but the entry here is under the alternative -ise, to place it next to the entry for **-ism**. Then see most of the following under their separate heads: **Albanianize, anonymize, authenticize, awfulize, Balkanization, cannibalize, catastrophize, customize, destabilize, fractionalization, infantilize, institutionalization, internationalize, Kuwaitization, marginalize, metaphoricization, negativize, operationalize, paratactization, polarize, politicize, pressurize, prioritize, problematize, proletarianize, quietize, revirginization, sanitize, sensitize, syntacticize.**

-ism Here are some of the -isms, of **ideology, lifestyle,** and **Political Correctness**: ableism, ageism, alphabetism, bufferism, collectivism, confrontationism, connectionism, credentialism, economism, electoralism, entryism, Europeanism, federalism, heightism, interventionism, masculism,

monetarism, multilateralism, nimbyism, one nation conservatism, populism, post-modernism, post-structuralism, psychologism, racism, reproclassicism, sectionalism, short-termism, statism, volunteerism, welfarism,
workaholicism. See separate entries for many of these.

issue A very important mode word, without which nothing can be raised,
aired, addressed, examined, or negotiated. It can signify a topic in politics,
or a theme in an **ongoing** social debate. 'Addressing the issues', or better,
'addressing *oneself* to the issues' is the correct thing to attempt; even more
satisfactory is 'firmly addressing [oneself to] the issues'. You may also
'speak to the issue(s)'. Issues imply debate and opposition. How to make
strawberry shortcake is not an issue; how to educate children raises a great
many issues. The framing of regulations and codes of practice for the
European Community involves major and minor issues – e.g. meat production and betting. 'The racing issue is more localised', says the *Independent*.
In American politics, a **hot button issue** is a matter of central or fashionable
concern, e.g. the greenhouse effect or deficit financing. With the definite
article, *the issues* are all matters of current concern, or all questions arising
out of a particular concern: 'Ever since Network 7 there's been a whole
welter of programmes that could take a story and deal with the issues in
10 minutes and you might do something more wrought but basically the
issues are yesterday's papers' – *Independent*. ' "Male" themes such as the
Cold War have receded, and "female" issues, including education and
health care, are uppermost' – *Independent*.

J

Jack the lad A cheerfully self-assured, possibly somewhat uncouth young
man. In Irish, a *jackeen*. This slang phrase turns up in journalistic assessments of politicians or other public figures perceived as youthfully brash.
See **laddish**.

jazzerati People well known as jazz musicians, or distinguished by their
knowledge of jazz. Based on *literati*; see **glitterati, numerati**.

judg(e)mental The word used to be 'censorious': always ready to pass
judgement, generally adverse. Goes along with **confrontational, confrontive**.
The judgemental by nature are confrontive in consequence: 'you are wrong'
leads to 'take that!' – a wigging begets a **handbagging**.

junk: junk bond, junk food, junk science All based on *junk* meaning
'rubbish'; possibly influenced further by the slang sense of *junk* as 'narcotic
drug'. A *junk bond* offers a high rate of interest but is an extremely risky
investment; junk bonds are commonly sold to raise money for take-overs
and buyouts. This is known as *junk finance*; *junk finance* frequently leads
to *junk debt*. *Junk food* is food that temporarily stills hunger but has little

or no nutritional value – potato crisps, 'nibbles', sweets. *Junk science* is pseudo-science, the arbitrary and selective incorporation of questionable facts into dubious theories: '[He] said that Dr X was frightening patients with "junk science" and misleading regulatory authorities in Britain and the US' – *Independent*.

K

K The **yuppie** word for one thousand pounds: 'People who take home less than fifty K just haven't made the cut' – *Independent* (see **make the cut**). In computerspeak, *K* signifies one *kilobyte*, i.e. 1,024 'bytes' of information. For senior Civil Servants, a *K* means a knighthood, which is a **mega** way of making the cut.

kebabbed (**vb**) Hacked, skewered and grilled; a culinary metaphor signifying, in political manoeuvres, more or less what Americans mean by 'hung out to dry' – i.e. left utterly defeated and humiliated. Hence the protest of Mr Neil Kinnock, leader of the Parliamentary Labour Party, during an internecine dispute: 'I'm not going to be kebabbed'.

key A fashionable prefix element, e.g. in *key issue, key role, key player, key question*, and many others. It combines the meanings 'most important', 'principal', and 'opening a way out of potential difficulties or confusions'. 'To die, to sleep – to dream – aye, there's the key issue', Hamlet might have said. See further **where it's at**.

keynote address, keynote speech An address or lecture given at the opening of a conference, often by an invited speaker, indicating the tenor and scope of the topics and **issues** about to be discussed. From the practice, in music, of sounding a note for a choir or vocal group. As a rule, the keynote speaker's 'doh' elicits nothing more harmonious than a 'so' or a 'me' from those who follow.

keynote species Eco-talk: a species of plant or animal upon which other species (including humankind) depend. Also, perhaps more appropriately, *key species*, with **key** in the sense described above.

kick into touch, to Sporting jargon, from soccer and rugby; a ball kicked into touch, i.e. over the sideline, is out of play. In political jargon, an inconvenient **issue** may be *kicked into touch* – that is, 'dismissed for the time being', 'postponed for later consideration'. 'It's a postponement of decisions [see **tactical voting**], it's a kick for touch, and you can't run a country on a basis of kicking for touch' – Neil Kinnock, interviewed by *New Statesman and Society*, 13 February 1987.

kick-start To give something the impetus of vigorous and decisive action, as in 'taking measures to kick-start the economy'. The source-jargon is motor-cyclist's talk; the engine of a motor-cycle is generally *kick-started*, by pushing down on a cranked pedal. 'Will the 20 December reduction in the federal discount rate prove sufficient to kick-start the US economy out of a double-dip recession, or will debt-deflation prove the stronger factor?' – *Independent*. See further **double dip recession** and **factor**.

knee-jerk reaction An instinctive reaction to social or political stimuli, as though (a) in religious genuflection, or (b), more probably, in response to a testing of the patellar reflexes. 'Mitterrand does not suffer from the knee-jerk anti-Americanism of his countrymen' – *Independent*.

Kuwaitization The creation of a small state enriched by one asset, governed by a small ruling caste, and protected by greater powers in whose financial or strategic interests its survival is desired. From the emirate of Kuwait, in 1990–1 the *casus belli* in the Gulf War.

L

laddish Cocky, brash, self-confident; like **Jack the lad**. 'At once scrub-faced and laddish, he's the kind of person you'd expect to see in an advertisement for shower gel' – *Independent*. 'Scrub-faced [fresh-faced] and laddish' = 'At once innocent and brashly knowing' (or *street wise*).

lame Inept, hence lacking in **credibility**; originates in Black English. 'In a lame effort to distinguish itself from ITV's *You've Been Framed, Caught in the Act*, BBC's outlet for home-video hilarities, tries to double as a game show' – *Independent*.

learning curve See Part I, p. 16. In educationese the 'learning curve' supposedly plots the student's advance through the continuous process of learning. This metaphor challenges the notion of learning as a series of *steps*; the beginner and the more advanced student are alike *on a learning curve*. It is always assumed that the curve tends upward.

learning difficulty This may be a euphemism, the **politically correct** way of referring to the **problems** of someone who is mentally **disadvantaged** or intellectually **challenged**. ' "Mental handicap" should be avoided. "People with learning difficulties" is preferred' – *Independent*.

-led Formative element in compounds, e.g. *consumer-led, export-led, growth-led*; signifies 'directed by a particular property or characteristic'. Expressions of this kind are a form of ellipsis or semantic shorthand, the meaning of which has to be elaborated from a **context**. 'It looked as though a stock-led recession had started' = 'It looked as though a recession characterized by a fall in the marketing of stocks had started.' The *-led* formations may be compared with those on **-driven**.

left field, out of   Familiar in American English, this expression, meaning 'quite unpredictable', 'coming from an unexpected quarter', or even 'preposterous', is relatively recent in British usage. The source is sporting jargon, and the reference is to the usual pattern of activity around the baseball diamond. The equivalent of *left field* in cricket would be the sector behind the batsman and the wicket-keeper; but I see little future for 'that's an idea from deep fine leg'.

left for dead   A foolish phrase used by sports commentators, meaning 'left far behind' (in a foot-race, when the **front runners** put on a spurt). Those who are *left for dead* cannot stay **in contention** and will assuredly not find themselves **among the medals**. Not the same as **dead in the water**. Proposals are dead in the water; runners are left for dead.

level playing field   See Part I, p. 31. The source-jargon is sport, the meaning 'conditions of negotiation or contest equable to all parties'. Compare **move the goalposts**.

lifestyle   Not exactly a 'way of life'; monks, nuns, scholars, poets, thinkers, hermits, and others who profess a way of life rarely if ever have a lifestyle. Lifestyles involve breakfast cereals, deodorants, mouthwashes, garden furniture, sportswear. An **up-market** lifestyle is expressed in material possessions and privileges; the kind of house you live in, your furnishings, the location of your holidays, your yacht, the number and make of your cars (it takes at least two cars to constitute a lifestyle), your winebin, your household complement of domestics and nannies, your social pretensions in general. The poor and the meek have no sort of lifestyle, except, possibly, in their **choice** of toilet paper and hair conditioner, or in opting for an **alternative**. Alternative lifestyles are nasty, brutish and unworldly. **Celebs** have ample lifestyles. **Essex men** and **suits** have commercial lifestyles. **New Age travellers** have alternative lifestyles. A dentist's advertisement placed in that accurate chronicle of rural England, the *Castle Donington, Kegworth, and Melbourne NuNews*, reads: 'A Healthy Mouth – A Happy Smile – Essential Parts – Of Your Lifestyle'. Toothpaste is a **lifestyle product** (see below).

lifestyle product   A manufacture designed to express pretensions to a **lifestyle**: e.g. a bidet, a shell suit, a gold chain, a microwave oven, a cordless telephone, a kimono, an exercise bicycle. In general, these products suit the lifestyles of **Essex man**, sometimes called *Basildon man*.

links   Links are an **issue**, as in 'links between the police and the social services'. The word denotes connections between institutions, and also, in the form **linkage**, the interdependency of political events. During the Gulf Crisis of 1990–1, there was said to be *linkage* between Arab readiness to participate in a Middle East peace conference and Israeli willingness to withdraw from territories on the West Bank and in the Golan Heights.

literally Figuratively, with emphasis; as in 'I literally died when I saw my tax bill'. (Out of seven dictionaries which I have consulted, three note the use of *literally* as an emphatic; which may suggest that it is becoming standard usage, and hence not an appropriate item for this glossary. Compare **basically**.)

long way, to go back a To have been friends for a long time. Borrowed into British usage from American, where it sounds natural and easy; in UK accents, it has the dying fall of oleaginous insincerity. People who enjoy **lifestyles** go back a long way with someone; common folk have old friends.

lookalike A *lookalike* was formerly a *double* in theatrical terms, or a *spitting image* in common parlance; in short, someone thought to bear a close physical resemblance to another person, usually a **celeb**, possibly a **royal**. Aspiring to 'look alike' is now a not unusual form of tribute and emulation; every neighbourhood nightspot and Karaoke Klub has its regular competition for Elvis Presley lookalikes struggling to be soundalikes and shakealikes.

M

macro- This, with its necessary partner, **micro-**, is a currently fashionable prefix-element. The source-jargon is techspeak (see Part I, pp. 79–81), but usage now extends into other, more general fields: *macro- (micro-) structure, macro- (micro-) economic(s), macro- (micro-) politics, -political.* There is a tendency for *macro-, micro-,* to replace *maxi-, mini-,* as modish prefixes, all the more modish for seeming 'scientific'. Thus the *Independent*: 'The questions involved in making such a macro-economic prognostication do not lend themselves to the *vox pop*.' This can be translated, or rendered down: 'Ordinary people will not ask the questions which lead to economic prophesying on such a large scale.'

make the cut To win the approval of a social group; to reach an acknowledged standard of success, e.g. to have an income of 70K and a Roller in the double garage, along with the wife's Morgan. Earlier *make the grade*, or simply *make it*. 'It is also the reason why most of Ford's models rarely make the cut with the cognoscenti' – *Observer*. 'People who take home less than fifty K just haven't made the cut' – *Independent*. Related to *cut it, hack it.* People who can't hack it seldom make the rich wife, let alone the Roller.

male bonding An expression of 'togetherness' between persons of the male **gender**; this occurs on fishing trips, on the football terraces, in locker rooms, in the Masonic lodge, at the Shriners' convention, in the charabanc on the way home from the works outing, and wherever two or three of the boys or *buddies* are gathered together to confide, confess, bless, blaspheme, smoke, joke, throw up, and devise rituals so astonishingly silly that no sensible person of the female **gender** would want to know anything about them.

male suprematism   Male dominance; see **mascul[in]ism**. See further **male bonding, new man**.

management skills   Simply, the ability to manage a business. When Adam Smith described Britain as 'a nation of shopkeepers', he meant that we are a corporate enterprise steered by people endowed with finely honed management skills.

mandatory sanction   In political language, an obligation (more honoured in the breach than in the observance) to place an embargo on trade with a country that has fallen into international disfavour. Usually in the plural. Usually meaningless.

marginalize   To assign (a personality or an **issue**) to a position of relative unimportance. 'The whole exercise had been an attempt further to marginalise the Jackson liberals within the party' – *Spectator*. See word forms under **-ise/-ize**.

market   Possibly the most important word in British English of the mid- to late twentieth century, denoting collectively the stock market, the commodity market, the money market, the export market, the housing market, the used car market, and all species of buying and selling. Markets are **driven** by *market forces* under the supervision of **market makers**, who help to influence *market sentiment* – meaning a feeling for money, as instinctive as the clutch of a boa constrictor.

marketeer   One who has faith in the wisdom of the market. Not infrequently a **market maker**.

market maker   A stock-jobber; one who undertakes to buy and sell securities, shares, etc., at notified prices which reflect *market sentiment*.

mascul[in]ism   A feeble riposte to *feminism*; the doctrine of male dominance, the assertion of male qualities and values. The adjective and agent-noun is **masculist**. 'The number of such cartoons [insulting men] is so small that . . . only a loony masculist would object to them' – *Guardian*.

measure   Something proposed; occasionally, something done. 'It is a short-term measure for people who need long-term support' – *Independent*. 'Though the measure [a Private Member's Bill in the House of Commons] received a first reading, Mr Cormack can rest confident it will never reach the statute book' – *Independent*. This long-established mode word is most effectively deployed in passive constructions: 'measures have been taken', 'measures are being considered', 'measures are about to be implemented', etc.

media director   A species of *agent* or *publicity manager*, engaged to puff a product or a person, in the press, on radio, on TV. 'Alexandre Lazare Lojpur comes from one of Yugoslavia's oldest Serbian families, according to Sarah Byfield-Riches, his optimistically named media director' – *Independent*.

media society   See under **information society**.

medilexic   A **fun** word (see **alphabetism**), defining someone whose surname begins with a letter in mid-alphabet. Messrs/Mesdames Lugg, Mudd and Nobbs are medilexics.

mega   Once a prefix in techspeak (e.g. *megawatt, megavolt, megaspore, megabyte*), this has come into general circulation, first with the denotation 'one million', and subsequently in a vaguer general senses of 'enormous', 'extremely important'. Thus *megabuck*, a million dollars, *megadeath*, a million deaths; then *megastar* (of stage, screen, television, the rock scene or the football field); *megadose*, a very large dose; *megaflop, megabore, mega-series* or *megathon* (in TV jargon, a portmanteau of *mega* and *marathon*, a long-running series). In youthspeak, 'It's mega' is tantamount to saying that it's def and brill.

meltdown   From nuclear technology where *meltdown* means the melting of the core of a nuclear reactor, the scientists' nightmare **scenario** of irreversible and destructive collapse; and so to other fields, as in *financial meltdown, economic meltdown*. The Stock Market crash of 19 October 1987 has been referred to as *meltdown Monday*.

metaphoricization   Figurative usage (of expressions that may already be figurative). *Economic meltdown* (see the entry above) is a metaphoricization. Metaphoricization is the hard work that theorizing critics make out of writers' easy play.

Mickey Mouse   Used attributively, means 'insignificant', 'trivial', as in *Mickey Mouse courses, Mickey Mouse subject, Mickey Mouse university*. 'He is not just a performer on television, but also a proselytizer about it, describing it as "our National Theatre", warning about the danger of it becoming "a Mickey Mouse medium"' – *Observer*. Considering what Mickey Mouse has wrought in our century of the common rodent, this seems an odd usage; I would have thought that Mickey Mouse was Maxi Mouse, and indeed fairly **mega**.

micro-   See under **macro-**.

militant   Adjective or noun, a political mode word. As noun, signifies an **activist**, usually a *left-wing activist*. As used in current British politics, *militant* is an abbreviation of *The Militant Tendency*, a sect on the left of the Labour Party criticizing the diplomacy of the party leadership and advocating a more **confrontationist** stance in politics. This group published a newspaper called *Militant*. Hence, 'she is a Militant', 'he belongs to Militant'.

milkaholic   See under -oholic.

minder   A sub-type of **carer**; specifically, a bodyguard. Politicians and **royals** have minders nowadays, but the original beneficiaries were crooks and the all-but crooked. The word became generally familiar during the 1980s as the title of a British TV comedy series about a seedy half-villain and his exasperated protector.

mini-   The prefix-partner to *maxi*, but rather more productive: e.g. *mini-series* (a short TV series); *mini-break* (a holiday of two or three days, usually at the week end, offered on special terms by hotels and travel agents); *minibus, minicab, minicomputer, minidose, minipill*. In some ways, *mini* is becoming the formal antonym of **mega**, rather than of *maxi*; see, for example, *megadose* and *minidose*.

minimalism, minimal art   In painting and sculpture, the reduction of the work to simple geometrical shapes and flat colours, 'minimizing' the illusion of something expressed or represented.

mode   In techspeak and pseudotechspeak, an executive state of the system or machine, e.g. 'print mode' in your friendly word-processor, 'shampooing mode', 'wet pickup mode', 'dry mode' in your implacably malevolent carpet cleaner. In the socio-political vocabulary, a *mode* is a way of organizing or going about things. 'When the Alliance fell apart, it became a conventional wisdom that Britain had entered into a three-party mode' – *Independent*. 'Back in Tokyo ... Mr Sakurauchi was forced to slip into *takemae* mode and the adoption of a front for public consumption by issuing his "clarification"' – *Independent*. (In Japanese, *honne* and *takemae* are social conventions; *honne* means saying what you like in the presence of friends, *takemae* means dissimulating in your public utterances.)

model   An academic's mode word. A *model* in mathematics, in the sciences, in linguistics, in social and economic theory, is the hypothetical pattern, the propositional design, the algorithm or **framework** defining procedures of investigation and discussion. An algebraist, for example, might adopt a Boolean model; a theoretical linguist a Chomskyan, or transformational-generative model. In laxer usages, it is a rough-and-ready synonym of **approach, context, strategy**.

monetarism   This is a word as big as **market** and **entrepreneur**. It is a philosophy, the primary tenet of which is that if inflation is to be contained, the supply of money must be controlled, while the economy is entrusted to the operation of *market forces*. These should regulate the demand for wages (especially in the public **sector**), the provision of subsidies, and any form of public **funding**, while governments curb the foolish pretensions of the impractical, the woolly-minded and the tender-hearted, whose dreams go beyond the rational giving and getting of **value for money**.

money mechanism, also **funding mechanism** In finance, a system that arranges the supply of necessary capital to a venture or undertaking. The supply of funds to a medical practice, for instance, requires a *mechanism*. The old, vague, limping, technologically inadequate term was 'arrangement'.

motivation, motivational On *motivation*, see **commitment**. In general, sportsmen have *motivation*; others have more or less compelling reasons for getting out of bed and pushing on with their business. ' "I'm having motivational problems," he said after a first round defeat in Sydney' – *Observer*.

mould, break the A craftsman's metaphor that has got into the cant of politics. Breaking the mould means, roughly, throwing off conventions and precedents in order to produce something unique, for example a political party. (The formation of the now defunct Social Democratic Party was said to have 'broken the mould of British politics'.) The metaphor is drawn from the process of casting, in plaster, clay, or metal; if the mould or cast is broken, the product cannot be further copied, and the point of breaking the mould (unless it be done by accident) is to ensure this. As often happens, there is a mismatch between the ground of the metaphor, strictly interpreted, and its applications. Strictly speaking, a political party that 'broke the mould' would not offer an **innovative** challenge to other parties; it would merely impair its own potential for growth and reproduction. This is a long way from the old shop talk of workers in foundries and kilns, who would occasionally say, in praise of a peerless man or woman, 'When God made them, He broke the mould'. That is good native English. But 'break the mould of British politics' is aboriginal journalese.

movers and shakers In the jargon of politics, finance, commerce, and the **markets**, the *movers and shakers* are the people who make things happen. The phrase is apparently – and most oddly – an echo of a line in Arthur O'Shaughnessy's poem 'We are the Music Makers'; *We are the music makers, / We are the dreamers of dreams, / Wandering by lone sea-breakers, / And sitting by desolate streams; / World-losers and world-forsakers, / On whom the pale moon gleams, / We are the movers and shakers / Of the world for ever, it seems.* There cannot be many lone sea-breakers or desolate streams on the floor of the Stock Exchange, but that is one of the places where the movers and shakers are to be found.

move the goalposts Change (or keep changing) the object of an argument, negotiation, etc., so that an opponent cannot hope to 'score', i.e. accomplish anything, make a point, conclude a demonstration. Indispensable in politics; useful for academics caught in tricky (losing) games of logic.

multi- Another important quasi-prefix, along with *maxi-*, **mini-**, **macro-**, **micro-**, **mega-**. Things with many purposes are multipurpose things;

buildings and scholarly hypotheses are multilevelled (the common characteristic being **structure**); multi-racial societies are multi-cultural and multi-**ethnic**; my carpet cleaner, besides having a wet pickup **mode**, has 'multi-directional castors', enabling it to slide and spew in every which-a-way. Lateralism may be *multi* as well as *bi* and *uni*.

N

naff   In current British English, this word is the thumbs-down for all seasons. Mechanics use *naff* in the sense of 'useless', 'broken down', as earlier generations have used 'clapped out' and 'kaput': e.g. 'Trouble is, guvnor, your starter motor's naff, innit?' But when social arbiters pronounce something *naff*, they mean 'vulgar', 'tasteless', *kitsch*. 'There may be a recession in the States . . . but people are still buying naff goods. Indeed, the things they're offered are naff beyond the dreams of Essex man' – *Observer*. The naff goods listed by Simon Hoggart in his column include 'an Elvis musical box in "fine bisque porcelain" . . . which plays "Heartbreak Hotel" when you lift the lid', and 'a set of 24 porcelain herb jars, each in the shape of a village building'. Now that *is* naff.

negative   In radio communications, an emphatic **no**, intended to be audible above any background noise. Not always effective; some cab-drivers have taken to saying **negatory**. In dispute, shouting *negative!* is a rhetorical **strategy** comparable to bellowing *no way!*. As an adjective, *negative* commonly denotes 'unconstructive', 'unhelpful', as in 'a negative attitude'. Note the phrase **negative feelings**, in cruder times called 'bloody-mindedness', now the **politically correct** attribute of people with **attitude problems**. 'I have negative feelings about him' does not mean 'I am unable to like him'; it means 'Having access to my own emotions, I perceive in myself a regrettable inclination to whack him in the gob at the first excuse'. *Negative feelings* are positively baleful. 'The prisoners are not a soft touch. Nearly all have been imprisoned for violence – rape, child molesting, robbery and murder. Many have committed violence in other prisons. Yet in Grendon, they learn new ways of handling negative feelings and are given a new view of authority: prison staff who wear uniform, set boundaries, but also care' – *Guardian*.

negativize   To be unconstructively critical; to insist on pointing out the drawbacks or *negative aspects* of a proposal or undertaking; compare **awfulize, catastrophize**.

nerd   Without drawing too fine a distinction, a **dork**.

networking   This occurs in commercial as well as in sociological jargon. In sociology, *networking* signifies the making of a complex social group, like a larger version of the family, through the creation of a 'network' of encounters (formal or informal), interactions (professional or nonprofessional), exchanges of correspondence, telephone calls, etc. In commerce, the process is similar but the purpose is wholly professional. It used to be called 'making contacts'. See also **cold calling**.

New Age This has nothing to do with Virgil's fourth Eclogue (*magnus ab integro saeclorum nascitur ordo*), though the **resonance** is pleasant for us college folk. As an adjectival phrase it means, roughly, 'devoted to the proposition that materialist society is sick and dying, that the old regulatory social conventions have had their day, and that a life of untrammelled joy, unburdened by possessions or oppressive customs, lies before those with courage to avail themselves of it' – in short, subscribing to the incorporated screwball beliefs of the high-minded, the hippy and the hobo. The epithet is frequently associated with the word *traveller*, which is **up-market** for 'tramp'. But there are signs of a freer movement: 'Myself and a few others went off in the direction of educational camps... if you like, New Age camps' – *Independent*. The educational value of a New Age camp might lie in **consciousness raising** and **getting in touch with one's feelings,** as well as *telling it like it is*, to the strains of guitar or ghetto blaster, while the convivial **spliffs** go round.

new man One mercifully devoid of the customary attributes of the male **gender** – selfishness, conceit, violence, a slothful aversion to housework – which arise out of **masculist** assumptions of male dominance; educated to accept **gender balance** and *role reversal*, to make a bed, make a soufflé, make love, or go out and make money, and do all these things gracefully. Some observers doubt that this paragon could ever exist. 'She's quite clear though, that whatever she reared her "New Man" son for, it was not to dwindle into a toy-boy to a woman more than twice her age...' – *Independent*. 'The New Man... sounds suspiciously like one of those fictional stereotypes dreamed up by an adman after a long lunch' – *Independent*.

Nimbyism In the acronymic base of this plangent piece of political jargon, the letters stand for *Not in my back yard*; the principle of Nimbyism being that any building project, road scheme, proposed railway line, airfield, power station, etc., designed to benefit the nation, raise the standard of living, and give **value for money,** may be enthusiastically supported as long as it is kept well away from the supporter's own property. We are all nimbies now; 'The Nimby syndrome prevails', announces a headline in the *Independent*.

numerati Formed on *literati*, and meaning 'people who are *numerate*, i.e. can do their sums'. The word-ending is of course the plural *-i*, but other creations on this model are formed as though *-ati* were a suffix. See **glitterati, jazzerati**.

O

objectify To make objective, to state objectively – as though it were possible, other than in mathematical notation, to escape the taint of subjectivity. Not to be confused with the once fashionable *reify*, which means treating abstractions and concepts as though they were things.

obscene A primary meaning of *obscene* is 'filthy', 'indecent', as in 'obscene publication', 'obscene photograph', 'obscene language'. This meaning is broadened and perhaps weakened in many modern **contexts**, where it signifies 'thoroughly objectionable', 'abhorrent' (to the speaker or writer); thus poverty is obscene, war is obscene, the greed of speculators is obscene. Even ideas may be obscene: 'The idea that a ruler who has systematically executed every possible opponent should now set himself up as a champion of Arab rights and democracy is obscene' – *Observer*.

-oholic/-aholic One of the best modern examples of a productive *false* suffix. The model is *alcohol-ic*, from which a suffix element *-oholic, -aholic* is inferred. Thus **chocoholic**, 'addicted to chocolate', **creamaholic, milkaholic, clothesaholic**, 'unable to stop buying clothes', **shopaholic**, 'helplessly driven into boutiques and craft shops'; and **workaholic**, 'unable to stop working', the most firmly established after *alcoholic*, and perhaps the most likely to survive as a standard item in the lexicon of twentieth-century addictions. (The word was coined in 1971 by an American author, Wayne Oates, and is now listed in most dictionaries.)

one nation conservatism Political cant: a modern version of the nineteenth-century conservatism represented by Benjamin Disraeli. It suggests that the Conservative Party and its policies might satisfactorily embrace the interests of the whole nation, from **crusties** to company directors. This attractive proposition would seem to offer us all a release from the quinquennial embarrassment of going to the polls – if we were all Conservatives there would be no point in setting up the booths – but it is fundamentally flawed. Conservatism depends on the existence of two nations; else what is left for conservatives to conserve?

ongoing Continued, protracted, persistent, as in 'an ongoing debate', 'ongoing negotiations', 'ongoing issue', 'ongoing problem'. Essentially a socio-political epithet, not much used in other fields, for example medicine or the language of the emotions: it would perhaps be unidiomatic to have 'an ongoing axillary abscess', 'an ongoing lust for Lady Jane', or 'an ongoing pain in the backside' – even though, in the latter **metaphoricized** instance, there are certainly public events and personages that might aggravate a persistent condition.

on hold Kept in abeyance; the saying used to be 'action deferred'. 'Sir Kenneth Bradshaw ... said yesterday that plans for both hotel and golf course had been put 'on hold' by the Department of the Environment' – *Independent*. The phrase is standard in telephone operators' jargon; a call may be 'put on hold' while the intended recipient is otherwise engaged.

on song Birds and sopranos are *on song* with winsome melodies; athletes and football teams are *on form* with winning ways; that is, until sports-casters are moved to **metaphoricization**, after which runners, golfers, darts players, cricketers, triple jumpers, chess masters *et hoc genus omne* are interminably *on song*. It goes with **asking the questions.**

on stream This dates from the discovery of oilfields in the North Sea; when the first barrels were piped ashore, the oil was said to be *on stream*. (The origin of the phrase is uncertain; it is perhaps some publicity person's invention, on the model of *on tap*; Guinness is 'on tap', oil is 'on stream'.) The expression is now a package phrase, available for the description of things other than oil – e.g. for services, facilities, or **funding.**

on the back burner Comparable with **on hold.** The *back burner* on a cooker is often less powerful than the other burners, and is hence suitable for dishes that require a low heat, or can be left to simmer, or 'warm over'. The figurative sense of *putting (or leaving) something on the back burner* is keeping a project in reserve for later attention. It is, however, slightly different from **on hold**, in that *the back burner* implies **ongoing** if reduced activity, whereas *on hold* may imply indefinite suspension.

on the back of On the basis of, using something as a foundation. The figure is that of climbing up on someone's back: 'Since the late 1970s Iraq has built up a formidable expertise largely on the back of technology purchased from Western and Eastern bloc countries' – *Observer*.

on the pace In sporting jargon, keeping up with **the front runners; up to speed;** hence, in any field of activity, staying in the forefront of things.

open government Politicians' shop talk. *Open government*, noblest article of democratic faith, is actually a condition of utmost secrecy, based on the *need to know* and the *right to know*, which members of the general public (in Great Britain, upwards of 50 million souls, men, women, and tots) do not have. Those who *need to know* are very discreet in their assessments of other people's *right to know*, because on their discretion depends the security of *open government*. The recent proliferation of **charters** is possibly a response to the aggrieved **perception** of members of the general public that they have no *right to know* what they *need to know*, even though it may be better *not to want to know*. See further **accountability; economical with the truth; porky.**

operationalize In politics, to put into operation; in science, to find means of measuring and quantifying a concept, so that it may be tested.

opt in and **opt out** Political shop, related to a concept revered among Conservatives, of **choice**. Schools may *opt out* of the traditional arrangement that puts them under the control of a local authority, and *opt in* to recently introduced provisions allowing them direct management of their own budgets. So also with medical practice; partners may opt for a self-budgeting *trust*. When used attributively, the phrases are usually hyphenated: 'The opt-out plan will now go to Ian Lang, the Secretary of State for Scotland . . .' – *Independent.*

overbedded, overbedding In the jargon of hospital management, the provision of more beds than can be filled by patients. 'London is over-bedded and has been for many years. This overbedding will only increase in future years' – *Independent.*

over the top This well-worn package phrase is wholly unconnected with the First World War expression that meant climbing out of a trench to attack the enemy. It means 'exaggerated', 'hyperbolical', 'flamboyant', 'too, too much': 'Events such as these are high kitsch, celebrated in a no-holds-barred, over-the-top manner' – *Independent.* In general usage, those who express themselves with enthusiasm and eloquence are said to be 'going over the top a bit'; it is a quite unBritish thing, except for football hooligans, who also go over the top in the First World War sense.

own goal An *own goal* in football occurs when a defender unintentionally kicks the ball into his own side's net. In politics, an own goal is a blunder (commonly verbal) that puts the politician's own party at a disadvantage. See **foot, to shoot oneself in the:**

P

package A commercial-political mode word, figuring usually as the filler-noun in phrases, e.g. *package deal, package of proposals, care package, pension package, package holiday.* The sense of *package* is that diverse elements are included in the deal, the proposals, etc.; a package holiday includes the cost of travel, arrangements for board and lodging, and possibly the entitlement to join certain parties, courses, or excursions.

paradigm A rather elderly mode word, this, but still going the rounds among the **chattering** classes. From its source in grammar and linguistics (where the elements of a *paradigm* are finite in relationship to a given function, e.g. the syntax of the noun), *paradigm* has slipped into the general, loose sense of 'characteristic pattern', 'typical example'. It can also mean 'plan', 'set of proposals', 'political programme', as in this *Guardian* account of proceedings at a Republican Party convention: 'The platform preamble, pulled as an all-nighter by James Cicconi, a Baker aide, and

James Pinkerton, the New Paradigmer, is filled with references of "our new paradigm" and "profound change".'

parameter(s) In mathematics, a parameter is a potentially variable quantity which is taken as constant in a particular functional context. In general usage the word commonly occurs in the plural, with the sense of 'definable bounds', 'limiting conditions', **constraints**: 'In practice, to operate within the ill-defined parameters of the public interest is to serve a hybrid of vested governmental and commercial interests and pay lip service to ill-informed judgments from unaccountable advisers and "gurus"' – *Observer Magazine. Parameter* is a smart, quasi-scientific piece of jargon which might pass for a card of admission among the **numerati**.

paratactization Here is a word to enchant Holofernes or Dr Teufelsdröckh. In grammar and rhetoric, *parataxis* means the arrangement of a succession of clauses without connecting conjunctions: e.g. 'The night was cold, I was tired of waiting, I went home', instead of 'The night was cold and I was tired of waiting, so I went home', or 'Because the night was cold and I was tired of waiting, I went home'. To *paratactize* means to create *paratactic* constructions: for 'God will forgive human beings for their silly mistakes', read 'To err is human, to forgive divine'. The partner of *parataxis* is *hypotaxis*, meaning the creation of structures with incorporating and subordinating devices. 'She left the web, she left the loom, she made three paces through the room' is *parataxis*; *hypotaxis* would be 'She made three paces through the room, in doing so leaving the web, which consequently involved her in the abandonment of the loom'.

patriarchy Feminist jargon for the tradition of the dominant male, together with the social and intellectual systems supporting and maintaining that dominance – not least the systems of marriage and the family. Families are thought to be *phallocentric*, i.e. governed by father and all he stands for. Language itself is frequently alleged to be one of the most powerful devices of the patriarchy (see Part I, p. 56). One might suppose the combative counter to the patriarchy would be a *matriarchy*; but in fact it is the *sisterhood*.

Pepsification The introduction (into a country, region, chain of stores, etc.) of branded **junk food**. From *Pepsi-Cola*, or simply *Pepsi*, a well-known soft drink. 'On the summit fringe there is new evidence of what has become known as the Pepsification of Moscow' – *Daily Telegraph*.

percentages, to play the A now somewhat elderly package phrase, even in British English – where, however, it is still useful to sportscasters describing how snooker players and kindred athletes conduct their **strategies**. The phrase also occurs in the language of politics and the jargon of investment – *playing the market*. Playing the percentages means not incurring undue risks or attempting anything spectacular, but making what experience has shown to be the sensible and reasonably profitable move. The source-jargon is the language of gambling, probably at the roulette table, where some results might be predicted as a matter of X-per cent likelihood.

perception This has been a mode word in British English since the 1970s at least. Meaning 'how things are seen or understood or interpreted' (by the man in the street, or your average Cabinet minister, or women, or foreigners, or stockbrokers), its context is usually political, as in 'the British perception of developments in South America'. It is a clever word, bringing with it intimations of shrewdness and **credibility**. Perceptions are generally *informed* or *sophisticated*.

performance A mode word in finance, commerce and political economics. The performance of a share is its yield; of a company, its turnover or annual profit; of an economic policy, its statistically measurable results: 'This dismal performance for overall living standards has been explained by two factors . . .' – *Independent*. (See **factor**.)

performance art Acting, dancing, playing the fiddle, clowning, miming, pretending to be an armchair, marching with a partner from Land's End to John O'Groats, in lockstep, carrying a telegraph pole. All such things qualify as *performance art*; unlike **conceptual art**, or **installation art**, or just painting.

photo opportunity Time set aside for press photographers to take pretty promotional pictures of politicians, **royals**, or **celebs**. It is a moot point whether the opportunity is conceded by those photographed, or offered by the photographers; but it is apparently profitable to both sides. 'The Palace seems to want television in one of two ways: either the carefully controlled documentary or pre-arranged photo opportunities of royalty out and about' – *Independent*. A slightly older expression is *photo call*. See further **sound bite**.

pilot project This was once called a 'trial run'; and before that, a 'first attempt'. Pilot projects habitually beget **feedback**.

plonker Crudely speaking, a *berk*, or **wally**; or more precisely, *prick*, and even *dickhead* or **dork**; for *plonker*, like these, signifies 'penis'. As a term of more or less amiable abuse, it became popular in Britain through the TV comedy called *Only Fools and Horses*; Del, the principal figure in the series, repeatedly calls his brother Rodney a *plonker*.

pole position In motor racing, the *pole position* is that of the first car on the *starting grid*. The phrase is coming into general usage with the sense 'leading', 'in front of competitors'. A likely candidate for election to the leadership of a political party may be described as being in pole position.

P(olitical) C(orrectness) See Part I, p. ●●. Political Correctness, or *PC*, involves social attitudes with linguistic symptoms. It means using words and expressions which will (a) display your own social credentials as one who has a **sensitive** respect for women, or homosexuals, or people of non-European race, or the disabled, or the mentally retarded, or the chronically sick, or the elderly and aged, or the undersized, or the oversized, or vandals or drunks or ram raiders or drug addicts – among others, and (b) not give offence to anyone belonging to any of these groups. Thus *chairman* gives way to *chair*, and *blacked* (as in 'the UDM has been blacked by the other unions') to *boycotted*. PC usage is currently making deep inroads into the language of affliction. An item in the *Independent* (22 January 1992) reports on an Employers' Forum on Disability, and specifically on a book called *Disability Etiquette*: 'The forum argues that the word "handicapped" should not be used because it carries connotations of "cap in hand", while "invalid" equates disability with illness and could be construed as "not valid".' And further: 'Do not say victim of, crippled by, suffering from, afflicted by; say person who has, person with, person who experienced.'

political will The determination in government to do what is morally right or administratively necessary, though it be politically imprudent (because it does not guarantee the taxpayer **value for money**, and will be unfavourably remembered at the next election or street riot). Other words for political will are 'guts', 'decency', 'integrity'. 'Above all, what is needed is a recognition that the City's morals are sick – and the political will to do something about it' – *Observer*. It should perhaps be called *the political won't*.

politicize To raise political consciousness; to make politically aware; to stir up out of their sleep envy, resentment, hatred, greed. Commonly a transitive verb, as in 'his mission was to politicize the cleaning staff/the workers in the garment industry/the Afghan tribesmen'.

pollster Formed on the model of gangster, mobster, youngster, hipster, huckster, doomster, gloomster, *pollster* signifies one who conducts a *poll*, or statistical enquiry, into (usually) the voting intentions of the public at a general election. Pollsters are regarded with some deference before the event and with some contempt afterwards, if their predictions prove to have been misleading. This may justify the residually pejorative note in the word form.

poll tax See **community charge**.

pollute A standard verb which, however, takes on the colouring of jargon when it is used intransitively; as when urban councils or heavy industries seek *permission to pollute*, i.e. to tip noxious substances into convenient watercourses.

pollution A source of concern for all who care for the **environment**, *pollution* affects the atmosphere (through emissions, of smoke, dust, or fumes), seas, lakes and rivers (through the discharge or spillage of toxic substances and liquids), and the earth itself (through chemical sprays, illicit dumping of toxins, etc.). The word becomes modish when it is applied to loud music, smoking, foul language and **unacceptable** public behaviour. Each of these things may be an *irritant*, but none is a *pollutant* in the primary sense. However, swearing may be considered *pollution*, much as unemployment can be described as **obscene**; a misuse gradually becomes an accepted usage. Whence, **noise pollution**: 'Noise, he says, is now recognised as the world's worst form of environmental pollution, and yet, he claims, "We live in an ever-noisier world"' – *Guardian*.

pontificating classes A superior, oracular sect of the **chattering classes**. '*Time and Tide*, an illustrious title that once vied with the *New Statesman* and *The Spectator* for the attention of the pontificating classes, is to cease publication...' – *Independent*.

populism A political style, rather than a system or a philosophy; in essence, the appeal to 'ordinary people', the populace being supposedly a repository of wisdom and integrity not known to bureaucrats and political mandarins. The *Penguin Dictionary of Sociology* defines it as 'a distinctive form of political rhetoric that sees virtue and political legitimacy residing in "the people"'.

porky A piece of political clubmanese, this is simple rhyming slang: 'pork pie' > 'lie', hence 'porky'. 'He's telling porkies' = 'He's being **economical with the truth**', 'He has produced *an inaccurate précis*'. No member of any British establishment ever lies (well, hardly ever), but anyone can tell a little porky from time to time. In a letter to the *Independent* (11 November 1989), a loyal supporter of Mrs Thatcher took indignant exception to the headline *An honest woman lying to save her own skin*, and suggested that 'there are many other more subtle ways of conveying the same message'. Perhaps *An honest person tells porkies to save her bacon*?

positive Constructive, helpful, sympathetic, as in 'positive criticism', 'positive suggestion', 'positive response', 'positive attitude'. 'Here is a prison... where the atmosphere is relaxed, inmates are polite, positive but questioning, and there is [*sic*] no graffiti' – *Guardian*. The old ballad exhorts us to accentuate the positive, ee-liminate the negative, latch on to the affirmative, don't mess with Mister In-Between. This is known as **getting in touch with your feelings**.

positive discrimination Discrimination in favour of minorities, or of individuals representing categories thought to be at a social or professional disadvantage: e.g. the appointment of black people applying for positions traditionally held by whites, the recruitment of more women into a largely male workforce, the granting to the disabled of opportunities for advancement equal to or greater than those available to the able-bodied. The phrase is a kind of oxymoron, since *discrimination* is commonly read as a negative act – discrimination *against*.

post- In the modern lexicon a fairly productive prefix, e.g. *post-modernist*, *post-structuralist*, *post-bang* (see **deregulation**), *post-lingual deafness* (deafness occurring in someone who has the power of speech), *post-punk* (following after the youth cult called *punk*, see Part I, p. 78: 'a world which had spawned various post-punk types' – *Independent*).

post-modernism In art and architecture, the stylistic successor to twentieth-century movements now allegedly bankrupt or exhausted, e.g. abstract painting, action painting, expressionism, minimalism, brutalism, etc. Post-modernism retrieves and paraphrases or re-states traditional styles and motifs; is decorative, figurative, and colourful; is plausibly piecemeal, without governing concepts; tends towards pastiche; creates an idiom rather than an art, and is regarded by many as empty and fraudulent. A contributor to the *Guardian*'s 'Notes & Queries' column has neatly described post-modernism as 'today's interpretation of yesterday's vision of tomorrow'. Literary post-modernism appears in the numerous fictions exploring the past from the standpoint of the present, and in the growth of 'self-referentiality' – the convention that permits authors, as they write, to comment on the process of writing, so that they are not telling a story so much as demonstrating the possibilities of story-telling.

post-structuralism Although *structuralism* has an important technical meaning in sociology and linguistics, *post-structuralism* refers primarily to recent movements in the theory of literature. Structuralism formulates principles of encoding supposedly discernible in literary works, thus providing a method of interpretation; the implication is that to rehearse the structure exhaustively is to exhaust the meaning of the work. Post-structural **approaches** to the study of texts treat this implication as suspect; 'meaning' cannot be captured and closed in this fashion, and texts have open, virtually infinite ways of meaning. See **deconstruction**.

posture A mode word meaning 'attitude', to some extent replacing *stance*: 'The perfect posture is regret at the changes that have overtaken Val [*Val d'Isere*, a skiing resort] in the last few years' – *Independent*.

potential As a noun, a useful filler-word (a 'thingummy' word, like *character* and *nature*); e.g. *sales potential, growth potential, export potential*. 'For the UK, this gives a diversified, secure future with major export potential' – *Independent*. Some meanings of *potential* are 'possibility', 'chance', 'opportunity'. In athletics, *He has not reached the limits of his potential* means 'He isn't running as fast/jumping as long/vaulting as high/throwing as far as he might'.

pre- A word-forming element, perhaps not as productive, currently, as its counterpart, **post-**, and much less busy than **pro-**. Note, however, nouns like *preschooler* and *preteen* (respectively, a child below school age/below teen-age).

presentation For public relations people, this mode word has elegantly replaced the earlier 'pitch' or 'spiel'; a *presentation* is a sales talk with graphics, display sheets, videos, brochures, addressed to a boardroom congregation of **suits** and *power dressed* consumers of **designer water**. The word has got into educationese, as a synonym for 'conference paper', 'address', 'lecture'. In a slightly different development, it denotes 'representation', 'negotiation': 'So the week went on, driven as much by the logistics of modern warfare as by diplomatic presentation' – *Observer*.

pressure A mode word, particularly among sportscasters, this evokes the psychological strain of the big occasion. 'The pressure is getting to him', they say of tennis champions double-faulting for the fifth time, snooker virtuosi missing easy pots, or darts players fumbling for a final double. They may also say *he is feeling the pressure* or *he is under pressure*, even *he is pressurized*; and these things may be said of (for example) golfers, though hardly of (for instance) concert pianists. However intense Mr Ashkenazy's demeanour at the piano, he can never be *under pressure* like young Mr Hendry at the snooker table, or Mr Faldo putting for a birdie to level the scores at the seventeenth. Money, however, that sensitive commodity, can be under pressure: 'Every day that sterling avoids severe selling pressure, the danger of a crisis recedes' – *Independent*.

pressure group In the shop talk of politics-in-general, a *pressure group* is a group of like-minded people (consumers, constituents, party members) having common goals or aspirations (in commerce, public service, con-stitutional reform, etc.), in pursuit of which they are ready to *pressurize* the appropriate department of government or administration. This quite elderly piece of political jargon grew out of the use of the verb *press*, in 'press for higher standards of food production', 'press for political reform', etc. *Press*, however, has been almost insensibly displaced by *pressure* (as verb) and *pressurize*; so that a *pressure group* is now one that exerts some form of coercive influence, or **clout**, rather than one which merely 'presses for', or 'urges the necessity of', change or reform.

prioritize To set in order of priority; to establish which of the first things are first to be considered. In educationese, *prioritize* goes along with **problematize**; stalwart companions, they march together, like fife and drum, at the head of the Duke of Baloney's Heavy Word Brigade.

privatize/-ation Now a quite old-fashioned political *-ize*, this replaced, doubtless for reasons of **ideological** acceptability, the earlier *denationalize*. *Denationalization* meant taking things away from the nation; *privatization* signifies putting them into safe private hands (after taking them away from the nation).

pro- A recurrent element in the formation of adjectives relating to objects of contemporary debate; e.g. *pro-lifer*, one who opposes abortion, *pro-family* (with the same general sense), *pro-choice* (supporting a woman's right to have an abortion if she so chooses).

proactive In the jargon of business, *proactive* means 'anticipating events', 'making things happen', rather than waiting for events and responding to them. **Movers and shakers** are *proactive*. In vaguer senses it means 'stimulating action' and correspondingly 'taking an active part': 'Mr Bennett argues that games are proactive – the players have to react and respond to what is happening on screen – and are therefore an improvement on watching television' – *Independent*. 'However, speaking on BBC radio yesterday, Mr Lilley appeared to rule out one of the report's main recommendations – the need for a beefed-up DTI taking a more proactive role in supporting industry' – *Guardian*. This is one of those usages that might be described as pronauseating if not actually proemetic.

problem Here is the pan-Euro-American mode word, a standard item in the Western dictionary. A *problem* is a difficulty, a weakness, a vice, a personal frailty, an inconvenience. 'He has a *drink problem*' = 'He sleeps on the kitchen floor'; 'You have an *attitude problem*' = 'You should not have thrown the manager down the lift-shaft'; 'She has a *credibility problem*' = 'She is **economical with the truth**', 'She tells **porkies**'; 'He has a *motivational problem*' = 'He is work-shy'. There are also problems in mathematics, science, philosophy and chess, but these are not problems in the true, **politically correct** sense. People who say they have no problems have a problem.

problematize In academic enquiry, to begin the elucidation of problems by stating what the problems are; if necessary, to justify a thesis by inventing problems. For some professors, this word is a forlorn hope, the vanguard of an assault on a monograph. See **prioritize**.

procedure This trusty old mode word, a comfortable abstraction, plods in tandem with **measure**. Measures are taken; procedures are *outlined* or *laid down* or sometimes *recommended*. In academic jargon and educationese, *procedure* is generally synonymous with *method*.

process A modish filler of 'thing' phrases, as in *democratic process, peace process, education process, European process, talks process*. 'Talks process' = 'holding talks'; 'peace process' = 'making peace'; 'European process' = 'building Europe'; 'education process' = 'teaching and learning'; 'democratic process' = 'voting'.

productivity A political talisman of the 1980s, the word *productivity* has been used with reference to the work done by individuals, by institutions, by the nation at large; and the product has been concrete or abstract, real or notional, factual or verbal. Thus we have heard of the 'productivity' of farms, coal mines, insurance brokers, students, dinner ladies, ambulance crews and undertakers. Productivity is allegedly measurable; e.g., journalistic productivity can be measured by counting words, the productivity of a university department by counting the number of students successfully completing degree courses, and the productivity of a mortuary by establishing the turnover of cadavers. As an example of the irremediably unmeaningful, this word is about to be overtaken by **subsidiarity**, a new inanity for a new epoch.

proletarianize   In politics, to refer all questions to the interests of the proletariat; to assert the primacy of the working class. 'The country seems to be caught in the grip of a militant trade union psychology, with everything politicized and proletarianized' – *Independent*.

property-owning democracy   Prominent in the jargon of the British Conservative Party, *property-owning democracy* denotes the happy condition of people free to saddle themselves for the greater part of their working lives with the burden of buying a house, thereby establishing a real stake in the affairs of the nation. This is an example of **choice** at work; and in this the British are more democratic than the citizens of other Western countries, so many of whom are obliged to pay rent when they might have the satisfaction of taking out a mortgage. The following quotation illustrates the conjunction of this egregious piece of cant with other expressions of opportunistic philosophy: 'She [Mrs Thatcher] set us on towards – dramatically towards – an open society, a freer society in which people have more choice, more opportunity, more of their own money to spend and, increasingly, a property-owning democracy' – Prime Minister John Major, reported in the *Independent*.

psychologism   In sociology, a tendency, deplored by strict practitioners of the science, to explain social structures in terms of individual psychology. 'For example', says the *Penguin Dictionary of Sociology*, 'adherence to religious beliefs is sometimes explained in terms of the psychological need for a way of coping with death.' That seems reasonable, but is apparently bad sociology.

public interest, in the   This phrase, with its legal/constitutional **resonances**, is designed to elicit a **knee-jerk reaction** from patriotic citizens. It provides a reach-me-down defence for scandal-mongering journalists ignoring the call for **self-regulation** and pleading the public's *right to know*. Much depends on the interpretation of *interest*: 'the . . . defence would have been that publication was in the public interest rather than merely of interest to the public . . . It remains our contention that there was a genuine public interest in the story' – *Independent*. Note the importance of **genuine** in that sentence. It is one of a small number of valuable voucher-words:

classic enhances, **acceptable** excuses, **genuine** reassures and redeems. The surrey with the fringe on top (in *Oklahoma*) had 'seats of genuine leather'; the story with the fringe on top has 'genuine public interest'.

punter The racetrack provided the original meaning of this slang expression, which meant 'a gambler', 'one who bets on horses' (generally on a modest scale, with some expectation of a more than modest recompense). The movement of meaning has been generally pejorative, working down through 'bargain hunter' and 'prospective consumer', towards the simple notion of 'participant' or 'practitioner'. The following quotation refers to a proposed TV programme on 'musicals' about political dictators: 'In the end we turned it down because you were going to be given a royal opportunity to humiliate a lot of innocent punters in front of the camera' – *Observer*. In such contexts, *punters* has the sense of 'mugs', 'suckers'.

put it about, put oneself about This package phrase occurs in social as well as in sporting contexts. In its dual form it is ambiguous. 'She puts herself about' = 'She takes the trouble to be seen in the right places with the right people'; 'She puts it about' = 'Her charms are more or less freely on offer'. Correspondingly, 'He puts himself about' = 'He bustles up and down the field of play vigorously challenging opponents'; 'He puts it about' = 'His fist and boot are more or less freely on offer'.

Q

quality time The private citizen's prime time; the hours good men and women devote to their children, or even to their spouses. Quality time is meaningfully occupied. In quality time good things are done, and people **get in touch with their feelings**. I am told that 'career women' value their careers all the more because time spent away from the family only serves to intensify the quality of quality time. (One crowded hour of glorious domestic life, as it were, being worth an age of rattling round the house.) But it seems that not all women believe this. 'The idea of "quality time" is laughable. As far as kids are concerned there is only being there and not being there' – Nora Ephron, quoted in the *Observer*.

quietize From American usage, a transitive verb meaning 'to make [a room, house, etc.] sound-proof'.

R

racial equality Something for **politically correct** people to proclaim, meaning that citizens of diverse races are equal before God, the law and the employment agencies. The principle is so obviously **acceptable** that only a flawed democracy would need a word for it. However, the American

Declaration of Independence states 'We hold these truths to be self-evident, that all men are created equal, etc.', not 'We hold this truth to be self-evident, that racial equality exists' – a proposition which in any case the subsequent history of the United States would have repeatedly falsified.

racket abuse A foul fault invented by the organizers of International Tennis; it consists of dropping, hurling, battering or generally maltreating your racket in moments of pique after losing a point or falling victim to a poor call. Semantically, may be compared with **child abuse**, if *abuse* signifies 'maltreatment'; or with **solvent abuse** if *abuse* is tantamount to 'misuse'. The phrase is almost as silly as the behaviour it denotes.

radical Sir Arthur Quiller-Couch once said that he called himself a radical because he had a love of his country so deep that it went to the roots. In political jargon the association of radicalism with patriotism continues; radicals and subversives live in different sections of the underground. *Radical* suggests fresh, new thinking and unsentimental concern for efficient and beneficent solutions. Note the phrase *radical chic* – meaning the style appropriate to an elegant radicalism. Someone with radical chic is a **designer** radical.

raft A collective term, stylish and burly. Do your arguments have a *thrust*? Why not push them out in a *raft*? 'Read the Heseltine texts, where he sets out in detail the raft of government fiscal proposals pulling companies and developments to the South' – *Guardian*.

rave, raver In youthspeak, a *rave* is tantamount to a **festival**, or possibly an **acid house** party. A *raver*, called of old a *head-banger*, is one who attends a rave, passes round the **spliffs** and the **XTC**, moves in approximate time to the music, leaves used condoms all over Farmer Giles' bottom-land, and generally enjoys enraging the populace into the wee small hours. In this sense it has overtaken an earlier usage; *a right little raver* used to mean 'an extremely pretty girl'.

real terms (in) A confident statement of absolute value inferred from dubious **parameters** of relative value, as in 'We pay four times as much for X as we did in 1982, but in real terms it costs the same or even less, taking into account the purchasing power of the average family income and the price of a decent dinner for two at the Dorchester'. Then determine the value of X to three places of decimals, and post the result to the Chancellor of the Exchequer.

recovery This word is so usual in our daily intake of phrases that it may be necessary to remind ourselves that here economic jargon has a source in medicine. Even so, *recovery* scarcely reads like jargon – until it begins to keep figurative company with *round the corner*, with *in sight*, and with the *light at the end of the tunnel*. It also has *green shoots*. Recovery means an **upturn** out of recession; and of course requires **growth**.

recycling In reference to a well-established social and **environmental** practice, of collecting and treating waste material – e.g. paper – for further use, this is a fairly old new word; its current interest may lie in its figurative application to non-material things, e.g. ideas, policies, writings. Many a scholarly paper has been recycled in the form of a lecture; or vice versa. This is the nuance that used to be expressed by *re-tread* or *re-mould*; *a re-tread spinster* = 'a divorcee', *a re-mould doctorate* = a textbook. In fact, the word has come out to play. Thus the *Independent* on 7 January 1992: 'The British launch of the new year – widely seen as a public relations disaster – has been accompanied by predictions of such deep gloom, disaster and tedium, that we've considered calling for the year's immediate withdrawal from circulation and recycling as 1993.'

relativism, cultural To the question 'Is it culture?', we answer 'Well, it's all relative, isn't it?'. Cultural relativism defies cultural absolutism; if you like Shakespeare, well and good, but soap powder commercials are cool, too – each in its own way is cultural, relatively speaking. 'The waspish debate recently opened up by David Hare's blast at television's cultural relativism really rumbled into life years ago, when films like Wall's "My Way" and *Arena*'s profile of the Ford Cortina were first broadcast' – *Independent.*

relevant As a modish attributive, this does not necessarily mean *relevant*. It means, consistent with the speaker's **perception** of how things ought to be; therefore, 'worthy of note', as in *relevant* **issues**, *a relevant argument*. In some usages, e.g. 'This film is relevant', it approaches the meaning of French *actuel*, German *aktuell*, i.e. up-to-date and spot-on and absolutely the thing to go with **in terms of** a thoroughly modern **lifestyle**. In that sense, *Neighbours* or *Twin Peaks* may be more relevant than Shakespeare. See, however, **relativism, cultural**.

renewable As an eco-noun, this denotes a permanent resource, such as the power of the wind, or the waves of the sea, or potentially recoverable land. A letter to the *Independent* refers to 'an imaginative scheme to promote markets in different types of renewables for electricity generation – hydro, wind, bio-mass, washes and land-fill and sewage generation'. (*Bio-mass* refers to fuel – e.g. methane – derived from a mass of organic waste material.)

reproclassicism In architecture, the decorative use of classical styles and motifs; a feature of **post-modernism**. The coinage is more than a little disparaging, the element *repro* suggesting *repro[duction] furniture* – hence something pretentious or false.

resonance A mode word most useful for the almost infinite resonances with which it can be made to resonate. It means an overtone, an aftertaste, an echo, a harmonic; a fugitive vibration; something suggested, reflected, recollected, but not explicitly stated; a twanging at the back of the collective mind. Thus, from the *Independent*: 'The phrase "poll-tax" has historical resonances'; 'The breakfast menu . . . was a document full of resonance yesterday'; and (in a book review) 'Without that allegorical resonance the final scene at a Demolition Derby . . . resolves nothing'. All who cherish the ambition to speak **designer** English should possess themselves of this word without delay.

revirginization Behold, I show you a mystery: *revirginization* means the restoration of *psychological* virginity, the attempt, by religious or moral precept, to persuade young women to be chaste, though hunted. The deed appears to be as improbable as the word. Thus, a doctor speaking at a conference on the spread of *HIV*: 'The female condom was an important step. There was no evidence that youngsters who started having sex would stop, she said. "Programmes of revirginisation won't work"' – *Independent*.

royal This word-form, beloved of journalists, is a noun, meaning a member of the British Royal Family; the collective term *royalty* no longer serves to stir hearts or sell newspapers, and a word for the individual Windsor was evidently wanted. Members of the royal families of Norway, Sweden, Denmark, Holland, and Spain are no more than *Euro-royals*, and do not qualify for the adulation or the abuse ritually heaped on the genuine article, i.e. the heads of state, stuffiness and steamy stories in This Great Country Of Ours. 'Pictures of grinning royals on ski-slopes don't tell the whole story of what goes on in Klosters, the Swiss ski resort' – *Independent*. A *royal* is a kind of **celeb**; and a celeb, in some cases, is a form of **Essex man**; and Essex man, as he appears in the **tabloids**, is first cousin to some of the *royals*, as the tabloids depict them.

run-up As in 'the run-up to the election', 'the run-up to Christmas', this means a period of increasing activity before a particular event. It may derive from the shop talk of the racetrack, where jockeys taking part in flat races give their mounts a 'run up' to the starting gate. But if that is indeed the figurative origin, it is hardly discernible in the following: 'One senior housebuilder said that the market was absolutely dead after the brief flurry in August in the run-up to the deadline for the stamp-duty exemption' – *Guardian*.

S

sab, sabbing *Sab* is short for *saboteur*, specifically a *hunt saboteur*, an **animalist** who **targets** foxhunting, with the intention of disrupting the activities of the hunt. In a wider sense, *sabbing* refers to any attempt to prevent the alleged maltreatment of animals; e.g. by breaking into laboratories, by releasing experimental animals from captivity, or by resorting to such 'terrorist' activities as the planting of explosive or incendiary devices. However, not all animalist movements condone sabbing.

safe sex   Sexual intercourse – heterosexual or homosexual, vaginal, anal, or oral – in which the appropriate partner takes the precaution of using a condom. Thought to be an effective precaution against the contraction of *HIV* (*Human Immuno-deficiency Virus*) and the subsequent onset of *Aids* (*Acquired Immune Deficiency Syndrome*). Often presented as the antonym of **casual sex**, *safe sex* being 'sensible', and 'thoughtful', a matter of taking wise precautions when you do the **fun** thing, whereas *casual sex* suggests a reprehensible incapacity for planning your evening in advance.

sanitize   Generally, 'to clean up', 'to expurgate', 'to remove potentially distressing or offensive, albeit realistic material'. A *sanitized* view of war is presented by some films. The meanings 'censored', 'edited', 'bowdlerized' are also involved: 'Terry Eagleton observes that this wish to downplay the Marxist component of [Walter] Benjamin's work is particularly strong in the United States, where "Benjamin has really been captured by the professors, who have sanitised him and turned him into an industry"' – *Independent*.

satellite   An item in the shop talk of *telecommunications*; e.g. *satellite broadcasting, satellite television, satellite dish* (the receiver-aerial, mounted on the wall or roof of a house, which enables the subscriber to view programmes transmitted via the 'satellite' transmitter put into orbit round the earth). The phrase 'satellite television' seems to be undergoing a typical process of abbreviation, e.g. 'You will be able to see it on satellite'. Note also *satellite surveillance*, the use of a satellite as a device of **espionage**, to monitor events in another country.

scenario   A mode word; recurrent in politics and militarese. A *scenario* is the particular set of conditions, the **framework**, the **context** in which events are to be enacted, putatively or in fact. Political commentators and military strategists postulate scenarios for General Elections or Armageddon. Wisdom prescribes the anticipation of *the worst possible scenario*; the explorer foresees the possibility of finding himself in a leaking canoe in crocodile-infested waters; the election candidate makes provision for the night when it rains, vandals set fire to the polling station, and all the cars break down. These are *last ditch scenarios*.

scenic route   *Scenic route* begins with the shop talk of guide-book writers; the 'scenic route' is the most picturesque way for the tourist to travel, with opportunities to stop and admire the view. The scenic route is, of course, far from being the shortest. In general usage it has come to mean 'the long way round, with pauses, distractions and delays'. Thus, of a footballer who had played for several teams before returning to the club where he started: 'W. began his career with Everton...and has taken the scenic route back here to Goodison Park' – ITV broadcast.

sectionalism   In politics, a narrow concern with the interests of a particular region, social class, industry, etc.

sector   Military jargon translated into political shop talk, as in *private sector, public sector, corporate sector*; meaning respectively those parts of the economy or **infrastructure** that are controlled by private interests, those that are directed by central or local government, and those otherwise known as 'business'. In soldiers' talk a 'sector' (e.g. in the First World War) was a part of the front line; now the word has been taken up on the economic front.

self-image   The view of ourselves, by ourselves, that governs our behaviour and our relationships, personal or professional. 'He has a poor self-image' = 'He is pathologically modest, considers himself worthless, behaves as though he had acne (which he has), and is incapable of making a decision.' Of persons with an unduly **positive** self-image, the Scots say that they have 'a guid conceit of themselves' – which is a much better way of putting it.

self-regulation   A power entrusted to the press, of controlling its own behaviour and refraining from the infliction of embarrassment and insult on undeserving citizens. This is as fanciful as relying on the fox to go easy on the chickens. The same privilege is exercised by the institutions of the City of London. But there, too, 'self regulation has proved a hypocritical sham. It is time that the flakier inhabitants of the City were pursued with the energy, skill and resources deployed by the Securities and Exchange Commission and similar regulatory agencies in the United States' – *Observer*.

sell-by date   In storekeeper jargon the *sell-by date* specifies a date before which perishable goods (notably food and drink) must be sold. In figurative use, the phrase denotes the terminus of any power or excellence. 'He's past his sell-by date' expresses what used to be meant by 'He's over the hill', i.e. he has seen the best of his useful days and is fast becoming a **wrinkly** or even a **crumbly**. 'My wits are approaching their sell-by date' = 'I'm going ga-ga', 'My internal computer is down.'

sell short   To sell below the **market** rate; hence to misrepresent the **value** of something. Akin to *short-change* (vb), meaning not to give **value for money**.

sensitive   At first, people, feelings and spots were *sensitive*; then the adjective could be applied to topics; now it is the turn of **issues** and **areas**. Calling an issue *sensitive* means that you are too cowardly to speak about it without first establishing your own sensitivity. Disability, unemployment, and Aids are all sensitive issues – not for the disabled, the jobless and the afflicted, but for the **chattering classes** who need to speak about them. In politics and militarese, sensitivity is synonymous with secrecy, as in *sensitive files, sensitive communications*. In art criticism, *sensitive* is equivalent to *namby-pamby*. Even money can be *sensitive*, and dealers are devoted to assuaging its feelings: 'The pound will be sensitive until the general election' – *Independent*. An **area** may be *sensitive*: '. . . will member states [of the European Community] accept interference in such a sensitive area? [laws on gambling]' – *Independent*.

sensitize Generally transitive, 'to make sensitive', whether the object of the operation be a person or an **issue**; persons can become sensitized *to* the issues.

serious money Money in very large sums – much larger than the £1,000 that sounds quite serious enough to your average professor emeritus or district nurse. 'Add in the £2 billion of tax cuts the Chancellor seems to be contemplating, and we are beginning to talk serious money' – *Independent*. Note the idiom – 'to *talk* serious money'. The frivolous pence, cents, spondoolicks and bawbees of little semi-serious folk are handled, fingered, palmed, grasped, rubbed, counted, exchanged, but serious money is *talked* – which is what makes it so damnably serious. As to its origin, the expression is perhaps an instance of the 'transferred epithet', i.e. from 'a serious offer [of money]' or 'a serious proposal [to raise money]'. The phrase has been used as the title of a play by Caryl Churchill (1987).

set piece In football (soccer or rugby), the *set piece* is a movement beginning from a fixed position (e.g. a 'corner', a free kick, a scrum, a line-out). Here sporting shop talk has raided another jargon; in large firework displays, the tableaux set up on scaffolds and wire frames are 'set pieces'. The common element is fixity. Thus in political life, any ritual or fore-ordained procedure may be described as a set piece – e.g. the response of the Leader of the Opposition to the so-called 'Queen's Speech' made at the opening of each British Parliament.

sexy Spectacular, exciting, stylish, fashionable, newsworthy, picturesque. Dutch football, *nouvelle cuisine*, trips to the Caribbean, star wars and liver transplants are sexy; English soccer, boiled cabbage, bargain breaks in Brixham, domestic disputes and appendectomies are not. Said of a journalist who liked a good story: 'What is saddening about Danny is that examination of his surviving notes and papers shows a sad story of misspent energy and misdirected investigation – but all of it the sexy type of material of which good conspiracy theatre is constructed' – *Independent*. Said of a stylish, attractive woman employed to read weather forecasts: 'Wincey Willis . . . the most naked attempt to make weather sexy – a sort of isobarmaid' – *Listener*. According to Jonathon Green's *A Dictionary of Jargon* this usage was coined by journalists (specifically, by the *Sunday Times* 'Insight' team) as early as the 1960s.

shelf life 'The average new novel', I was once told by a publisher, 'has a shelf life not much longer than [that of] a bunch of ripe bananas.' This illustrates the general use of a phrase that began in shopkeeper's shop. The shelf life of food is (fairly obviously) the period for which it can stay on the shelf before it begins to go bad; the shelf life of anything else – a book, a political policy, a personality – is the time it can hope to claim the public eye before the public begins to look elsewhere.

short of Catch-phrases turning on the words *short of*, and indicating some degree of mental disability, are numerous and increasing. Some examples: *one card short of a deck*; *two teacups short of a service*; *one sandwich short of a picnic*; *one cherry short of a fruit salad*; *one groove short of a record*. There are many more, suggesting the impulse of individual creativeness rather than the dreary collective tendency of common jargon.

short-termism The philosophy of solving problems in the short term – that is, of clearing the way for tomorrow and letting next Friday look after itself.

significant This modish adjective shares some of the territory of **relevant**. Authors and their works are *significant*, which sometimes means 'important' and sometimes 'indispensable' and sometimes 'crucial' and sometimes 'highly interesting and informative'. To **make the cut** with the **chattering classes**, a book should be relevant to contemporary needs and make a significant contribution to the analysis of current **issues**.

simplistic One day someone will have the courage to say 'naively simple', or perhaps 'misleadingly simple', when the *cognoscenti* are talking about *simplistic arguments* and *simplistic solutions*. In the meantime the simple things in life will go on being objects of simplistic evaluation; to say that money is the root of all evil, for example, is a simplistic analysis of a moral **issue** (though how true, heaven knows).

situation This darling of the educationists hangs around with **context** and **scenario**. We find it in *the classroom situation*, the *mixed ability situation*, the *distance learning situation*, the *audio-visual situation*, and many another case, instance, position, scene, scenario, setting, set-up, state of affairs, etc., requiring a handy prop-word to fill out a phrase. Some might say 'the distance learning thing' or the 'mixed ability stuff', but teachers are happy to turn a thing into a scene and a scene into a situation, and a situation into an area extending to a dimension.

sliced bread, the best thing since Ready-sliced bread – the godmother of *convenience foods* – came to us some decades ago (according to the Federation of Master Bakers, it is a British invention dating from 1937), and despite its plastic consistency and negation of all flavour has proved a boon to those who spread sandwiches, make toast, or cannot cut into a cottage loaf without endangering their thumbs. Consequently, any perceived landmark, not only in our domestic culture, but in our social and professional experience, must qualify for the appraisal, *the best thing since sliced bread.*

Sloane Ranger   Unlike the Lone Ranger, the heroic film cowboy from whom they take their name, Sloane Rangers are urban, upper-class, affluent young Londoners, living in the neighbourhood of Sloane Square. The phrase is sometimes playfully contracted to *Sloane.* Male Sloanes may include *Hooray Henries*, well-bred boobies reminiscent of the type immortalized by P. G. Wodehouse in the characters of Bertie Wooster and his friends.

slumpflation   A portmanteau of *slump* and *inflation*, meaning a depression in the economy accompanied by inflation. There is an antonymic form, *boomflation.*

smart   In modern techspeak, *smart* means endowed with the artificial intelligence of the printed circuit. A *smart weapon* guides itself to the target; a *smart card* is a credit card with a 'memory' of the transactions conducted, designed to protect the cardholder from fraud.

smart money   Money invested (or wagered) by knowledgeable people who are not deceived by appearances. The 'investment' is commonly figurative: as in 'Labour is strongly favoured to win the election, but the smart money is on the Conservatives'. Compare **serious money**.

software   See **hardware**.

solvent abuse   Popularly called *glue-sniffing*; the inhalation of vapours from some types of glue and household adhesives, as well as from volatile fluids such as lighter fuel and petrol. Practised in the main by children and teenagers, with the object of inducing a 'rush', or trance-state; often leading to fatal results. Also known as **substance abuse**, particularly if the toxic agent is a solid, e.g. a powder.

sound bite   A word for politicians and mediafolk, this means the usable quotation, the snatch of speech that may be conveniently extracted and reported. Like the **photo opportunity**, the *sound bite* represents a potential conspiracy between the public figure and the journalist, ensuring in the one case a favourable representation and in the other a story with good punchlines. Some political speeches and interview utterances are prepared with the 'sound bite' in view. Thus, of Ross Perot (an American politician briefly contending, in 1992, for presidential honours): 'No candidate has relied so exclusively on the much-derided sound bite' – *Independent*. The word figuratively combines the senses of 'something taken at a bite, a mouthful', and 'a unit of information' – as in the *byte* of computerese.

-speak A useful suffix, like *-ese* or the more derisive *-babble*, for designating styles of shop talk and professional language; e.g. *techspeak, youthspeak, rockspeak*. These coinages reflect a debt to George Orwell, whose *prolespeak* (in *1984*) was probably the first example of the *-speak* pattern.

spectrum As a mode word, commonly turns up in the phrase *across the spectrum*, which may be 'the spectrum of political ideas', 'the spectrum of religious beliefs', or even 'the spectrum of choice'. It has the general sense of diversity within unity, or of gradations variously realizing a central concept. Compare **across the board**.

spin Political managers' shop talk for what used to be called an 'angle' or a 'slant' – i.e. the bias, direction, or propagandist turn that can be taken from political events and used, offensively or defensively, in debate. Possibly a metaphor from the pool table; or from the baseball pitcher's use of spin to flight the ball; or, in British derivation (for the usage is American in the first place), from the bowler's use of spin to tease and deceive in cricket. **A spin doctor** is someone employed to devise favourable versions of *spin*, the word *doctor* here signifying (a) a healer, and (b) one who 'fixes' or 'contrives' (as in 'doctoring the evidence'). The word *spin meister* also occurs.

spliff Formerly known, in youthspeak and drugbabble, as a *joint*; a cigarette made from marijuana.

spokescrat A high-ranking spokesperson. 'And though the Foreign Office was reported to have expressed some flickering interest in Macaulay's effort, a spokescrat tells us: "We've not actually commissioned or funded it"' – *Independent*. For the word form, compare **artocrat**.

stabilization fund Financial jargon: a loan (or gift) of money, enabling a country in political difficulties to bring its economy under control. 'Like Russia, it [Bulgaria] had no reserves and no stabilisation fund' – *Independent*. Conversely, a country may be **destabilized** through the withholding of financial support.

stand-off A state of hostile confrontation in which neither party dares strike the first blow or fire the first shot. The term is quite old, but has been recently revived in connection with the Gulf War (1991). In old Western films, the expression *a Mexican stand-off* described that heroical-comical scene in which opponents, having drawn and pointed their pistols in the same instant, slowly backed away from each other.

starters, for The phrase is well-established in the meaning 'to begin with'; Americans may say *for openers*. The British expression involves – whether intentionally or not – a kind of pun, 'starters' being the popular word for the first course in a meal (e.g. 'We're having chilled soup for starters'). 'For starters they complimented me on the taste of my electric cooker' –

advertisement for *COOK ELECTRIC* in the *Observer Magazine*. The portent of the phrase, however, is commonly hostile; quarrelsome responses begin with 'how's this for starters?', or even 'here's a knuckle sandwich for starters'.

state[-]of[-]the[-]art   The song says 'Everything's up to date in Kansas City'; for which, to be idiomatically state-of-the-art, read 'Everything's state-of-the-art in Kansas City'. In the 1960s and 1970s, 'the state of the art' meant the current position in scholarly or scientific enquiry (e.g. *Linguistics: the State of the Art*, the title of a learned paper). The phrase then began to be used adjectivally (and with hyphens) as in 'state-of-the-art presentation', 'state-of-the-art theory', but most frequently with reference to technological **hardware**, a usage which recommended itself to advertisers and publicity persons: thus the latest record-player, laptop computer or contour-clinging battery shaver is deemed to be *state of the art*. 'However, perhaps the real criticism of *Gamesmaster* is not that it tends to corrupt... but that more imagination could have gone into presenting state-of-the-art technology' – *Independent*.

statism   Yet another trooper in the great legion of *-isms*. *Statism* is the philosophy of rigid control by the state – of administration, institutions, and above all the economy. See **command economy**.

stockbuilding, stockpiling   Originally from military jargon, and meaning the amassing of weapons, *stockbuilding/stockpiling* is established in the vocabulary of the **market** and refers to the planned acquisition, by a dealer, of particular stocks.

stock-lending   This involves raiding the piggy-bank to fill the trouser pocket, with every intention of putting the money back eventually, before anyone notices. On the money exchanges, it takes the form of borrowing shares in order to float a transaction in the market. This practice came to the notice of the general public during the discussion surrounding the imaginative accountancy of the late Robert Maxwell, a bold entrepreneur who used his employees' pension stocks to raise finance from the banks. Commenting on the general assumption that this sort of thing is not only indecent but surely illegal to boot, a reader of the *Independent* observed: 'Far from being an underhand mode of operation, stock-lending describes the process by which company shares are lent to stock-exchange market-makers in order to facilitate the speedy settlement of share transactions...' From which it may be apparent that the small investor could most prudently resort to the old teapot, the tobacco-jar, the biscuit-tin, or, at a venture, the sock under the mattress. There is no stock-lending from your cast-off Jaeger footwear.

strategy   This is a mode word of the first water – and the second, and the third, and all degrees to the nth; so watery is it, in fact, that it signifies almost nothing and almost anything, which is the final test of modishness. The general meaning is 'plan', with the bracketed implication ('of attack'). Educationists love it (it goes with **framework** and **approach**) and politicians are not averse to it. Thus William Waldegrave, reported in the *Independent*: 'It [a fund of £8m] does not provide the basis for a coordinated national strategy to address and prevent homelessness.' Only in the cheerless jargon of Whitehall could homelessness be 'addressed' by a 'strategy'.

street cred A necessary commodity for those who wish to survive in the inner city; *street cred* (in full, *street credibility*) means the confidence, the self-assurance, the reliability, the plausibility and the manifest willingness to take care of oneself that will win the respect and trust of other denizens of the street. Or of the office. Or of the profession. Or of the House of Commons. Or of the Senate of the United States. See also **credibility**.

street-smart Those who have **street cred** – in brief, those who are *street* – must *ipso facto* be **street-smart**, or, as they occasionally put it, **streetwise**; meaning *au fait* with the ways of the street, office, profession, etc. 'While Yates is politically street-smart, in the past he has not exactly gone out of his way to avoid treading on other people's sensitivities' – *Observer*.

structural unemployment A political economist's euphemism, suggesting that a great many people are out of a job because that is how the system necessarily works; a free economy incorporates losers. 'Britain, though plagued still by slow growth and high structural unemployment, is more competitive than a decade ago . . .' – *Independent*.

structure A grand mode word, one of the giants of the first division, discursively broader in scope than **framework** and correspondingly less meaningful. Language has structure; and so does argument; and agreements; and university courses; and perceptions and poems and skeletons and sentences and molecules and all sorts of set-ups. Structures may be unitary or binary or polymorphic or irregular; structures are structured, and therefore structurally accessible. Readers will note the rhetorical structuring of this entry. So much for structure.

student A word rashly commandered by (British) journalists, who often use it instead of 'pupil', to describe learners below the age of 16. Even primary schools are described as having students; nor are their infant departments denied the right; and perhaps this voucher of academic status will presently be conferred upon toddlers mouthing their first sentences. This is not exactly jargon **as such**, but it illustrates a well-known tendency in This Great Country Of Ours to tinker with names and feel better for it. To call a class of noisy nine-year-olds *students* is possibly a form of **political correctness**.

style counsellor Also known as a *taste maker*, this is a person who advises great ones and **celebs** in matters of dress and personal appearance. The taste maker is the natural beneficiary of the **market maker**, as the progress of **monetarism** begets new generations of **Essex men** and **suits**. The thought that anyone should make a living in this way, at the end of the twentieth century AD, baffles and forbids further comment. But see **colour-coordinated**.

subsidiarity A politician's word, now in common use and baddish odour. A quotation from the *Independent* explains its meaning: 'The commission says that it is concerned to promote the principle of subsidiarity, under which decisions are taken at the lowest possible level.' This is in reference to the administration of the European Community, and the principle that member states should be free to settle local questions locally. Wags have begun (June 1992) to refer to this word, which many people detest as much for its frequency as for its form, as 'the S-word'. Its use in political talk is recent, but it has a longer history in business administration, and in the pastoral terminology of the Roman Catholic Church. The following passage from the *Independent* shows how *subsidiarity* fits comfortably into context with other gems of jargon – **democratic deficit, input, issue**: 'The commission says that it is concerned to promote the principle of subsidiarity, under which decisions are taken at the lowest possible level. Many of the EC's staunchest supporters are worried about its democratic deficit, the fact that EC regulations and directives emerge without direct, popular input. In the case of drinking water, these two issues come together.'

sub-text The lines read between the lines. The source-jargon is (for the nonce) literary criticism, where it denotes the complex of inferences, assumptions, etc., necessary to the reading of a literary work, but not made explicit in the text. In general usage it has come to mean, loosely, 'what they don't tell you'. (See **agenda, hidden**.) The form **sub-theme** occurs: 'The sub-theme is that Fairbrother and Hick are preferred not just because they have fewer years behind them . . . but because they have been successful in one-day cricket' – *Guardian*. Further, with the yet looser meaning of 'incidental consequence': 'The sub-theme is that, with zero inflation, unions will be cowed still further' – *Guardian*.

suit A *suit* is a man in a suit; a man of entrepreneurial or financial consequence, a businessman, a broker, a banker, whose dress represents his status and power. Usually in the plural, *the suits*, i.e. the powerful men in the City. The usage is comparable to the century-old designation *the frocks*, meaning 'the men in frock coats', the politicians and civil servants in Whitehall, usually as opposed to the soldiers.

summilexic Aherne, Baker, and Chateaubriand are *summilexics*, persons whose surname initials place them fortunately at the beginning of the alphabet. See **alphabetism**.

summitry In political shop talk (or politico-journalese), *summitry* is the diplomatic art of arranging 'summit' conferences – that is, international meetings of statesmen and senior politicians.

surgical strike More militarese, in the euphemistic manner of the General Staff. A *surgical strike* is an attack, usually from the air, which is aimed at purely military targets – e.g. troop concentrations, gun positions, arsenals – and designed to avoid **collateral damage** in the form of civilian personnel, housing, hospitals, etc. The figurative comparison with surgery relies wholly on the status of the skilled and compassionate doctor as a folk-hero, and on the perception of surgery as something strict but 'clean'.

sustainable In military jargon this appears to mean 'supportable', 'capable of being supplied with fuel, provisions, etc.': 'These [amphibious craft] are logistically more sustainable than air-lifted troops' – *Observer*.

sweetener A word of discreet elegance; this is businessbabble for 'a bribe', though of course it is not called a bribe; more of an incentive. Those who deal in unimaginably large sums of money never bribe anybody; like poker-players, they merely sweeten the pot.

syndrome Back in the 1950s, the weighty word for the well-informed was *dichotomy*; now it is *syndrome*. In the language of medicine, a syndrome is a combination of signs and symptoms pointing diagnostically to a particular disorder. For the show-talking jargonist it is a pseudo-scientific way of referring to any state of affairs, habit, practice, or rooted belief: 'the wet socks syndrome' (in dinghy sailing – picked up from a BBC radio broadcast), 'the early-to-bed-early-to-rise syndrome', 'the all men-are-potential-rapists-syndrome'.

syntacticize In linguistics, to refer an utterance, sentence, etc., to the rules of syntax; to make something syntactic.

T

tabloid A newspaper of conveniently square, small-paged format (easy to read in the bus or tube or any confined space, easy to tuck away into a pocket); with many pictures, bold print, short sentences, minimalist paragraphs; strident in style, often sensationalist in content. (See **bonk journalism**.) The opposite of a *tabloid* is a **broadsheet**.

tactical voting An electoral **strategy** for the undecided or faint-hearted; it means placing your vote to keep the opposition out, rather than to put your own side in; e.g., to vote for the Yellows, even though you are a Red, in the hope of discomfiting the Blues. This never works. See **kick into touch**.

take on board To *take on board* means 'to assimilate', 'to incorporate into one's own way of thinking', 'to take account of', 'to accept'. Insights, criticisms, arguments, points of view, objections, considerations, are taken on board. Things taken on board can be **handled**. The source-jargon is (presumably) maritime, with reference to the taking on of cargo. The antonym of *take on board* could be *throw overboard*, but is more likely to be *jettison*.

talk up (and talk down) Twin phrases, meaning to speak with the intention of promoting attitudes, and fostering facts, **positive** or **negative**; a form of word-magic or semantic sorcery. Talking will make it so. 'Talking Britain down' means speaking about This Great Country Of Ours in a way that will encourage foreigners to perceive it as less Great than we know it to be. 'Talking down the pound' means depreciating its value against the Deutschmark, with a few ill-chosen words. But good warlocks can *talk up*: 'In September they heard the Chancellor, Norman Lamont, and the Prime Minister, talking up the economic recovery' – *Independent*.

target In a common noun–verb transfer, *target* means 'aim at', 'set one's sights on', and like those expressions is used both literally and figuratively. 'This would enable them to target all the bases in Saudi Arabia, as well as the whole Gulf' – *Independent*; 'Is there anything wrong when a woman with the money, the confidence and the social freedom that women have fought for, uses it to target a young man and buy his time and attention?' – *Independent*. In the passive, this becomes a phrasal verb, *target on*: 'The bomb was targeted on the band of the Blues and Royals, playing at St Albans civic centre' – *Independent*.

target-rich environment A militarism from the reporting of the 1991 Gulf War, this means (apparently) a place with plenty of troops, weapons, vehicles, bridges, ammunition dumps, power stations, etc., just waiting to be obliterated; the very location, indeed, for a series of **surgical strikes**, or some **interdiction bombing** with little or no **collateral damage**.

targetry The science and method of defining targets; whence, more broadly, the definition of aims. In the language of political economy, *growth targetry* = 'estimations of the level of economic expansion to be achieved'.

tax haven A place where capitalists, developers, entrepreneurs and miscellaneous scoundrels may keep their money in safe protection from the clutches of any Inland Revenue Department. The best tax havens are *offshore*, on palmy islands set in blue seas. The suggestion of piracy or freebooting is a not inappropriate **resonance**.

technical recession One might have thought, in the manner of Gertrude Stein, that a recession is a recession is a recession, but it appears that some recessions are more recessive than others. There are recessions proper and there are technical recessions. Thus, from the *Independent*: '... Germany has had what Whitehall calls a "technical recession"', and 'A recession is defined technically as two consecutive quarters of a falling output'. It is this technicality, no doubt, that enables finance ministers to announce that the recession is **bottoming out**, that there is *light at the end of the tunnel* and that **recovery** is *on the way* if not *round the corner.*

technology Keep this word, along with **ideology**, in your toilet-bag of traveller's terms; never go anywhere without your state-of-the-art *logos.* But the meaning of *technology* is weakening, broadening – flattening out – until soon it will mean not much more than mere 'technique', 'method', 'process': 'In a further blow to morale in the industry, British Coal announced the end of its clean coal-burning technology project at Grimethorpe' – *Independent.*

tectonic shift In geology, *tectonic shift* refers to a movement of the 'plates' that make up earth's outer crust, and that from time to time grind against each other, causing earthquakes and volcanic disturbances. It seems, however, that the phrase may be going figurative: '...some sociologists claim to detect a tectonic shift in natural living patterns' – *Independent.* The same *Independent* article uses the phrase *lifestyle earthquakes* to describe profound changes in social behaviour.

terminal Final, and therefore fatal, as in *terminal illness, a terminal case, the management of terminal patients.* These medical euphemisms have all but driven out 'fatal illness', 'a death', 'care of the dying'. The adverb *terminally* occurs, in *terminally ill* (as well as humorously, in *terminally stupid/mean/insensitive*), and the verb *terminate* comes in handy when 'switch off the machine' might be hard for the practitioner or the patient's relatives to **handle.**

Thatcherisms Lady Thatcher's trenchant contributions to the phraseology of British English are quite numerous, and make useful conversational counters for citizens occasionally grasping for self-expression. Here are some, noted over the years: *There is no alternative, or TINA; rolling back the frontiers of the state; safe in our hands* (in reference to the now moribund National Health Service); *the oxygen of publicity* (on which the Irish Republican Army purportedly thrives); *there is no such thing as society* (manifestly untrue); *there is no such thing as a free lunch* (quite).

thirtysomething This was the title of an American TV series about a group of up and running professional folk, all in their thirties. They were wholesome and *sympatisch* to the point of nausea. The phrase has caught on, as a label that immediately pictures the product – 'He's thirtysomething', 'She's one of those thirtysomething women, you know?'

throughput An old comedian used to tell us that books had frontispieces, backispieces, and inbetweenispieces. So machines, computers, systems of calculation, etc., have **input**, output, and *throughput. Throughput* is inbetweenisput, the volume of input becoming output.

time warp In cosmology – or perhaps only in science fiction – a time warp is a kink in the time–space continuum which would bring the putative time-traveller back on himself again and again. (As though the continuum were given a twist, like a Möbius strip.) The figurative, weaker meaning of *time warp* is a state of geopolitical backwardness in which some nations are thought to be almost inescapably caught: '. . . a generation of Middle Easterners caught in a time-warp of nationalist anti-Western hatred' – *Observer*.

tokenism The principle of allotting a minimal, or 'token' representation on any committee, board, or governing body, to persons otherwise having little democratic **clout** – e.g. Afro-Asians and women. Male administrations have their token woman; white delegations have their token black.

top up As a verb, this means to supply additional resources (usually in the form of grants, loans, credit); so governments may offer to *top up* the pensions of the needy. As a noun, **top-up** (customarily hyphenated) denotes the additional payment, loan etc.; the pensioners may get a top-up now and then. The usage is figurative, from the act of replenishing a glass – or as the Americans say, 'freshening' a drink. As an image it is more attractive than **trickledown**; I would rather have my pension topped up (cheers) than wait for it to come down in beads and droplets from the seats of the mighty.

toy boy Otherwise a **bimboy** or a **himbo**, a personable young man fortunate enough to have attracted the interest of an affluent, generous and comfortably passionate older woman, something that happens to relatively few of us. For 'passionate older woman' read, as **gender** requires, 'passionate older person'. 'Yet, even reduced to the classic 'toy-boy' scenario, this situation remains a puzzle' – *Independent*. (Note, in one sentence, *classic*, *scenario*, and *situation*.)

tranche The word is etymologically related to 'trencher', and ought to mean a 'slice' or 'cut' – which, in a way, it does. In financial jargon, it means an issue of shares, usually supplementing a previous issue; in wider application it refers to whatever occurs in regular stages – the intake of recruits to a profession, the volume of a product released onto the market. It is a word not well suited to British sinuses.

transsexual A noun, the weaker meaning of which is 'one who habitually behaves like, and wishes to be accepted as, a person of the opposite sex'; the stronger meaning being 'one who has undergone surgery to change external sexual characteristics into those of the opposite sex'. **Political correctness** might seem to call for a word form on the basis of **gender** (e.g. 'cross-generate'), but the displacement of *sex* by *gender* has not occurred in this instance; possibly because sexual characteristics are considered to be purely physiological, whereas 'gender' involves the whole personality.

trash Shakespeare used this verb, but in the sense of 'to discard, reject'. In more recent usage it suggests 'destroy', 'break up': 'The worst of the alienation dates from the Battle of the Beanfield in 1985, when the police in Wiltshire trashed part of the annual convoy travelling to the Stonehenge gathering, which had been outlawed' – *Independent*.

trawl As a verb, this is replacing (or 'metaphrasing', see Part I, p. 11) earlier uses of 'sift', 'comb', or plain 'search': 'Headhunters are trawling the field for candidates from within and outside television' – *Independent*. The mind boggles.

trickledown A noun denoting an idea once popular among business-persons and economists of Thatcherite tendency, that if the rich were left to themselves to make money, without irksome legal constraints and the burdens of excessive taxation, some of the profit would eventually *trickle down* to the poor, who would await its arrival in God knows what postures of abject gratitude. The image is so gross, not to say **obscene**, that one wonders at the mental furnishings of those who could devise such a word.

triumphalism The practice of triumphing and letting the world know you have triumphed; possibly to the extent of kicking your opponents while they are down, on the principle that there is no percentage in kicking anyone while they are up. This quotation refers to the defeat of Iraq in the 1991 Gulf War: 'The complacent triumphalism of Washington insiders is understandable, given that they think that the whole business was a roaring success' – *Observer*.

turn the economy round Halt the *flight from sterling*; *steer a course out of recession*; promote *growth*; water the *green shoots of recovery*; *put the country back on its feet* and *get the nation working again*.

twilight course In educationese, a training course for teachers, held in after-school hours. The phrase has a soft romantic air, not usual in the jargon of pedagogues. Would a twilight course held at teatime include a sandwich course?

U

underclass A class of human beings so low, so degraded in the socio-economic scale that there are no letters (e.g. **DE**) to describe them. Members of this class live under protest, labour under delusions, sleep under bridges, and die under tragic circumstances. (See **cardboard city**.) 'One obstacle to this [an "investment-led recovery"] is a large underclass with little to contribute either as producers or consumers. They need to be brought back into society by massive targeted government generosity' – *Guardian*.

underpin   A verb, meaning 'to support, buttress, prop'. The source-jargon is the language of the civil engineer and architect; buildings, etc., may need to be underpinned. The extended usage is illustrated by the following: '... it became clear that economic sanctions demanded underpinning if Iraq was to be prevented from lashing out with further force' – *Observer*.

under the cosh   To be *under the cosh* is to be taking a beating, usually in some sporting contest. The origin is street jargon, and the phrase may date back to the 1950s, when the so-called 'cosh boys' – louts armed with bludgeons – were busy in the back streets of British cities. Recent usage suggests an extended sense, 'to come under censure': 'Dostoevsky ... T. S. Eliot ... and Henry James were just a few to come under the Nabokovian cosh' – book review in the *Independent*.

universality   In TV broadcasting, the principle of offering (a) a service presenting programmes of every kind, and (b) a service available to all, without payment of charges over and above the licence fee. Thus – 'Subscription is described by senior BBC officials as "destroying universality"' – *Observer*.

unrealistic   Common in popular usage with the meaning 'insufficient', 'inadequate', or 'disproportionate', as in *an unrealistic price, an unrealistic rent*. The reference is usually to money (occasionally to expectations) and the suggestion is generally 'too little', though 'too much' is possible. 'An extra £8m in government funds over the next three years to help mentally ill people sleeping rough in London was condemned by charities yesterday as unrealistic and inadequate' – *Independent*.

up-front   The adjectival usage, e.g. *an up-front sort of person, she's absolutely genuine and up-front, it's all up-front – what you see is what you get*, is a development from **up front** as an adverbial phrase meaning 'on offer', 'in advance' (of payments, funds, etc.: *there's a lot of cash up front*). As an attribute, *up-front* suggests 'frank, open, not given to secrecy'.

up market   Here is the territory of the rich and successful, the entrepreneurial and the quite prestigious; e.g. company directors, estate agents, turf accountants, literary pornographers and **celebs** of various kinds, including some **Essex men**. Car manufacturers move *up market* when they design vehicles for people who need a third car for the home help to do the shopping in. The adjective is hyphened – *up-market*, as in 'definitely an up-market buy, this property will set you back a cool two hundred K'. See **K**. See also **AB**; and **C1, C2**; and **DE**. See also **down-market**. See further **upwardly mobile** and **yuppie**; to say nothing of **lifestyle**.

up to speed   Commentaryburble, meaning up there among the **front runners**, staying **on the pace**, definitely **in contention** and even likely to be **among the medals**. Sometimes used colloquially (and negatively) in the sense of 'unsatisfactory', 'not of the required or expected standard'; e.g.

'His recent work just hasn't been up to speed.' (This resembles the development of the old prizefighting idiom *up to scratch*.)

upturn Mr Micawber expected that something would turn up; economists professionally read the **indicators** for an *upturn*. 'A substantial upturn in oil production is largely behind the projected increase in government revenues' – *Independent*. An upturn is a sign of **recovery** after an economy has been **bumping along the bottom.**

upwardly mobile Now a well-established phrase, this has the general sense of 'rising ambitiously in the world', a process usually associated with youth, whence *young and upwardly mobile*, whence, possibly, **yuppie.** Upwardly mobile people migrate **up market.**

V

valid On this modish specimen of cant, made for the pusillanimous, Nigel Burke (*Spectator*, 16.3.90) aptly comments: 'A word that is useful for condoning some proposition or policy when you are too yellow to judge its truth or falsehood.' That is arguably a valid observation. Thence we have the *valid argument*, the *valid perception* and the *valid stance*, all of them **sensitive** responses to the **issues.** *Valid* is a horse from the same questionable stable as **relevant.** *Valid* is a runner that has been got at. *Valid* is dodgy.

value A word to be treated with suspicion when it occurs in political **contexts**; prod it, and it will crumble. It does not mean *value*; it means electoral percentage, or what's in it for the party? It can be forced into temporary significance with the support of other words, in package phrases bawled at conferences or read from teleprompters by careerists on the campaign trail. The current favourite is **family values**, an expression as **naff** as a porcelain herb-jar. Other examples of this queasy cant are **Victorian values** and **value for money.** Meanwhile, back at the Texan ranch: 'Elements within the media, the entertainment industry, academia and the Democrat [*sic*] Party are waging a guerrilla war against American values' – Republican Party manifesto, quoted in the *Guardian*.

value for money A primary idiom from the political jargon of the 1980s, *value for money* is the *ultima ratio* of governments bent on rolling back the frontiers of the state, establishing the authority of the **market**, and making **choice** available to all socio-economic groups. Even football teams may give value for money: 'In value for money terms, Oldham's games are well worth watching' – television commentary. But it is from the public **sector** that value for money is expected, and, indeed, exacted: 'Speaking on Channel 4 News, Kenneth Clarke, the Home Secretary, said a reduction in resources would be inconceivable, but warned: "It is obvious that we are going to look for value for money. Policemen are already experiencing change, are expecting change. I hope they want a modern police force that commands public confidence and that demonstrates the value for money it's giving" ' – *Independent*.

Victorian values This refers to the admirable principles of self-help, thrift, family unity, respect for law and order, thought to characterize Victorian times. It manages not to refer to child labour, child prostitution, drunkenness, urban squalor, disease, hypocrisy, philistinism. The phrase is sometimes attributed to Baroness Thatcher of Kesteven, who certainly used it more than once in her quest to Put The 'Great' Back In Great Britain, but while it suits her rhetorical style it was probably in existence long before she took it up.

video This is becoming important as a phrase-forming epithet, as in *video game*, a game in which the field of play is the computer's Visual Display Unit, the episodes, obstacles, etc., being supplied from a special **software** programme; and *video nasty*, a film of horrific or sadistic content, designed for showing on a domestic television set. The abbreviation *vid* now exists, and from America, as soul-mate to the **couch potato**, comes the *vidkid*, the young person obsessed with video games.

virtual reality Not, as might be supposed, the state that most of us live in for most of the time until death draws our attention to things as they truly are, *virtual reality* is a form of electronically governed experience, the technological creation of a context of sound, vision, sensory orientation, so powerful as to present the illusion of reality, or at any rate of real toads in imaginary gardens.

volunteerism The practice of volunteering for social work; the equivalent, among today's **yuppies**, of the 'good works' which gave occupation to affluent ladies and gentlemen in the nineteenth century.

W

wally A disparaging word for a simpleton, an innocent. The source is the personal name Walter, persons so called being known for their ingenuous behaviour, amiable gullibility and want of **street cred**. *Wally* has generally replaced *Charlie* (which in its day may have been considered disrespectful to HRH the Prince of Wales), and 'Charlie' has ousted – or outstayed – the equally scornful *Tony*. (In the 1950s, an advertisement for a home hairstyling kit called *Toni* showed a photograph of two women, and asked 'Which twin has the Toni?' – inviting the waggish response 'Which twin *is* the Tony?') *Percy* and *Herbert* have enjoyed sporadic popularity; and *Hooray Henries* still walk the London scene. (See **Sloane Ranger**.) British troops in the Falkland Islands (1985) called the inhabitants, whose demeanour they perceived as rustic and slow, *Bennies*, **Benny** being an amiably half-witted character in the (now discontinued) TV soap opera, *Crossroads*. Onomastic insult has a long history. From the early nineteenth century we have *jessie* (from 'jessamy', an affected dandy); from a century earlier, *namby-pamby* (a maudlin or excessively sentimental person; from the name of *Amb*rose Philips, a writer of genteel verses). *Jessie* is still current in British dialect speech (mainly in the north of England) with the meaning 'effete person, of little practical competence' – to describe a man as *a right jessie* being almost as much of an insult as calling him *a wet nellie*, or *a big girl's blouse*.

wannabe(e) A noun, meaning someone with (usually vain) aspirations to be someone else, somewhere else; as in *I wannabe famous*, *I wannabe rich*, *I wannabe a star*, *I wannabe a fashion model*.

welfarism The belief in schemes of social welfare, creating a **benefit culture** or **dependency culture**, and discouraging the development of *self-help* and the cultivation of **Victorian values**.

where I'm/he's/she's/we're/you're/they're/coming from Knowing where someone is coming from means understanding what makes them tick, or perceiving what sort of people they are, or having some grasp of the psychological bases of their conduct and opinions, and consequently knowing their 'angle' or the 'line' they are likely to take on any question. It does not mean knowing where they were born. Knowing where a politician is coming from is tantamount to knowing what his (or her) game is. 'At least we know now beyond peradventure which corner the Prime Minister is coming from' – *Guardian*. (See **corner, fight one's**.)

where it's at This inane phrase signifies nothing more than 'the point', 'the nub of the matter', 'the essential question'. As Hamlet says, 'To die, to sleep, to dream – aye, that's where it's at'. It can also denote a **happening** place or a **fun** pastime, as in 'going to **raves** is where it's at'.

whistle-blower See **blow the whistle on**.

wildlife A word that is busily aggregating its own jargon. As a noun, it refers collectively to creatures in the wild, whose **lifestyle**, courtship rituals, mating habits, domestic arrangements and reproductive ingenuities may be observed at disconcertingly close quarters by **couch potatoes** and others watching TV *wildlife programmes*. As an attributive, *wildlife* refers to anything or anyone involved in the study and marketing of the notion of wildlife: *wildlife programme*, *wildlife specialist*, *wildlife enthusiast*, *wildlife safari*, etc. Wildlifery (wildlivelihood?) is a department of **eco**business.

wimp A timid, irresolute, ineffectual male person; a right jessie; a big wet nellie; a bit of a **wally**, really, not to say a **dweeb** or a **nerd**. But also a person of mild, conciliatory demeanour, conservative dress, and indecisive utterance. The adjective is *wimpish*; there is a noun, *wimpery*, and a verb *wimp out* (comparable with Am. *chicken out* and Brit. **bottle out**). Eric Partridge records, as nineteenth-century 'lower class coll.', the expression *wimmeny-pimmeny*, meaning 'dainty, elegant'; and in Cambridge undergraduate slang of the 1920s, *wimp* signified a young woman.

workaholic See -oholic.

wrinkly A noun, in youthspeak; a contemptuous usage, indicating a *senior citizen* or elderly person whose skin is wrinkled, but who, being as yet alert, mobile and tolerably continent, cannot after all be patronized as **crumbly**.

X

X-words The first of the x-words, or unmentionables, was probably the *C-word*, i.e. *cancer*. Political discourse has produced the *L-word* ('liberal', anathema to conservative Americans), the *H-word* ('hostage', not to be lightly mentioned in Middle Eastern politics), the *F-word* ('federal', 'federalism', concepts heartily detested by British negotiators opposing political integration into Europe), and most recently the *S-word* (**subsidiarity**). It is not wholly accidental, or inapposite to the drollery of journalists, that the *F-word* and the *C-word* have other **resonances**.

Y

young fogey Based on earlier *old fogey*, which meant an elderly gentleman of set habits and pronounced, often reactionary opinions: some retired colonel, ancient Master of Foxhounds, superannuated magistrate or embittered professor emeritus. A *young fogey* is an *old fogey* in his thirties or early forties, when he ought to know better. Tweed jacket, trilby hat, brown owl feather; waistcoat (pron. 'weskit') with pocket watch and albert; countryman shirt; regimentally barbered; staring countenance; threatens mischief to anyone who pronounces 'involve' as 'invoalve'. Given, in short, to **bufferism**. There is no question of **gender politics** here; fogeys in any age group are exclusively male.

youth style Not for young fogeys; rather for the *rock scene*. It includes dress, appearance, manners, *ambience*: 'The show's camp heavy-metal gothic settings . . . reflect what is by now a clichéd Eighties youth style' – *Independent*.

yuppie See **upwardly mobile**. The formation is acronymic – whether on young **urban professional** or on young and **upwardly mobile person** – plus the **-ie** suffix which has a disparaging **resonance**. *Yuppie* has spawned other, semi-humorous, formations, for example **buppie,** *yeepie* (*youthful energetic elderly person involved in everything*) and *yottie* (one whose affluence extends to the ownership of a yacht). A female yuppie is a *yuppette,* a Russian yuppie is a *yupski,* yuppie language (for instance, saying *yah* for 'yes') is *yupspeak.* A BMW (in yupspeak, a *Bimmer*) is a favoured *yupmobile.* The Y-*word* (see **X-word**) is everywhere. Inevitably, a verb, *yuppify,* has developed, and with it a further noun, *yuppification.* These relate, as a rule, to the transformation and up-marketeering of housing estates once tenanted by citizens of socio-economic classes **C1** and **C2,** now refurbished and sold off at scandalous prices to **AB** folk. Places once **gentrified** may await further *yuppification.*

Z

zap   'Zap!' exclaims the text of the comic strip, onomatopoetically evoking Captain Marvel's corrective response to his insolent enemies, who, being zapped, give no more trouble. In space fiction, the good captain zaps his foemen with a ray gun, or a 'fazer', in compact form not at all unlike the remote control unit with which, in the 1980s, viewers were enabled to change the programmes showing on their TV screens. Hence a new way of zapping – skipping around the channels with a *zapper* (which ought to mean the agent, but in fact means the instrument). Heaven's gift to the *boob tuber* or **couch potato** is the *zappable* TV set.

zero   Adjectival prefix in many current phrases, especially in militarese and in economic jargon: e.g. *zero option* (the proposal to abolish all nuclear armaments), *zero growth, zero inflation, zero-sum.* 'Sunday opening may prove a zero-sum gain for the groceries industry' – *Independent.*

Postscriptural and
Bibliographical Note

As alps upon alps arise, so there must always be furthermores beyond
furthermores; because new words appear every day, because new social
phenomena take shape, new cults displace old cults, new catch-phrases
take the air; most of all, perhaps, because an observer's consciousness of
jargon sharpens and deepens, becoming receptive to the new, certainly, but
also newly receptive to the old, to those expressions (e.g. *in the public
interest, diplomatic initiatives*) which have been in the language long
enough to beg the questions we ought to be asking of them. The study of
ingrained phraseology should be the first object of the critic and historian
of jargon, but I know of no book that properly undertakes such a task.
I have occasionally approached it in the present book, but have shied
ironically away, in a kind of moral and aesthetic horror, fearing to find
that in its current state our language consists entirely of jargon, of phrases
unpacking phrases, the fabric becoming more threadbare all the time.

Books on new or recent words are more easily found, for those whose
aspiration it is to keep lexicographical records in a thoroughly comprehensive way. They should turn to Jonathon Green's *Newspeak; a
Dictionary of Jargon* (Routledge & Kegan Paul, 1984), and to his larger
and invaluable *Dictionary of Jargon* (1987). Recent compilations are the
Longman Register of New Words (vol. 1, ed. John Ayto, 1989; vol. 2,
1990) and *The Oxford Dictionary of New Words* (ed. Sarah Tulloch,
Oxford University Press, 1991). Both of these are excellent collections,
produced by teams of workers, and having the great virtue of supplying
examples from the press and other current sources for each entry. They
also furnish explanatory notes, in some cases amounting to *scholia*; the
Oxford Dictionary is outstanding in this respect. Somewhat earlier compilations are those by Clarence L. Barnhart, Sol Steinmetz and Robert K.
Barnhart, *A Dictionary of New English, 1963–1972* (Longman, 1973),
and *The Second Barnhart Dictionary of New English* (Longman, 1980);

and, for a polemic treatment of jargon, Kenneth Hudson's *The Dictionary of Diseased English* (Macmillan, 1977).

On a specialist topic, Edward Tenner's very amusing and very informative *TechSpeak, or How to Talk High Tech* (Kogan Page, 1989) is to be recommended; I have also learned much from Kerstin Klasson's *Developments in the Terminology of Physics and Technology* (Stockholm, Almqvist & Wiksell, 1977). Technical abbreviations are exhaustively listed in Eric Pugh's *A Dictionary of Acronyms and Abbreviations* (2nd revised and expanded edn, Clive Bingley, 1970) and in the same author's *Second Dictionary of Acronyms and Abbreviations* (Clive Bingley, 1980). Other useful compilations of shop talk may be found in the *Penguin Dictionaries* series; for sidelights on jargon in the past, readers should consult *The Penguin Dictionary of Historical Slang* (ed. Eric Partridge, abr. Jacqueline Simpson, 1972, most recently 1986). A valuable nineteenth-century source is John S. Farmer's *Slang and its Analogues, Past and Present* (4 vols, Routledge & Kegan Paul, 1890; repr. New York, Kraus Reprint Corporation, 1965). On underworld language, the principal source has to be Partridge's *A Dictionary of the Underworld* (Routledge & Kegan Paul, 1949). On swearing and terms of abuse, see Hugh Rawson's *A Dictionary of Invective* (Robert Hale, 1989), or, still better, Geoffrey Hughes's *Swearing, A Social History of Foul Language, Oaths and Profanity in English* (Blackwell, 1991); on religious – specifically, puritan – jargon, consult M. van Beek's *An Enquiry into Puritan Vocabulary* (Groningen, Wolters-Noordhoff, 1969). All these have been of auxiliary value to me, though in some instances I have to acknowledge a general interest rather than any specific debt. The major source, however, is our broadsheet press, the repository of so much of the wordage that comes, reader, out of your own mouth. *De te fabula*; this is your story.

Index

An index to a book already furnished with a detailed Table of Contents and a discursive glossary might appear to resemble what is known in carmanspeak as an optional bolt-on accessory. This index, however, excludes references easily accessible from the Contents page, and (for obvious reasons) does not re-list Glossary items. It includes (a) words relating to specific or recurrent themes, e.g. **cant, ideological function, suffix**, (b) names of persons, real or fictional, to whom some allusion is made, e.g. **Galbraith, Hamlet, Quayle**, (c) literary or academic sources, e.g. **Byron, Partridge, Sheridan**, and (d) some references to ephemera, e.g. brochures, advertisement copy.

Throughout the book, as I have noted in my preface and again in my Bibliographical Note, there are brief illustrations drawn from broadsheet newspapers. To have indexed these (as I at first intended) would have been to create one or two absurdly long entries. I leave the reader to identify from the Glossary (a) the newspaper regularly delivered to my house during the period of composition of this book, (b) the papers or periodicals I commonly buy and study, and (c) those sources which I have come upon casually, as a common-room loafer or TV lounger presciently equipped with a stub of pencil and a scrap of paper. I cannot imagine that, for want of indexing, these items will lie irrecoverably doggo in the coverts of my text.